BUILT ON A ROCK

A Memoir of Family, Faith and Place

JERRY D. NEAL
WITH JERRY BLEDSOE

Down Home Press, Asheboro, N.C.

ISBN 0-9767829-0-1
Library of Congress
Control Number: 2005933909
Printed in the United States of America

Book Design by Beth Hennington
Cover Design by Tim Rickard

Down Home Press
P.O. Box 4126
Asheboro, North Carolina 27204

Distributed by:
John F. Blair, Publisher
1406 Plaza Dr.
Winston-Salem, North Carolina 27103

For my parents, Albert and Bertie Neal,
whose lives inspired this book
and gave me the values I cherish.

For my wife, Linda Stewart Neal, whose love
of my parents and constant encouragement
and support were crucial in writing this book.

And for my family and friends who embrace
and spread the example set by my parents.

Acknowledgments

Many people made significant contributions this book. Special thanks go to:

My dear sisters, **Betty Pope** and **Diane Cavin**, who in reviewing this book traveled back with me to our childhoods and many happy memories. My aunt, **Frances Hill**, whose memory of my father's move to Randolph County with her and the rest of his family untangled a mystery for me. My pastor, **Randal A. Quate**, for reviewing the book and for his wonderful participation in the dedication of the plaque on my parents' rock. **Spencer Ahlmer** who gave me insight to a part of my father I would not have known otherwise. Thank you for the friend you were to my father during a difficult time and through the remainder of his life. **Kathy Adams**, my assistant, for the time spent in researching the details of my experiences and for the innumerable tasks performed in the process of completing this book. **Linda Duckworth** who has been invaluable in the proofing process. I appreciate your support and friendship. **Mary Farlow** for your support in proofreading this book and for your support of my previous book, *Fire in the Belly*. **Jamie Miyares** who not only helped in proofing the book and offered a fresh perspective on the story, but also provided a wonderful service in her research of book promotion. **Beverly Nelson** for taking on the task of checking my grammar and spelling. **Victor Steel** for the beautiful photography of Linbrook Hall. **Jerry Bledsoe**, my co-author. The conclusion of this book is bittersweet as I will miss the time spent together these past four years. It is rare to find such a friend as you.

Therefore whosoever heareth these sayings of mine, and doeth them, I will liken him unto a wise man, which built his house upon a rock:

And the rain descended, and the floods came, and the winds blew, and beat upon that house; and it fell not: for it was founded upon a rock.

—Matthew 7:24-25

Contents

Prologue

On a cloudy Friday morning in May 2004, I gathered with a small group of gifted people at an 850-foot-deep well I had drilled, a well that produced more than 100 gallons of water a minute, and that, when we finally hit our target, threatened to become a geyser. We were on a mission, and it had little to do with this well, although it and another, far shallower, were factors in it.

This was a family affair in every way. My son-in-law, Don Smith, husband of my daughter, Annette, was there, as was my brother-in-law, Mike Cavin, who is married to my sister Diane. Mike was in charge of this special mission.

My first cousin, Harold Loflin, arrived in a big Chevrolet truck, pulling a large steel trailer with a bright yellow John Deere 310E backhoe on it. He backed the big tractor off the trailer, as its irritating reverse beep ordered everybody near and far to clear the way. Then he put it into a forward gear, guided it next to the copper-roofed stone pump house, and set the machine's supports so he could begin to dig.

He gently lowered the big shovel and with his first swipe deftly and delicately uncovered a buried electric line that had to be moved. Harold is a master with a backhoe.

"He can part your hair with that thing," Mike said, and there was no question of that in my mind.

Owning a backhoe—this one was mine—and thinking that you can handle it with genuine expertise, even after training and extensive practice, is akin to buying a scalpel and thinking that you can become a surgeon. As much as I love sitting at the controls, I wouldn't have thought of operating the machine on a task as important as this.

With the electric line out of the way, Harold began to dig in earnest, placing the big shovel within an inch of the huge flat rock that was the object of our attentions, lifting bucketsful of dry, red clay and placing them to the side.

In many ways, it was a small miracle that we were gathered on this day, undertaking this job. The rock that we were digging out had special meaning to my mother and dad, especially my dad. It once had lain by the side of the road on which I live. It was just a narrow country lane then, muddy and rutted, with farm houses set far apart.

My mother has been dead nine years now, and my dad nearly three. The road had been paved for years, lined with brick, ranch-style houses; split-levels; and double-wides. Only a couple of the old farmhouses remained to remind us of the area's history. One of them was my grandparents' house, where my Aunt Gracie had lived until her death just ten days earlier at eighty-four.

The rock had disappeared from the side of the road more than thirty years ago, and my dad had always wondered what had happened to it. It was near an old house where he had lived as a teenager, while his family sharecropped. The house was owned by Jeff Rush, a sort of rough fellow, a farmer and sawmiller who traveled widely buying and harvesting timber. He was a colorful character in the community. He worked into his eighties, claiming he'd never had a headache and never taken an aspirin. He lived to be ninety-nine. His son, Clarence, later moved into the house where my dad had lived and reared his family there.

One day as my dad was driving past the Rush house, he thought about the rock and decided he would just stop and ask Clarence if he knew what had become of it.

Clarence knew exactly where the rock was and led him straight to it. The Rushes once had a hand-dug, rock-lined well, a well from which my dad had raised many a bucket of water in his youth. But it had gone dry. Clarence had to drill a new well and wanted to cover the old one so that no person or creature might accidentally fall into it. Dying in old, forgotten wells once was a common danger in our part of the world. Clarence had used the big rock to cap the old well.

My dad was pleased to see the rock and to stand on it again. He called to tell me about it. Later, we both were shocked to learn that Clarence had died of a heart attack only a few hours after my dad left. If he hadn't stopped when he did, my dad never would have known what had become of the rock that meant so much to him—and now to me. If he hadn't acted on that impulse, none of us would have been on this mission this day.

A time came when I was able to purchase the site of the old Rush house. The house had fallen long before, the debris later burned. Few traces of it remained. The land had grown over in briers and brambles, cedars and scrub pines. I cleared the property, except for the big oaks that once had shielded the house. I had the new well drilled for irrigation, and my cousin, Harold, had used the backhoe on which he now was working to move the rock my dad treasured and bury it in front of the pump house as a keepsake, a huge flagstone of memories.

Now it was to be moved again, and Harold had one side of its length exposed. I hadn't been present when he placed the rock there and wasn't aware of its full dimensions. Now I could see that it was thicker than I expected, eighteen inches at least, maybe twenty. Harold had to reposition the tractor to dig along the sides of its width, and they quickly were laid bare.

Mike was holding wide nylon bands, blue and yellow, each of which could support 10,000 pounds. The question now was how to get them around the rock so that Harold could lift it from the ground.

"You're the expert, Mike," said Paul O'Connor, a landscape architect, who also had an important role in this mission.

"I don't know about that," Mike said.

As Mike studied the problem, the sun popped out from behind the clouds, justification for the straw hat he was wearing. And Lloyd Bingham, a master stonemason, uncle to my wife Linda, showed up in his red suspenders nearly as bright as the sun. Lloyd's work with the rock would come later, but he wanted to judge its size for himself and see how things were going.

"What's the chance you can push it that way?" Mike asked Harold, motioning with his empty hand.

"I can get over there and pull it that way."

"If you can do that, we can get one band around it."

Paul and Mike spread a nylon band into one of the trenches and held up the two ends as Harold moved the tractor into place and gently tugged the rock onto the band.

"Can you raise it up some?" Mike asked.

Harold nodded and lifted one end of the rock so that more bands could be carefully spread beneath it. That done, Don, Paul, and a young helper swarmed the rock, crisscrossing and tightening the bands until the rock looked as beribboned as a birthday present. Paul was standing atop it, Don in the ditch beside it.

"Which end you want to pick it up with?" Paul asked.

"I have to get it on the front," Harold said, raising the machine's supports, then shifting into gear and turning around. Meanwhile, Don and Paul were adjusting the straps to balance the weight. Paul got chains of hardened steel from the truck, looped them through the bands, and attached them to the tractor's wide front bucket. Harold slowly raised the bucket until the slack was gone in the chains, then the big rock moved. Soil and clay fell away from its sides, and slowly, the rock rose until it barely cleared the surface. Harold backed up and laid it on the ground.

Now would come the tricky part—getting it onto the trailer. The rock was five and a half feet in length and lacked only two inches from being five feet at its widest point. Its thickness actually was only two inches short of two feet. Putting such a huge rock on the trailer would require lifting it higher than getting it out of the ground, and it had to be unhooked from the front bucket so that Harold could reposition the tractor as Paul moved the trailer into place.

On the first try, the rock was out of balance, and the left rear wheel of the tractor rose precariously off the ground before Harold could ease the rock back down. He extended the arm of the rear bucket for extra balance, and Paul and his helper climbed onto it to add more weight. Still, Harold couldn't lift the rock high enough to swing it onto the trailer.

"Anybody got any suggestions?" he asked.

"It'll lift it if we can move the chains back behind the bucket," Paul said. Then he and Don set to work doing that.

"I want to keep equal weight on these arms," Harold told them. "I don't want to twist them."

This time it worked. The big rock rested securely on one side of the sturdy trailer, and Harold drove it to my nearby shop, where we cleaned it with a pressure washer. He then took it the mile and a half to a new spot where we could complete this day's mission.

To lift the rock off the trailer, Harold used a trackhoe, a much bigger and heavier piece of equipment that crawls on steel tracks like a battle tank. It had much greater reach and far more capacity than the backhoe. But it hadn't been used in a while; the hydraulics weren't working perfectly, and its controls were a little jerky for Harold's precision. Still he plucked the rock from the trailer and lifted it high into the air. The bands and chains that swathed the rock had been rearranged so that it was hanging as if it were standing on end, broad and rounded at the bottom, narrower and slightly pointed at the top, a big slice missing from one side.

The rock twirled slowly, as Harold expertly swung it over a young Yoshino cherry tree and onto a base of steel rods and stone that Lloyd Bingham had erected earlier. Don and Paul grabbed it with gloved hands and guided it into position.

"Is that the way you want it?" Paul asked me.

"Set it down some more and lay it back a little."

"Is it leaning this way too much?"

"Yeah, it is."

"Let the weight down on it," Mike told Harold, "and see if we can lean it back."

It still wasn't quite straight, but Lloyd stuck a rock under one corner and that seemed to work until he fetched a level and held it up to its side.

"Third of a bubble off," he announced.

Don and Paul pushed on the back of the rock, and Lloyd adjusted the smaller stone beneath it.

"Okay," I said. "That looks good."

Even though it was as straight as possible, the natural cut of the rock made it appear skewed to the left.

"Lloyd, you happy with the way it's sitting now?" I asked.

He, after all, would have to complete the base and finish this job.

"Yeah, it looks good to me. It's just a little bit Yankee-doodle. Don't know how to straighten that, though."

Yankee-doodle or not, this was a proud moment for me, because this rock was more than a monument to my mom and dad, and to the importance and sanctity of family and place. It was the very foundation upon which my life and the story I'm about to tell were built—and now it represented a promise of a dream that, I hoped, would reach far beyond my own life.

Part I

Foundations

One

Randolph County, North Carolina, not only occupies a big part of my heart, but it lies at the very core of my being. At 801 square miles, it is one of the state's larger counties in area. Vast, hilly, and heavily forested, it is still mostly rural and sparsely populated, although it is only an hour's drive or less from the state's major cities, Charlotte, Raleigh, Greensboro, Durham, and Winston-Salem. Did I mention beautiful? It is that for sure.

It lies at the heart of our state, and I like to think of it as that. As rapidly as it is developing, it remains one of the least-affected areas in a state changing so drastically that natives who have been gone for a while no longer can find their ways around when they return—and feel lost for more reasons than that.

From the cupola of a ridge-top house I have built in the county's northwestern section, I can see for many miles in every direction, and with the exception of a few cell-phone towers, a distant silo, a rooftop or two, barely exposed, all that I see are trees on undulating hills, delicately pastel and flowered in spring, deep green in summer, brilliantly colored in fall, gray and bare except for the pines and cedars in winter, but beautiful no matter the season.

The Uwharrie Mountains fill a big part of my county. They are said to be one of the oldest ranges on the continent. Many millions of years ago, we're told, they were raw and rugged peaks of 20,000 feet and more, wind-whipped, snow-capped, pounded at the base by the sea. But now they are worn, aged, and gentled, barely deserving a description as mountains, and the Atlantic is two hundred miles away.

The highest of the Uwharries, High Rock Mountain, which is in adjoining Davidson County, is only 1,188 feet. Mount Shepherd, near which I grew up, and of which I have a spectacular view, is the second highest at 1,150 feet. The Uwharries are underlain by volcanic rock, including granite and a vast belt of slate, blue, gray, and green, layered with milky quartz that sometimes is pocked with gold, silver, copper, and other precious metals. There is not enough to justify serious mining any longer, although at one time that was a major industry. Our small section of North Carolina was the scene of America's first gold rush and once supplied all the gold to the Philadelphia and Charlotte mints.

Three shallow, rocky rivers make their tortured ways through our county. The Uwharrie and the Little are in the western section, only a few miles

This covered bridge, which exemplified the rural nature of Randolph County, once stood near my grandparents' farms.

from my house, barely creeks at that point. They empty into the Atlantic at Georgetown, South Carolina, through the muddy Yadkin and the much broader and darker Pee Dee Rivers. Our primary river is the misnamed Deep, in the central and eastern part of the county, which flows to Cape Fear and on to the Atlantic at Wilmington.

The Indian Trading Path, a trail from southeastern Virginia to western North Carolina, passed through what would become Randolph County, not far from where I live, and it brought the first white explorer to the area. John Lederer, a medical student from Germany with an interest in the native people, came to this area in 1670. Near the Uwharrie River, he encountered a group he called the Watary Indians but recorded little about them. Soon white traders were following this path to profit from the many tribes that populated central North Carolina, which was lush with growth and ranged by bison, elk, deer, bear, wolf, and cougar, among abundant other wildlife, much of it long departed, some of it extinct.

The famous English explorer John Lawson came to the county by a different route, from Charleston, in 1700 and wrote of his discovery of a large Keyauwee Indian town between the Uwharrie River and Caraway Creek, not far from my house. Its residents lived in clay-covered pole houses and had fields of corn, squash, and other crops. Suffice to say that our county had been settled for hundreds, even thousands, of years before the first Europeans came, and I have found arrowheads, pottery shards, and other traces of their existence all of my life.

The first white settlers began to come only a few decades after

John Lawson's visit. They were hardy and independent people, Scots-Irish, English, German. They came for land they could call their own, for opportunity, for freedom from religious persecution and government, as well as for personal reasons known only to themselves. Many were Quakers, but there also were Dunkers, Moravians, Mennonites—a large percentage of them pacifists—Methodists, and Baptists, too.

Randolph Countians, although they didn't know themselves as that, were among the first to rise up against British control, fighting the troops of Governor William Tryon in nearby Alamance in 1771, four years before the famous battles at Lexington and Concord in Massachusetts. Many of them later paid dearly with the loss of their homes and lives at the hands of the merciless, marauding Tory, Colonel David Fanning, and his men. Yet, the county was torn and at war with itself during the Revolution, as it would be during the Civil War when many Randolph Countians were opposed to slavery and secession and stood with the Union.

Randolph County came to be because of its very isolation. Guilford County, of which it was a part, had been formed from sections of Rowan and Orange Counties. But Guilford Courthouse, where a key Revolutionary War battle would be fought on March 15, 1781, now part of Greensboro, was too far away from people in the southern part of the big county, so the county was divided in 1779, and the southern half was named for Peyton Randolph of Virginia, president of the Continental Congresses of 1774 and 1775.

I'm not sure when all of my ancestors first came to Randolph. No genealogy of the family ever has been done so far as I know. But I do know that my roots here are deep. My maternal great-great-grandfather, John Hoover, is as far back as I am aware. He was a farmer, as most people in Randolph County were. He died in May 1923, and is buried in the cemetery at Mt. Zion Methodist Church only a couple of miles from my house. He had worked in his garden that day and gone into his house to rest. My mother, Bertie Dorsett, who was three at the time, discovered him sitting in a straight-back chair, mouth agape, dead. She ran to tell her mother that Grandpa had choked on his chaw of tobacco, but the actual cause of his death remains unknown. He was seventy-six.

Hoovers were widespread through our part of the county. They were of German descent, the name Anglicized from Huber. Andreas Huber migrated from Germany to Pennsylvania, then on to Maryland before his restless-ness brought him to the Uwharrie River with his wife and twelve children around 1763. He became Baptist, but his wife was Quaker, as were his children. He built a grist mill on the river, and his sons continued to run it after his death in 1783, until the mill was destroyed by floods years later.

The house where my great-great-grandparents John and Frances Hoover lived.

Mt. Zion Methodist Church cemetery, where John and Frances Hoover are buried.

Some of Andrew Hoover's descendants moved to Ohio in 1801, and one, Jesse Clark Hoover, went on to Iowa, where a son was born to him in 1874. That son, Herbert, would become president of the United States. No doubt, I'm a distant cousin of the man who is credited with bringing us the Great Depression, which, coincidentally, brought the other half of my family to Randolph County.

My father's family came from Guilford County, not far from the head-waters of the Deep River, along which my father fished and hunted as a child. They lived in Friendship Township, where my grandfather, James Virgil Neal, farmed twenty acres near Lindley Field, an airstrip where Charles Lindbergh landed not long after his historic flight across the Atlantic in 1927, later to become Piedmont Triad International Airport. My grandparents would go on to have eleven children, only three of them boys (one, Edward, died a month before his second birthday). My father, Albert, was the youngest of the three.

In addition to farming, my grandfather had to work at a furniture factory in High Point to support his big brood. He owed $850 on his farm, but his wife Ethel Miles, who survived polio as a child, was chronically ill with pellagra and other ailments, and he had to spend much of the money he earned on doctors and medicines instead of paying off his debt. With the coming of the Depression, Continental Furniture Company, where he had worked for many years, shut down, and he lost not only his job but his farm.

My dad talked often about that bleak January day in 1932 when his family had to take refuge in Randolph County in a house they never could call home, on land they never would own. They had few possessions: some furniture, household goods, clothes, a mule, a wagon, a cow, and a flock of chickens, all vital to survival.

A friend of my grandfather's, Shorty Ridge, had an old open-bed truck, and he volunteered to help the family move. One of my dad's sisters was grown and gone from home by then. My grandmother was eight months pregnant with her ninth child. She and her younger daughters crowded into the truck cab with Shorty. My granddaddy and the older girls rode in the back with the furniture.

Randolph County roads were muddy ruts at the time, and the going was slow and difficult. Not until well after dark did the truck reach its destination at the unpainted, four-room house with a rusty tin roof at the foot of a hill near the community of Flint Hill. A preacher named Hill owned the house and was allowing them to use it.

My dad was twelve at the time. He and his brother, Howard, two years older, had to make the thirty-mile trek in the wagon loaded with farm implements and burlap sacks filled with chickens tied by their feet, the milk

21

cow trailing behind. It was an exhausting journey, and my dad never would forget the misery of it. Numerous times the cow balked, refusing to take another step, lying down in protest. After letting the cow rest a while and enticing her with a little corn, my dad and his brother would pull and prod and plead until they got her up and moving again.

The two brothers didn't arrive at the forlorn house until well after midnight, making their way by lantern light. They were chilled to the bone. They still had to unhitch the mule, get it and the cow into the barn, free the chickens from the burlap sacks, and untie them. They slept in the cold barn that night with their daddy, Shorty Ridge, and the animals.

I only can imagine what was going through my dad's mind on that dismal day. But as bleak as the prospects may have seemed for him and his family, these events actually were delivering my dad to a lifetime of happiness. He just didn't know it at the time.

My dad finished the seventh grade and most of the eighth in a two-room school at Flint Hill before his family moved again in 1934, this time nearly five miles to the west to another house not their own. It, too, was small, unpainted, and weather-grayed. It had been built on stacks of field stones. It had a rusty tin roof, a stone chimney, a hand-dug well, and an outhouse out back. It was owned by a sawmiller named Jeff Rush.

But this house had a distinction that the previous one lacked. The rutted dirt road by which it sat curved sharply at that point, and less than a half mile beyond that curve was a similar farmhouse in which my mother had grown up, and where, having just turned fourteen, she still was living.

And in that curve, close by the road, was a big flat rock nearly two feet thick.

Two

I had a childhood privilege that few are accorded: a long and deep relationship with my great-grandfather. His name was Edd Walker Hoover. He was one of three children of John and Frances Hoover and, like his father, a get-by farmer. He never saw much of the world except for the section of Randolph County where he lived, but my experience with him told me that he probably knew that area more intimately than anybody.

Edd Hoover married a young woman who lived close by, Charity Briles. She had frailties that plagued her entire life and kept her from having more than one child, my grandmother, Myrtle, born in June 1896. Charity received an inheritance that allowed my great-grandfather to buy forty mostly wooded acres adjoining his father's farm in 1902. He used two mules and hand tools to clear enough land for crops, and built a small frame house that would forever go unpainted just up the road from his father's.

As a young woman, his daughter, Myrtle, was wooed by a farmer named Jefferson Dorsett, called Jeff. He was four years older, lived a couple of miles away, and attended her church. They were married in the fall of 1916,

and moved into a tiny cabin on land I now own not far from her parents' house. For years I searched for the remains of that cabin, and only recently found a portion of the chimney still standing deep in the woods, long hidden by a jumble of growth. They lived there for a couple of years before moving to another rental house closer to where Jeff had grown up, a mile or so away.

Myrtle had three daughters. The first was my Aunt Gracie, born in August, 1918. She never would marry. My mother, Bertie, came next, in March 1920, when my grandmother was twenty-four. More than eleven years would pass before my mother's

My grandmother Myrtle Hoover at seventeen, before her marriage to Jeff Dorsett.

23

younger sister, Beulah, was born in July 1931.

Myrtle would end up being a family nurse for much of her life. Her grandmother, Frances Hoover, wife of John, was five and a half years older than her husband and died in March 1913. John would outlive her by ten years, and during the last of those, as he grew increasingly feeble, Myrtle

The house where my mother, Bertie, grew up and where I had many happy times as a child.
It was the home of my great-grandparents, Edd and Charity Hoover, as well as
my grandparents, Jeff and Myrtle.

The barnyard across from my grandparents' house, where the mules
and the milk cow lived and where I loved to play.

and Jeff and their two young daughters moved into his house so that Myrtle could look after her grandfather while Jeff worked his land.

Following John Hoover's death, his farm was sold to a family named Carne, and the proceeds were divided among his children. By then Myrtle's mother, Charity, had fallen ill, and Edd asked his only child to move back home to help care for her.

Edd added a room with a separate entrance on the front of the house and a kitchen on the back to accommodate his daughter and her family. Jeff took up farming with his father-in-law. They never had a tractor and always used a pair of mules for breaking the ground and hauling.

My great-grandmother, Charity, suffered from edema of the heart, which then was called dropsy. She was bedridden for years and died on May 14, 1934, when my mother was fourteen and my grandmother not quite thirty-eight. My great-grandfather would live another twenty-four years with his daughter and her family.

My grandmother's own grandparents, John and Frances Hoover, had attended Mt. Zion Methodist Church, about a mile from their home, where both now lie in the church cemetery. As a child, Myrtle went to services there with her mother, but Charity later joined Poplar Ridge Friends Meeting, which occupied a simple wood structure, painted white, that her husband helped to build, although he didn't attend services himself. Myrtle, too, became a member there and was a devout Quaker, as were her three daughters. Poplar Ridge was a mile and three quarters away on Hoover Hill Road.

Across the road from the meeting house was a two-room frame building. It had a small belfry and a chimney in the middle with flues in each room for the wood stoves that heated it. This was Poplar Ridge School, built in

1879, where my mother and her sisters were educated. They walked the three and a half miles back and forth to school each day. The school year was much shorter then, because families needed their children on the farms in spring, summer, and early fall, when the crops had to be planted, tended, and harvested.

My dad, Albert, didn't return to school after his family moved into the house owned by sawmiller Jeff Rush in 1934, just before he turned fifteen. He had to take what odd jobs he could

My dad, Albert Virgil Neal at seventeen. Before he got the bike, he walked nine miles round-trip to court my mother.

find to help his family survive. My mother, who had just turned fourteen, walked past my dad's house twice every weekday on her way back and forth to school.

A lot of girls lived in that area. The Snyders, whose farm was west of my grandparents' and for whom the road on which my parents lived would be named, had many daughters. But Bertie Dorsett was the one who caught my dad's eye. He managed to find himself by the big flat rock in the curve one day when she was walking home from school with some of the Snyder girls, and there they met and began to talk.

Throughout the winter, the road usually was a mired and muddy mess, and the rock was a refuge. My dad began waiting there almost every afternoon, and romance soon blossomed. Courting was a more formal process then, drawn-out and closely overseen. And in the Randolph County countryside there was no place to go except church—or a big flat rock in the curve where they could sit and talk, laugh and dream.

After only a year in the sawmiller's house, my grandfather Neal was forced to move his family once again, this time to another small house in Flint Hill, four and a half miles to the east. This surely had a drastic effect on my dad and mom. He was almost sixteen then, she nine months younger, and they already were in love. But my dad was not to be deterred. He later recalled many times how he regularly walked the nine-mile round trip to meet his sweetheart at their rock.

The Great Depression didn't have as big an effect in rural Randolph as it did in cities and other parts of the country. Randolph County people were largely self-sufficient. They helped one another, and what they couldn't get, they usually easily could do without. As the dark decade of the '30s began to wind down, economic conditions started to improve a little, and my grandfather Neal got a job at Tate Furniture, a factory in High Point. My father also got a job at Tate Furniture when he was eighteen. He was making thirty-five cents an hour and felt as if he were rich.

Dad had a sister whom he adored. Her name was Jewel, and she was twenty months younger. He had closely looked after her when she was little. When Jewel was fifteen, while the family still was living in the Rush house, she got a bad cough that wouldn't go away. One day she started hacking up blood. The diagnosis was dire: tuberculosis. There was little treatment for it at the time, and she deteriorated slowly, spending most of her time in bed.

Jewel loved music, and after my dad started to work at Tate Furniture, he bought a big, battery-powered table-model radio for her on credit. She kept it by her bed and played it as often as the battery would allow. My dad would be a long time paying it off, but he always said that radio brought her a lot of comfort. Jewel suffered greatly but never complained. She died in

April 1938, at seventeen, and my dad never quite got over it. He talked about her often.

By that time, my dad had little question about the direction his own life would take. He was going to marry Bertie Dorsett. He did just that on October 21, 1939. He was twenty, my mom nineteen. His friend Clyde Ward and Clyde's girl-friend at the time rode with them to Danville, Virginia, just across the state line, and served as witnesses as they were married at the courthouse by a Baptist preacher named Francis Harrison, whom neither of them knew. My mother later remembered that she was wearing a lime-green suit. They had no time or money for a honeymoon.

Soon after the wedding, my mom and dad moved into a small rental house

My mother and dad before their marriage in 1939.

without electricity or running water less than a mile from my mother's parents, and there my sister, Betty Lou, was born in February 1941.

I always believed that my sister was delivered by Dr. Jefferson Davis Bulla, who treated everybody in our area, including my grandparents and their children. He called on his patients with horse and buggy and mixed his own medicines. His father, Archibald, was known as the doctor of the poor, because he treated the indigent and mentally feeble at the county Poor House in the Back Creek community.

Doc Jeff, who was born during the Civil War, lived in a two-story white house beside the grocery store in Hillsville, a community a few miles north of Poplar Ridge Meeting House. He kept up his practice until he was one hundred, a cigar usually clenched in his teeth. I remember riding by his house when I was in high school and he was in his late nineties and seeing him sitting on the front porch in bow tie, white shirt, and suit coat, even on hot summer days. He lived to be 103 and died in June 1965.

Maybe it was because Doc Jeff was such a memorable character in our community who was noted for delivering almost all the babies in our area that I got it in my head that only he could have delivered my sister. Maybe it was because he treated her for pneumonia when she was about eighteen months old. But after this book was written, my sister checked her birth certificate and discovered she actually was delivered by a doctor from High Point. What made my dad summon him, or how he did it, I have no idea.

Not long after Betty was born, my parents moved to High Point so Dad would be close to his work. They rented the first floor of a house at 126 Russell Street, less than a block off Main in downtown High Point, directly across the street from where my dad's parents now lived with their younger daughters in another rented house. For the first time, my parents had electricity and indoor plumbing. My mother's sister, Gracie, had taken a job in High Point, and she lived in the apartment upstairs with a friend, Florence Wall. Gracie always returned to her parents' house every Friday and remained until Sunday night.

I was born on Labor Day, September 4, 1944. My mother always considered that appropriate. Her labor began in the early morning hours, and my dad rushed her to High Point Hospital. He was a supervisor at work and had a problem that had to be taken care of first thing that morning, so he had to leave the hospital for a while. He got back at 7:30, ten minutes after my arrival.

My paternal grandparents, James and Ethel Neal, lived across the street from us when I was a small child in High Point.

Our nation was nearly three years into World War II at that time, and my dad had been exempted from the draft because he was married and had a child. Now he was twenty-five, with two children, but the need for fighting men was desperate.

Many Quakers were pacifists and conscientious objectors, but my dad felt an obligation to serve his country. He had been summoned for a pre-induction physical in June, nearly three months before I was born. He had passed it, but his induction was delayed until my birth. He left for fifteen weeks of infantry training at Camp Willard near Macon, Georgia, on September 30, when I was not yet a month old. He had no doubt that he was headed for combat. He came home for a week-long leave before reporting to Ft. Ord, California, on the Monterey Peninsula, one hundred miles south of San Francisco, where he would ship out to the South Pacific.

At the end of his leave, as he was about to walk off up Main Street to the train depot and a dangerous and uncertain future, he stood on the front porch on a cold morning at the end of January saying good-bye to my mom and sister Betty, who was nearly four. Mom held me in her arms. Dad was in uniform, his carefully packed duffel bag at his side. He knew what was on my mother's mind.

"Bertie," he said, "you see that bag. I'm going to pick it up, throw it over my shoulder, and I promise you that I'm going to come back and drop it on this very spot. You can bank on that."

Dad was at Ft. Ord for only a couple of weeks before boarding a Victory ship, the *Sea Pike*, with 1,200 other soldiers on February 23, 1945. He had no idea of his destination. He thought the ship might be joining a convoy, but he spent more than two weeks at sea before even seeing another ship. When he next saw land, he discovered it was New Guinea, where the ship stopped to pick up more troops, including a unit of black soldiers. On March 29, the ship's commander dropped anchor in Manila Bay in the Philippine Islands.

The city was still burning, and my dad could hear artillery booming in the distance. After more than five weeks on board the *Sea Pike*, he descended a rope net to a landing craft and made his way to shore. It was April 1, Easter Sunday, 1945.

Two distinctive peaks rose above Manila, and soon my dad would be fighting in those mountains in Company E, 149th Infantry Regiment, 38th Division. He never talked about his experiences in combat, and not until after his death many years later would I learn about them.

My mother worried constantly and prayed fervently while my dad was gone. The stress from anxiety and taking care of two small children alone on little money sometimes sent her to bed for two or three days at a time, but she always rallied, and in the end her prayers were answered. Church bells sounded throughout High Point on August 15, 1945, when the war finally ended, and people crowded into cars and rode around cheering and blowing their horns in celebration.

Another Victory ship delivered my dad back to California early in 1946, and he and many of his fellow soldiers came across country by train. My mother knew that he was coming but didn't know when he would arrive. Communication was not so convenient back then.

Dad was discharged at Ft. Bragg, near Fayetteville, on February 23, one year to the day after he had embarked for the South Pacific. He rode a bus to High Point. He intended to surprise my mom.

Dad smoked as a young man and had developed a nagging smoker's cough before he went into the Army. My mother was just finishing washing supper dishes when she suddenly heard that cough on the porch and dropped the pot she was drying. She ran to the front door, dish towel in hand, and there stood my father in uniform, knuckles preparing to knock, the duffel bag on one shoulder. He saw my mother's face, and with a smile and a dramatic flair, he lifted the bag and set it on the spot where he had left her thirteen months earlier. Then they fell into each other's arms, my mother crying with happiness.

My sister had missed my dad terribly and she raced into his embrace. I was almost eighteen months old and had been walking for six months or more, but I was wary of this stranger. I ran from him like a turkey, my dad always said.

Dad went back to work at Tate Furniture, and our lives fell into a routine. We continued to live in the house on Russell Street until I was five, and although I don't have a lot of memories of that period, I do have some that are especially strong.

A family named Cummings lived next door, the only other house on the block on our side of the street. They had a son, Van, who was a couple of

Mom and Dad soon after my dad returned from combat in the Philippines during World War II.

years older than I, but we became playmates. Van introduced me to two feelings I'd as soon have not become acquainted with—pain and jealousy.

One day we were playing with shovels and buckets in a sandbox my dad had built, and for reasons unknown—I'm sure it couldn't have been anything I said or did—Van whacked my blond head with a shovel, taking out a big hunk of scalp and sending me running, crying and bleeding profusely, to my mother. Pain, I discovered, lingers in memory long after it's gone.

Van's father was a crane operator and often was away from home for long periods. Van spent a lot of time at our house and became quite attached to my dad. My sister and I both were resentful about the attention my dad gave him. While it was an instinct I somehow sensed I shouldn't be indulging, it still was there and even now touches off twinges of shame, especially in light of what soon was to happen.

One day Van slipped away from home alone and walked a couple of blocks north on Main Street where a new building was under construction. He wanted to see the machines that were working there. I had a similar fascination with machinery and might have been tempted to tag along if I'd known he was going. A truck accidentally backed over him at the construction site and broke his leg. His father was away on a job at the time. Van was taken to the hospital where doctors decided to put him to sleep to reset the bones. It was a routine procedure, but Van never came out of the anesthesia. He was only six.

In those days, people in the South brought their dead home and displayed them in their coffins for grieving family and friends. Van's stunned parents did that. I never will forget the image of my friend, pale and still in that coffin, never to speak, or run, or play again. It made such a deep impression that I suspect it may have affected how I later paid scrupulous attention to what my parents said and always obeyed their rules and admonitions.

As a supervisor, my dad had to work long hours, ten a day, and often more, plus six hours on Saturday. He always was exhausted when he came home, his clothing and hair powdered with fine wood dust. Sunday was his one day of rest and that was devoted to family and faith.

My parents were deeply religious and completely dedicated to Poplar Ridge Friends Meeting, which my mother had attended all of her life and my dad had joined when they were married. We were there for every service unless my dad was working, or somebody was awfully sick.

Soon after returning from the war, my dad had bought a black, two-door

1936 Chevrolet, which was in dreadful condition. He had to work on it constantly to keep it running, and even then, it wouldn't go more than thirty-five miles an hour. The engine bearing expressed its distress with an awful clatter. But somehow that old car managed to deliver us down Randolph County's pitted and always muddy or dusty roads to services every Sunday morning.

Sundays were a

Soon after the war, my dad and mom took my sister Betty and me on a camping trip to the Cherokee Reservation in the Smoky Mountains. I wasn't afraid of the bears.

My sister Betty and I loved our parents' first car, a two-door '36 Chevrolet that wouldn't go over thirty-five miles per hour.

I must have been seven or eight when this Easter photo was made at my grandparents' house. I'm holding three fish called horneyheads that I had caught earlier in a nearby creek.

ritual for our family that I looked forward to with great anticipation for as far back as I can remember. Unlike a lot of kids, for whom church is an ordeal to be suffered through, I enjoyed Sunday services, but that was prelude to the best part of Sunday.

That was when we went to my grandmother Myrtle's house for Sunday dinner. In those days in much of the South the mid-day meal was called dinner, the evening meal supper. Sunday dinner at my grandmother's house was an event as sacred as going to meeting, but so much better. Heaven, surely, will be like it.

This was always a major production for my grandmother, two days in the making. She and Aunt Gracie began working on it Saturday afternoon. They continued into the night and got up at daybreak and started again. After services, they hurried home to add the final touches.

There were no plastic-wrapped packages of meats and vegetables from the supermarket ready to cook. My grandparents raised almost everything they ate.

Fried chicken was a Sunday dinner staple, but it required killing and plucking and cleaning. Country ham was always there. My grandparents bought baby pigs and raised them, and slaughter time came with the first freezes of November. The carcasses were hung, gutted, and cut into hams,

Diane shows off her Easter basket. In the background, Great-grandpa Edd and I are heading off for a walk.

shoulders, side meat, chops, and tenderloins. Much of this was salted, peppered, sugared, and cured for months in the smokehouse out back. Fat was rendered into lard in a big black cauldron suspended over a wood fire, a cauldron that I still have. The fat that didn't melt became crunchy "cracklings" to flavor cornbread. My grandmother made sausage, souse meat, and livermush, and what wasn't eaten fresh was canned in big blue Ball jars topped with glass-lined galvanized lids and boiled in an enameled stovetop canner. That canner was kept busy summer and fall as my grandmother preserved the vegetables and fruits that would see them through to the next growing season.

The big, white wood range in my grandmother's kitchen was fired from morning until night, and the spacious warmer above the cooking surface was never bereft of something delectable. Nobody ever came to my grandmother's house without her saying, "Wouldn't you like something to eat?" And if that person had any smarts at all, he or she would say, "Well, maybe I could have a bite or two."

That question never had to be asked at Sunday dinner, and the wood range never was busier, or more crowded. By the time all of us got to my grandmother's kitchen after church, the warmer would be filled with cornbread, chicken already fried, slices of country ham grilled to a light brown and aswim in red-eye gravy, and sometimes baked sweet potatoes with crinkled skins oozing their own caramelized sugar and begging for a dollop of my grandmother's hand-churned butter. The range's surface

My grandmother, Myrtle, cooked many incredible dinners on this wood range in her small kitchen.

33

would be covered with pots of potatoes, corn, peas, beans of several varieties, squash, cabbage, okra, turnips, and greens, or wild creecy greens, depending on the season. Every Sunday dinner offered five or six vegetables, sometimes three or more meats, and oftentimes deviled eggs and potato salad. In the spring, there might be leaf lettuce from the garden, wilted by hot bacon grease, and in summer thick slices of succulent tomatoes straight from the vine.

A big enamel coffee pot would be filled with water and raw grounds and set to boil when the biscuits went into the oven. My grandmother made huge biscuits, double-fisted, but as light and fluffy as the clouds that wafted above the house. When the biscuits came from the oven, it was time to take our seats at the table.

Small though the table was, it managed to accommodate us all. It was built of wide slabs of rough pine, covered with a patterned oilcloth. Grandpa Edd sat at the head of the table, my grandfather Jeff, whom I called Paw-Paw, at the other end. The rest of us filled in the sides, sitting in hand-woven, cane-bottomed chairs—my mother and dad, Betty and me, and my sister, Diane, when she grew big enough. My mother's sister, Beulah, would be there with her husband, Eugene, along with their two sons, Dwight and Harold, who were several years younger than I. Sometimes, if they were lucky, the preacher and other guests might join us, and some of the kids would have to give up their places.

My grandmother and Aunt Gracie didn't eat with the rest of us. They always waited until everybody else was full and had left the table. During the meal, they hovered, passing dishes that the table was not commodious enough to accommodate; shooing away flies in warm weather when the unscreened doors and windows were open; hurrying to fill cups and glasses with coffee, sweet tea, cold well water, buttermilk, and sweet milk, as we called milk that hadn't soured. The milk came fresh from their cows and was kept cool in the root cellar behind the house.

The root cellar had been dug several feet deep and was topped by a tin-roofed wood structure, built by Edd. Inside were two open metal tanks separated by an earthen walkway. Those tanks were filled with well water that kept milk and butter fresh, along with anything else that needed coolness. In summertime, an ice truck came from nearby Thomasville, and huge blocks of ice were put into the tanks.

The meal always began with a blessing, and nobody dared touch a fork until it was finished. My dad usually offered the prayer. As soon as amen was spoken, Grandpa Edd took the first biscuit, sliced the top off, and put a slab of country ham on the bottom. Then he unscrewed the lid from a quart Ball jar, poured molasses over the ham, put the top on the biscuit, and started to eat. He began every meal that way.

Grandpa Edd grew his own sorghum and hauled it by wagon each year to a neighbor's cane mill, where a solitary mule walking in relentless tight circles, harnessed to a cedar pole, provided the power to crush the stalks into sweet, greenish juice. After aging for a day in barrels, that juice was cooked in a big metal vat over a log fire. Stirred constantly with wooden paddles, it filled the air with sweet vapors. When it became golden and viscous, it was drained off, cooled, and poured into canning jars.

I always was invited along on molasses-making day, and I looked forward to it with the same delicious anticipation that I held for my grandmother's Sunday dinners. Usually, several other kids would be present, filled with the same excitement. After the molasses was drained from the cooking vat, a residue was left that hardened into candy, and we kids were allowed to scrape off and eat as much as we wanted, stopping only at the point of sickness—and sometimes not even then.

As good as that candy seemed, the greatest use of molasses that I ever encountered came in the spicy molasses cake that my grandmother made and topped with powdered white sugar. It was divine, and it frequently was to be found in the pie safe in her kitchen. The pie safe was a wooden cabinet, taller than I when I was a small child. The tin in its wood-framed doors had designs punched in it to allow air to circulate but keep flies from entering.

We never knew what delights waited behind those doors at Sunday dinner, but we were certain that they would be scrumptious. Fruit pies, custard pies, cream pies, brown sugar pie, buttermilk pie, pumpkin pie, sweet potato pie with toasted marshmallows. Cakes of all varieties. Cobblers, too. Oh, those cobblers. Blackberry was my favorite.

My grandmother always wore an apron at home and a bonnet whenever she worked outside. Every summer, she spent long hours in the hot sun, shielded by her bonnet, picking gallons of wild blackberries. She made jelly and preserves from them, and canned the rest so that we could have blackberry cobbler year-around.

We often had three or four choices of desserts at Sunday dinner, but the one to which I most looked forward was the big banana pudding topped with meringue, browned in the oven. I don't think I've ever since tasted anything as good as that.

All of Sunday was a pleasurable experience for us. After dinner, the grown-ups would sit and talk. On clear, warm days they often gathered outside under the shade trees, and neighbors and other family members occasionally stopped by to visit. My dad loved to laugh and tell stories, and these gatherings were always a happy time for him.

Sometimes I would wander off to the barn across the road to visit with the mules and cows, or to explore some other spot of interest. In the woods behind the house, well out of sight, were rusted hulks of two old Model T Fords, long since plundered for any serviceable parts. I was drawn to them and loved to play there. I'd climb into the front seat of one of those old cars; sit amid the spider webs, fallen leaves, twining vines, shed snakeskins; and pretend that I was driving, making all kinds of dramatic engine noises.

One Sunday when I was five and had my fill of driving, I decided to forgo the path back to the house and take what I thought would be a shortcut. When the house didn't turn out to be where I thought it was, I forged resolutely on, thinking it would present itself any minute, only to find myself deeper in the woods. I panicked when I realized I was lost.

I started running, but I was running in the opposite direction from the house, down toward the Uwharrie River. The farther I went without seeing any recognizable landmark, the more scared I got, and the faster I ran. I finally emerged from the woods on an old logging road, and down a long incline I saw a tall, lean, solitary figure walking in my direction. He was wearing overalls and an old, brown felt hat. It was Grandpa Edd.

My great-grandfather was a strong man who was still roofing barns in his seventies and at eighty kept the ditch banks near his house mowed with a huge scythe that took both arms to swing. But he had a calm, soothing, and reassuring nature. I raced to him, breathless and in tears. He seemed startled to see me.

"Why, Jerry, what in the world are you doing way down here?" he asked.

I could barely blurt out what had happened and how scared I had become. I had run at least a mile and a half.

Grandpa Edd calmed me, took my hand, and led me back to the house, where we discovered that the rest of the family had launched a frantic search after I'd failed to answer their calls. They had found my half-eaten cherry

sucker in the woods and knew that something had to be terribly wrong for me to have abandoned such a precious treat.

I got a lecture that day, but I never again had to be worried about getting lost on visits to my grandparents' house. Grandpa Edd saw to that.

A typical after-Sunday-dinner scene at my grandparents' house, when the family would gather in the yard to talk.

Posing in front of the well house are (left to right) my mother's younger sister Beulah Lee, her older sister Gracie, her mother Myrtle, father Jeff, an unidentified friend, and her grandfather Edd. My mother probably took the photo.

On future Sundays, after dinner was finished and the conversation had waned, my great-grandfather would come to me and say, "Jerry, I want to show you some things. Why don't we go for a little walk?"

I always accepted.

Those walks would continue for nearly a decade and would soundly root me on the land on which so many of my ancestors had spent their lives. I can't imagine the number of miles we must have walked on those Sunday afternoons, although the territory that we covered was no more than a few square miles. We walked roads, wagon trails, fields, backwoods paths, and the rocky banks of creeks and the Uwharrie River.

Grandpa Edd took me to springs bubbling from the earth, small hidden caves, unusual rock formations, trees growing in wild contortions, trees so big that they seemed invincible. He identified trees and told me what their wood was good for—white oak could be split into roofing shingles or stripped for basket making while cedar and locust made the most durable fence posts. He told me the names of wildflowers and pointed out herbs that could be used for healing.

At that time, hawks were the enemies of farmers, because they killed chickens and other livestock, and the state paid a bounty of twenty-five cents for a hawk's head and feet. Like many other farmers, my great grandfather, who loved songbirds, set baited traps atop tall poles for these predators. We frequently went to check those traps, but I never liked to see one caught.

Edd also set dozens of simple wooden traps for rabbits—gums, these traps were called. One year he had a goal of catching one hundred rabbits for the stew pot and frying pan, but got only ninety-five.

As we passed houses on these walks, Edd would talk about the people who lived there. He chewed Brown Mule plug tobacco. He would carve off a hunk with his pocketknife, deposit it in his jaw, and as he talked, he occasionally turned his white-haired head and spewed brown juice onto the ground.

I learned about all of my grandparents' neighbors on those walks, their habits, idiosyncrasies and the things they didn't want others to know. (One of Grandpa Edd's idiosyncrasies, was that he refused to use an outhouse. They were for women and children, he maintained. He had his own special spots in the woods, and we all knew better than to prowl there.)

One Sunday, I was taken to see the remains of a neighbor's corn whiskey still, buried in a creek bank. Thanks to revenuers, the owner was a guest of the federal government at the time, but Grandpa Edd assured me that as soon as he returned he'd be right back to old habits.

On those walks, too, he told me what he knew about our own ancestors who had lived so long on this land.

My great-grandfather has been dead now for nearly half a century, but those walks we took, the things he showed me and told me, and the closeness we came to share are still vivid in my memory. And now I can see how much they contributed to forging my own life; my sense of nature, place, heritage, family, and home; the values that all of these instill; and how they came to direct my life and my dreams.

I had a long and close relationship with my great-grandfather Edd.

Three

Just before I turned six in 1950, my dad moved us to another rental house, this one in Randolph County, but barely so. It was in the small town of Archdale, which was fast by the Guilford County line and closer to my grandparents but still convenient to his job in adjoining High Point. It was nothing fancy, just a white frame house but with more room than our previous one.

There were five of us by this time: my dad and mom; my sister Betty, who was three and a half years older than I; my sister Diane, who was two and just a toddler then; and me.

Not long after we got settled into our new home, I started school at Archdale Elementary. It didn't take me long to realize that school was a significant expansion of my horizons. It offered so many new opportunities, particularly for mischief. I have no idea of the origins of this sense of mischief with which I was afflicted, but even now, as I am entering my sixties, I've never fully recovered from it. By the time I started second grade, it was fully developed and began causing me trouble on a constant basis.

As I saw it at the time, however, the problem was my teacher. She had a total aversion to demonstrative education—and anything resembling fun. To her, a pea shooter wasn't an amazing example of the powers of air pressure. It was a dangerous weapon, no matter how innocuously employed, something that could put an eye out, a thing to be confiscated and destroyed at the loss of a hard-won nickel. A paper airplane sailing across a classroom was thought to be an intrusion on the educational process, not the wondrous lesson in aerodynamics that it truly was. This woman could get apoplectic over an exhibition of the theory of tension, the innocent stretching and releasing of a rubber band. A tug on a passing girl's pigtail was viewed as criminal assault instead of the innocent expression of affection that it actually was. And if anybody dared to whisper to a few seatmates something that provoked laughter…well, there was hardly a sin to match it.

Sheer deviltry was my teacher's definition of anything that she took to be amusement, and she had a sound solution for it.

High Point was a world center of childhood fun in one respect. That was because the FLI-BACK Company was in High Point. It made and shipped everywhere a toy that almost every kid I knew possessed at one time or another. A paddleball game. It consisted of a thin, rounded wooden paddle, maybe ten inches or so in length. A strand of rubber about two feet long was attached with a staple to the center of the rounded part of the board. A red rubber ball, about the diameter of a quarter, was fastened to the other end of the band. Hit the ball with the paddle and it would soar out to the stretchable length of the rubber band, then snap back to be hit again—or all to often missed. These things could be bought at any dime store for ten cents. Some kids spent endless hours mastering them, hitting the ball hundreds of times without a miss until the rubber band snapped. Serious competitions were held. We were easily and cheaply entertained in those pre-TV days.

My second grade teacher held a different idea of entertainment. She had one of these devices, too, but it was lacking the ball and band. I still remember the sight of it. A cowboy playing paddleball on a bucking bronco was stenciled in red on the back. As far as I could tell, the only competition in which my teacher ever engaged this paddle was seeing how many times she could whack it against the seat of my jeans. She set new records regularly.

From the day I first set foot in school, my parents warned me that if I ever got a paddling from a teacher or principal, I was assured another one when I got home. To complicate matters, my family and my religious instruction had instilled in me a strong sense of honesty and forthrightness. If I ever considered the possibility of not telling my parents the truth, guilt and the certainty that the Lord Him- self was taking note quickly over- came it.

I'm not sure that I got a spank- ing on my very first day in second grade, but it wasn't long afterward that I had to come home with a sense of dread and tell my mother that I had suffered an indignity that seemed hardly appropriate to the infraction, whatever it was. My mother kept her promise and was stern in warning. She did the same when I came home a few days later with another similar confession, and another soon after that. My dad didn't get involved in discipline unless it was a serious matter, and my mother didn't think it had reached that level yet.

But it soon got to the point that

My second grade teacher claimed that I looked so innocent to be so guilty.

she would greet me each afternoon with the same question: "Did you get a paddling today?"

All too often, I'd give a grim nod in the affirmative and get into the proper position.

After a while, my mother came to be concerned that perhaps the problem was as much with my teacher as with me. She wanted to have a talk with her, but first she wanted a record of evidence. I started keeping a calendar, checking only the days when I *didn't* receive a paddling. It had few checkmarks indeed. When my mother finally went to the school for a confrontation, she never forgot what the teacher told her: "He's such an innocent looking child to be so guilty." I would hear that refrain many times in the future.

If I were angelic in appearance, I fully acknowledge that I was often impish in behavior. I clearly remember calculating before some of my mischievous acts whether the fun would be worth the pain of the inevitable paddling to follow. And more often than not, I decided that it would be. I think my poor mother finally gave up the notion that paddling or stern warning could alter my prankish, fun-loving nature, but my need for such distractions grew less impelling when I began to discover interests that would spare my future teachers and fascinate me for a lifetime.

Anything mechanical caught my attention. That interest no doubt came from my dad, who was a very technical guy. He left Tate Furniture Company while we still were living in High Point and went to work at Alma Desk Company, which made office furniture, and there he became one of the youngest supervisors in the company's history. He studied the machines in the plant, learned how they worked, and discovered ways to make them function better. He was great at solving hardware problems.

An engineer would tackle a mechanical problem with mathematical calculations, but my dad, who had only an eighth-grade education, would do it by building models out of wood and using them to figure out the variables. He was the guy the company turned to when machinery broke or wouldn't do what it was supposed to do. He even designed a device to feed wood into a machine and got a patent for it.

For as far back as I can remember, I was intrigued by the magic of machines. What made a clock tick and tell time? What made an engine run and turn wheels? How did voices come through a telephone? Or music from a radio? I eventually would find answers to all of these questions on my own, but my earliest fascination was with engines.

My dad had a small gas-powered push lawn mower that no longer worked, and at my pleading, he gave me permission to take it apart and see if I could fix it. I still remember the sense of excitement that I felt at the prospect. I have no idea how many hours I eventually put into that project, but it stretched over months and occupied my mind like nothing else. I carefully disassembled every piece down to the tiniest screws and springs. I cleaned them and laid them out in order, noting if they were broken or damaged.

Then I began meticulously putting it all back together again, the greatest puzzle I'd ever undertaken to solve. I made a lot of missteps and mistakes, but I didn't let them fluster me. I retreated and started anew. I was bound and determined to make this thing run again. I think my dad was secretly proud as he watched the slow progress. He later told me that I was the most patient person he ever had encountered.

I never thought of myself as being particularly smart, but even at this early age I knew that I was different because I had a strong curiosity that other kids didn't seem to have. And once that curiosity drew me to a problem or project, I had another fortunate characteristic that set me apart: a strong will to persevere until the problem was solved or the project completed. No matter how long it took, no matter how difficult it became, I simply wouldn't quit until I had figured it out and gotten the job done.

The reward for that was incredible. I'll never forget the moment that I pulled the rope on that old lawn mower engine and it coughed back to life. My sense of accomplishment is still impossible to describe. And my dad's obvious pride made me want to accomplish more.

Even today, I think that curiosity and perseverance are far more valuable than sheer intellect.

I later adapted that old lawn mower engine to run on kerosene, which was cheaper and far more available since we heated with it and I could drain it from the big tank beside our house. But to tell the truth, it never ran well on that fuel. While my interest in engines has continued to this day, my youthful attentions soon turned to something that fascinated me even more.

World War II veterans with honorable service were eligible for what became known as the GI Bill, which was drafted by Congress to provide education to help returning soldiers make their way in a post-war economy. My dad had found his career in furniture and had a job waiting as soon as he returned, but he thought it imprudent not to take advantage of the GI Bill. That legislation would pay for tuition, books, and other expenses for college studies, industrial and agricultural training, even correspondence courses. Beyond that, it paid a monthly stipend that by 1948 had come to be $75 a month. At a time when people with full-time jobs earned $35 or $40 a week, that was not to be ignored. My dad signed up for a correspondence course in radio repair.

I never asked why he chose radio. Maybe it was because of that radio he had bought for his sister, and the memory of what solace and company it had given her as she lay coughing and dying of tuberculosis. Maybe it was because of the importance of radio to our family's entertainment. Almost nightly we gathered around the console radio to listen to such shows as *Amos & Andy*, *Jack Benny*, *Our Miss Brooks*, *The Shadow*, and *Inner Sanctum*. Because of my dad's sense of humor and love of laughter, he especially enjoyed the comedy shows.

The GI Bill not only paid for tuition and books for my dad's radio repair course, it also paid for a volt meter, a signal generator, and other essential equipment. Our new home in Archdale had a couple of finished attic rooms, and my dad used one as his radio repair shop. That room, with its enchanting electronic equipment and broken down radios, drew me like a magnet.

I quickly learned that the lessons in some of my dad's radio repair texts were elementary enough for a third grader to understand, and I engrossed myself in them. Whenever my dad was working on old radios, I was there watching and peppering him with questions. He showed me how to use the equipment and how to keep from shocking myself and standing my hair on end. I started asking family and friends if they had old radios that no longer worked that they might be willing to allow me to dig into and fix. Or at least try to fix. I tore a lot more apart than I repaired in the beginning, but I was learning more with every one.

In the midst of this early radio fever, I happened onto a book in the school library one day about Alexander Graham Bell, and I became completely entranced by it. The book contained elementary diagrams of the first telephone, and they seemed easy enough that I got the idea that I could build my own phone. I committed myself to this notion as deeply as I did to tearing apart that old lawn mower engine and putting it back together again. If you're creating the first telephone, as Bell did, it does little good, of course, to make only one. Effectiveness demands two. So I set out to follow Bell's example. My plan was to put one phone upstairs and another downstairs and talk to my parents or my sisters.

A telephone contains three basic elements—a microphone, a speaker, and a power source. I had batteries for a power source and speakers from old radios I had torn apart, but microphones were another thing altogether. I was going to have to create my own.

The microphone that Bell used was composed of granulated carbon with a metal diaphragm above it. A voice created sound waves that were picked up by the diaphragm as vibrations, which caused the carbon to react, compressing and decompressing as the vibrations passed through it.

Carbon is a conductor of electricity. A current from a battery, passing through a wire attached to the diaphragm, would flow through the carbon, picking up its reactions to the vibrations. A connector at the other end of the carbon cylinder would pick up the varying current representing these vibrations and carry it through a wire to a speaker, which recreated it as a voice.

I knew from my reading that dry-cell batteries, the kind used in flashlights, had shafts of carbon at their centers. I also knew that my great-grandfather had dumped a lot of old batteries in the trash piles in a gully behind his house over the years. On a Sunday visit, I scrounged through those trash piles and salvaged carbon rods from some decomposed batteries. They were about the diameter of a pencil, but shorter. I put these in my pocket and took them to school. When nobody was paying attention, I emptied a pencil sharpener of its wood shavings and ground these rods to dust, which I carefully dumped into an envelope and sealed as if it were secret treasure.

Back at home, I drilled a hole in a block of wood that didn't penetrate the entire block. I put a wood screw into the bottom of the hole, so that it stuck out the other side. I filled the hole with carbon dust, then took the lid from a can of Maxwell House coffee and tacked it across the hole. I attached copper wires to the edge of the coffee can lid as well as to the screw protruding from the block of wood. One wire led to a battery that would provide the necessary electric current and the other to a salvaged speaker. Another wire led from the speaker back to the battery, creating a circuit. The coffee can lid was a little thick to be an effective diaphragm, but if I yelled loud enough into it, I actually could hear my voice coming faintly from the speaker.

Understand that there was no need for a second such phone at this stage because I had to yell so loud that I could be heard anywhere in the house

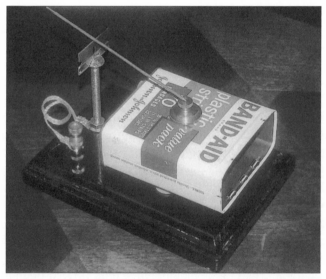

A replica of one of the early telephones I made. This one employed a Band-Aid box, a razor blade, and a pencil lead. I can't imagine why Alexander Graham Bell didn't think of it.

without benefit of the extra appliance, but I was really excited because I had mastered the theory and proved that it worked.

I spent a lot of time trying to improve on this primitive phone. In another of my inspired experiments, I used a metal Band-Aid box, a razor blade, and a pencil lead that I extricated with a pocketknife. I removed the lid from the box and laid the box flat on a table. I taped the razor blade to the bottom of the box so that it rose above the side. This would serve as a fulcrum for the pencil lead.

I balanced the pencil lead on the razor's edge so that one end of it rested at a spot on the side of the box from which I had scraped the paint to make a connection. I cut a tiny notch in the pencil lead to hold it in place. I attached one end of a thin wire to the razor blade and another to a battery. I connected another wire to a second spot on the box from which I had scraped the paint. This wire led to a speaker. A third wire, from the speaker to the battery, completed the circuit.

This was a highly delicate instrument, but I could speak into the box and the pencil lead would pick up the vibrations and pass them on through a varying current to the speaker, from which my voice miraculously emerged. Later, using salvaged parts from a number of devices, many of them military surplus, I would build some sophisticated phones that worked very well over a distance of several hundred feet, a much greater distance than Bell's early experiments. I actually could spy on people with them, primarily my sisters, hearing what they were saying out of my presence, although it rarely provided me any leverage or advantage.

My dad dreamed of having his own house. He had been thinking about it for several years and trying with little luck to save for it. He planned to design and build it himself, and he wanted it to be in the community where he and my mother had grown up and met. He found out that an elderly couple at Poplar Ridge Friends Meeting named Marsh wanted to sell off some of their land, and he negotiated with them to buy five acres on a narrow, unnamed dirt road only a half mile off Hoover Hill Road, a little over a mile and half from Poplar Ridge. The price was $500, and my dad had to borrow the money from his boss, Charles Hayworth, who owned Alma Desk Company.

He planned to build the house himself, and he designed it just as he designed equipment at work. He created a scale model out of wood. My dad was a frugal man with few resources, so the design was simple and practical. The house would be small, just five rooms. It would be constructed of wood on a concrete slab. It would have two wings. At the front would be three rooms: a bedroom for my sisters on one end; a living room in the center, the largest room in the house; and a kitchen and dining room at the other end. The back wing would be smaller, indented on each side from the front wing, giving the house the shape of a shortened T. It would have only two bedrooms, one for my parents and the other for me, separated by a single small bathroom.

The roof would be unusual, flat, with wide overhangs for aesthetic appeal and to provide shade and coolness in summer. It would be covered with several coatings of tar and graveled. It also would have a lip around the edge to retain water. In effect, it would be a shallow pond about two inches deep. My dad's theory was that the water would hold heat in the house in winter and help to cool it in summer, and that would turn out to be so.

Unfortunately, we later would discover, it also would have other unforeseen qualities. In winter, it would freeze, and sometimes the ice would crack with the sound of a rifle shot, usually in the middle of the night, startling us from sleep. In spring and summer, our roof would attract tree frogs by the hundreds, and they would set up such a racket that it was hard to sleep some nights. My dad would tell me to go quiet the frogs, and I'd have to climb a ladder with a flashlight and a broom and wade around swatting them away.

The roof of the model was removable so that my mother and dad could plan where furniture and appliances would go. I can remember taking off that roof and looking down into that model—our own house—and imagining that I already was living there.

Most of the five acres my dad bought were wooded, but about an acre on the northeast corner of the tract once had been a farm field, now

The little flat-roofed green house my dad built when I was nine was the only house my parents ever owned. Both lived out their lives there.

overgrown by sedge, briers, honeysuckle, scrub pines, and cedars. Dad and I spent our Saturday afternoons there for several weekends late in the summer of 1953, hacking away at the wild growth, dragging it into piles, and burning it.

Every chance I got, I'd slip off into the woods to explore, leaving most of the work to my dad. Water for the house would come from a nearby spring. My dad dug it out and put in a big concrete pipe so the water would collect and remain clear and we could pump it to the house. By the time I'd started fourth grade, the field was cleared and my dad had staked out the site where the house would sit, about seventy feet back from the road.

Dad's job required him to work six hours every Saturday, but as soon as he got off he'd head to the country to work on the house. I often went with him but usually was of little help. A friend from Poplar Ridge Meeting, Charles Coltrane, was a carpenter, and he helped my dad square up the foundation, prepare the base, install the necessary pipes for plumbing, and put in the bolts to secure the walls before a concrete truck came to pour the slab.

Building the house was an agonizingly slow process. By the next summer, it still was incomplete. A lot of interior work remained to be done, and my dad was growing impatient. He hated paying rent when he could be putting that money into his own property. So he hired a crew to help him finish the house.

We moved into it late in August 1954, shortly before my tenth birthday. Part of the rush was because my sisters and I would be attending different schools in Trinity, just down the road from Archdale at the original site of Trinity College, which had long before been moved to Durham, where it became Duke University. My parents didn't want us to start the new school year in Archdale only to have to be uprooted a short time later.

We all were excited about moving into the new house, even though it was smaller than the rental house where we were living. The most impressive room was the living room, which my dad had paneled in knotty pine, which was stylish at the time. It was bright and airy, with two big windows, one on each side of the front door. A brown oil circulator sat near the back wall in the center of the room to provide heat for the whole house. My dad had designed and built much of our furniture, using the machines at the plant at night with his bosses' permission and bringing the parts home to assemble.

Walls in the rest of the house were of sheetrock. The ceilings throughout were square panels of a product called Celotex. Linoleum had been glued to the floors in the three front rooms, but my dad didn't have money enough to put linoleum in the back rooms, so we had to make do with bare concrete for a good while. Our prettiest room, by far, was the small bathroom in the back of the house. It was tiled in pink, my mother's favorite color. The broad vertical wood boards on the exterior of the house were painted pale green, my dad's choice, a color it remains to this day. He painted the front door brick red, so it would stand out to passersby.

Symmetry and balance were of great importance to my dad. I guess you could say he was almost fanatical about it. If a gravel flew up from a truck tire and chipped the windshield of his car, he would patch it, then make an identical chip on the parallel spot at the other side of the windshield and patch it, too. Balance. It was a big part of his life in many ways.

That balance could be seen in the design of the house, and even more so in the landscaping that he would create around it. He carefully measured and calibrated every aspect. In the yard we had two of everything. He planted a pecan tree a certain distance from the house at a specific angle, then planted another identically on the other side. He did the same with fruit trees, shade trees, shrubs, and flowers. If one tree eventually died, he didn't just cut down the dead one; he took away the live one on the other side as well, so as not to destroy the symmetry.

Seven weeks after we moved into our new house, we had an unwelcome caller. Her name was Hazel, and she was ferocious. She arrived on the morning of October 15, after cutting a swath of death and devastation through the Caribbean. Hurricane Hazel hit the coast at the North Carolina-South Carolina line at high tide with winds of 140 miles per hour. She headed inland due north, her fury little spent, her eye passing within seventy miles of Randolph County.

We never had experienced such wind or torrential rain. The rain came in such great sheets that we hardly could see through the downpour. The roar of the wind and the rain that battered the house was frightening. I remember looking through the glass of the side door and catching glimpses of ghostly pine trees at the edge of our land almost horizontal in the wind. Limbs flew through the air and tumbled along the ground, and many trees were toppled. We quickly lost electricity, and it would be days before the lines were repaired. Our little house, snug to the ground, stood up well against the storm, and because my dad had cleared the land for a good distance around, we had no worry of damage from falling trees. But we did discover one flaw with his design.

The concrete slab on which the house was built was almost level with the ground, which became so quickly saturated that the rain pooled and the wind forced it beneath the front door. We had to pack towels at the bottom of the door and run back and forth to the kitchen to wring them out to keep the house from flooding. The storm moved fast, and by nightfall, when we had to turn to candles for light, the worst of it was over. Not until the next day could we begin to clean up. The water left a mark about two inches high on our front door, and for many years afterward, my dad would point it out to visitors and tell the story of our adventure with Hurricane Hazel.

We, however, were among the lucky. Hazel killed nineteen people in

North Carolina and seriously injured two hundred more. In some beach communities—Holden, Long, Ocean Isle, New Topsail—nearly every structure was destroyed by the wind and the greatest tidal surge residents of the area ever had seen. Hazel lost little of her strength as she rapidly moved northward over land, wreaking unimaginable damage through the heart of Virginia, and on into Maryland, Pennsylvania, New York, and even into Canada. More than four hundred people died, thousands were injured, and many more thousands left homeless. Hazel became one of the most destructive hurricanes of all time.

No other houses were near ours, only woods. And as excited and proud as I was of our new home, I soon developed homesickness for our old neighborhood in Archdale. I had three good buddies there whom I missed intensely, and although my dad sometimes would take me back to play with them, it never was enough, and never was the same again.

I also felt like an outsider at my new school, although I did know some students there from our church. I don't know whether it was the isolation of our house, the absence of my friends, the newness of my school, or that my interests, which demanded solitude and concentration, were consuming more and more of my imagination, my time, my energy—or if it were something else that I couldn't perceive—but our move to the Randolph County countryside marked a drastic change in my life. I suppressed my impish, outgoing, and once paddle-attracting nature, and began to withdraw into what now seems an unnatural but lengthy period of timidity and exceeding shyness.

Four

While we still were living in Archdale, I came down with a severe malady from which I wondered if I would survive. Measles. My body was consumed with rash and fever. I'd never been so sick. I don't remember how many days I stayed in bed, but I do recall that for the first lengthy period in my life, I had no desire for food of any type—not even my grandmother's oven-browned, meringue-topped banana pudding.

Not long after I recovered, I was hit by a new, more frightening threat. Suddenly, one night, I couldn't breathe. I was gasping desperately for air. Few experiences are more frightening. And the more frightened I became, the harder it became to breathe. Whether the measles had any role in triggering the asthma attacks that would afflict and imperil me for years I don't know, but I never suffered them before the measles.

These attacks actually grew worse when we moved to our own little house in the country. Pollen clearly was a culprit, because the attacks occurred far more frequently in spring, and again in late summer and early fall when ragweed became a real problem. Dust, too, was a factor, because I often suffered attacks after encountering dusty situations.

After my first attack, my parents took me to a doctor in High Point, who prescribed medicine to take when an attack hit. But the medicine offered little relief and made me so sick to my stomach that it worsened the situation. These fearful bouts usually happened at night, and my mother would stay up tending to me.

In our part of the world, we had a sure-fire treatment for situations involving breathing, colds, and many other afflictions. Vick's Vaporub was made in nearby Greensboro. My mother would set a pot of water to boil on our new electric range, scoop a dollop of Vick's from its blue jar, and drop it into the boiling water. She would have me breathe the steam with its searing vapors of menthol, camphor, and eucalyptus. It would momentarily open my breathing passages and set panic at bay.

My parents even tried country folk remedies suggested by family and friends. One my sister Betty told me about was putting rabbit tobacco in my pillow case.

When these attacks occurred, I'd be awake and sick all night from the medicine the doctor prescribed. I wouldn't be able to go to school the next day. My mother had taken a job at a hosiery mill in High Point to help with expenses, and after being up all night with me, she would drop me off at my grandmother's house and go on to work. My grandmother would comfort and baby me and fix whatever I wanted to eat. Soon I would be sleeping while my mother worked her shift at the mill without benefit of rest.

The worst attacks occurred during ragweed season. My dad theorized that the country air harbored more ragweed pollen than would be found in town, and that getting me away from the source would be a partial solution to the problem. When I suffered an attack at night, he would put me into the car, drive me to downtown High Point, and park beside the Tobias store near the depot by the mainline Southern Railway tracks. There we would sit all night watching the trains pass as my breathing eased. In those days lots of passenger trains came and went, and to this day, I still love watching trains. Sometimes my breathing would ease by two or three in the morning, other times not until dawn. My dad would drive me back to Randolph County, get an hour or two of sleep, or sometimes none and all, and go straight back to High Point to put in nine or ten hours at Alma Desk.

I suffered these attacks for more than two years before a doctor in Greensboro finally diagnosed my allergies and concocted a serum to deal with them. I got shots twice weekly for two years, and by age fifteen, asthma no longer would be a problem.

We had been in our house only a year or so when my dad started a new project. He built a small shop a couple of hundred feet behind the house at the edge of the woods. He constructed it from wood he salvaged from discarded shipping crates at work. It was about eight by ten feet, with two small windows and a flue for a little wood heater. He added open bays with angled roofs on each side, where lawn mowers and other equipment could be kept out of the weather. One bay would have sufficed for the equipment we had, but that would have thrown the structure out of balance.

The shop would become my haven much more than my dad's, but it also was a place where we would share a lot of private time together. In years to come, we would make a ritual of cleaning up the shop every Labor Day, while listening on the radio to the Southern 500 stock car race in Darlington, South Carolina. We cleaned as legendary drivers such as Curtis Turner, Fireball Roberts, Fonty Flock, Buck Baker, and Lee Petty, who was from Randolph County, battled for position in unbearable heat and mounting excitement.

My dad wired the shop for electricity and built a worktable and compartments for his tools. Although he had long since given up repairing radios, he had kept all of his testing equipment, and the shop was the natural place for that.

I was fascinated with all things electrical and was constantly prowling through books and magazines for more knowledge on the subject. But my primary interest in it was as a means of communication—telephone and radio.

After the telephones I built from military surplus parts had grown sophisticated enough to be useful, I strung a wire from the shop to the house so that communication would be possible without shouting or going out into the weather. I spent a lot of time in that shop, and most of the messages that came my way from that phone line were routine: supper was ready, it was time to go to services, or I'd better get in the house and get my homework done.

My interest in matters electrical had turned me into an inveterate collector of wire, primarily copper, one of the best conductors of electric current. I searched constantly for unwanted wire and scrounged for it wherever I went. I found it from many sources and in many conditions and gauges. I would spend many hours unwinding yard after yard of delicately fine copper wire not much thicker than thread from abandoned radio speakers. My bedroom and the shop became piled with all sorts of wire, copper and otherwise, insulated and not, a matter of some exasperation and concern for my mother, and, no doubt, my dad, too, though less so.

One Sunday after services, my mother was standing outside the meeting house chatting with a group of women who were discussing the activities in which their children were involved. Sports were mentioned, religious functions, working on cars. My mother remained silent until one woman turned to her and asked about my interests.

"Oh," she said, a little uncertain just how to answer, "Jerry messes with wires."

That would become a standard joke line at our house. My dad loved repeating it, adding emphasis to the word "wires" so that it came out "wa-a-rs."

I was eleven when I began to delve into the work of Guglielmo Marconi, who entranced me as deeply as Alexander Graham Bell did a few years earlier. I came to Marconi exactly as I did to Bell—through a book from the school library. Marconi, the son of an Italian father and a British mother, had created the electronic telegraph, becoming the first person to send messages over radio waves in 1895.

As devoted as I was to wires, Marconi soon replaced Bell as my primary hero, because radio—sending signals, voices, and music through the air to faraway spots—was even more magical than the telephone. The book that I checked out gave a brief description of Marconi's original experiments, and I decided to replicate them.

I checked out more books and studied Marconi's experiments in detail over many months. He had used an electromagnet spark-gap transmitter to send his first messages by Morse code. He had discovered that collapsing a magnetic field generated a high voltage spark that created a broad band of radio frequencies that could carry signals over great distances if harnessed to an antenna.

What I needed to recreate these experiments was some high voltage, and I thought I knew where I might find it. Out in the woods, my grandpa Dorsett still had those old Model T hulks that had attracted so much of my attention when I was younger. He also had outbuildings filled with old tools, parts, and junk.

I went prowling in those buildings one weekend and came across a couple of old ignition boxes for those abandoned Model Ts. They were made of wood, had Tesla coils inside (named for Nikola Tesla, the man who invented the electric motor), and had points on the top that would vibrate and break a current. They were used to step up the voltage from a Model T's six-volt battery so that a spark could be created to fire the engine. I figured that one of these ignition boxes would be just the thing to give me the voltage I needed.

My granddaddy was happy to let me use them, and I brought them back to my dad's shop and set to work. I had a Lionel electric train set that I got for Christmas, and I used the transformer from it to supply the current I needed.

I hooked the transformer to the coils in one of these boxes and found that I could generate several thousand volts, enough to make a heck of a spark. That spark would jump about an inch, and it announced itself not only in sight and sizzle, but in smell as well. Such electrical discharges produce ozone, a blue gas that is highly pungent, as anybody who ever has been in the vicinity of a close lightning strike can testify. My dad's shop came to smell constantly of ozone, and I suspect that I did, too.

This spark-generating business worried my mother, who feared that I might electrocute myself, or set the shop on fire and be immolated in a conflagration of my own creation. My dad wasn't as concerned. He believed that the future lay in electronics. He also knew that with my asthma I never would be able to survive in the dusty furniture industry, which dominated our area, so he was relieved that my interests were leading me toward a career path different from his.

While this spark that I was generating created radio frequency energy, it wasn't going very far because it needed an antenna for range. To solve this problem, I got two thin metal sheets about three feet long on each side, and mounted them several inches apart on a wooden frame. I searched the woods, found a slender, sturdy, dead tree about thirty feet long, and dragged it back to the house. I nailed the frame with the two metal sheets to the top of the tree. I connected sturdy wires to the tops of each of the metal sheets and suspended two metal balls about an inch apart between them. I connected wires to the bottom of each metal sheet that led to the igniter coils. Another wire led from the igniter coils to my Lionel train transformer, which, if theory proved accurate, I could plug into an electrical outlet and start sending radio signals much as Marconi did.

I used a post-hole digger to make a hole deep enough to support the dead tree with my amazing apparatus mounted at the top, and once everything was in place, I was ready for my great experiment to begin. I plugged my transformer into an outlet in the shop and ran back to my pole to find a steady blue spark springing between those two metal balls, creating a loud buzz that was a joy to a boy's heart. I was sending radio signals somewhere. Those two big metal sheets were acting as an antenna, directing my signals out into the air. But how far?

My grandparents, Myrtle and Jeff, had an early, battery-powered, portable radio. This was before transistor radios were readily available. They let me borrow their radio, which was operated by tiny tubes, to test how far my signals were reaching. This was possible because my transmissions were overriding every other radio signal coming into the area, creating nothing but a big buzz on every radio within their range. All I had to do was turn on the radio and walk until the buzz faded away. When I could pick up regular radio signals, I was at the end of my mastery.

I spent many days walking through the woods in every possible direction, listening to the amazing buzz I had created, which would be immensely annoying to any ear other than my own. Fortunately, we were so isolated that few people lived close enough to be affected, and if any of our neighbors were irritated by having their radio reception disrupted, I never heard about it.

The problem with Marconi's spark-gap transmitter was that it only could be used to send messages by Morse code, and I didn't know Morse code. Neither to my knowledge did anybody I knew to whom I might want to send a message. I wanted to transmit voices and music so that people I did know could hear it. What I wanted was my own radio station, and now that I had proven that I could master Marconi's fundamentals, I didn't see why I couldn't create a radio station, too, although many formidable obstacles lay in that path.

As I started eighth grade just as I turned thirteen,the shyness and introversion into which I had begun retreating after our move to the country had grown dramatically deeper. These conditions were enhanced by the solitude required by my radio experiments and the work that lay ahead if I followed my new dream of creating my own radio station.

My shyness prohibited me from associating with many other students. None of them shared my preoccupation with the accomplishments of Guglielmo Marconi, and no doubt would have thought such a person more than a little strange. My shyness and my interests had driven me into a self-imposed and self-fulfilling state of fear. In just six years time, I had made a 180-degree turn from my mischievous, attention-loving, second-grade self into a person who fervently prayed just to blend in and never attract notice.

I lived in dread of being called on in school to answer a question, read a passage, or, heaven forbid, give an oral book report. I literally trembled at the prospect. When it happened, I would be seized by panic. My stomach would seem to flip up into my chest. I would rise uncertainly, stand unsteadily, and struggle for breath. My brow would break into sweat, my face flash beet red. I would grasp desperately for elusive words, stutter and stumble, and finally sink back into my chair, defeated and shamed. Sadistic pleasure being not uncommon to early teens, some of my classmates would laugh or giggle, and make merciless comments after class, worsening my shame and my fear.

At Sunday meeting, I was certain that the minister was going to call on me for a prayer. I kept one in my mind from the time we headed to meeting, going over and over it throughout the service, just in case. It was quick and to the point. "Lord, help the sick. Lord, help the needy. Lord, give us clarity of mind." I should have added freedom from anxiety, but that would have been stretching my chances of getting through it all. I only got to deliver that prayer a time or two, and although I panicked and stuttered and stumbled, it wasn't quite as bad as my embarrassments at school, because nobody laughed—at least not aloud. And afterward, some people even went out of the way to compliment me, reassurance of the kind nature of the faithful.

My situation was not helped any by one of my eighth grade teachers. I'll call her Miss Cranky. She was a stickler for doing everything in a proper and dignified way, perhaps because so many of her country-bred students seemed utterly unaware of accepted standards of conduct.

I'm not talking here about blatant, excessive bad behavior. I'm speaking of things that might not even strike the mind of a reasonable thirteen-year-old as being wrong. If a person happened to be in a hurry, for example, and took two steps at a time going up a stairway, and Miss Cranky saw that person—which was unfortunate enough to happen to me—she summoned that person sternly back to the bottom, lectured him on proper ascension, and instructed him to proceed one step at a time in an acceptable manner under her watchful eye. Every time since that I've been tempted to take two steps at a time on any stairway, I hear her voice in the back of my mind, "Jerry Neal, you get back here."

At one point during the school year, however, I happened to become involved, quite innocently, I might add, in an incident in which there was no question of improper behavior. I simply went into the boys' restroom for the purpose for which it was intended, but arrived at an improvident time. Quite a few boys were in there waiting their turns and goofing around.

Some were older, much bigger, and far more raucous than I. One was a huge, raw-boned country boy who was not known for his civility. I'll call him The Intimidator. I am, after all, a NASCAR racing fan. Lots of boys were scared of The Intimidator and kept their distance.

Several boys were washing their hands at the sinks, and one of the bigger boys splashed some water in the direction of the boy at the next sink, who splashed back, setting off a water fight, with lots of splashing and dodging, hollering and laughing. The Intimidator quickly commandeered one sink, cupped his ham-sized hands, filled them with water, turned toward another boy, who fled for the door, opening it just as The Intimidator let go. A big glob of water sailed right past the shoulder of The Intimidator's intended target into the hallway.

A gasp. A sputter of absolute indignation. A voice.

"I want everybody in there out in this hallway this minute!"

Miss Cranky.

Stunned silence befell the boys' restroom. Panic set in—and not just in me. Miss Cranky was a terror.

"I mean it!" Miss Cranky said in her sternest voice.

We all looked desperately from one to another. The Intimidator took charge. "Anybody tells," he said in a low but threatening voice, "I'll whip your tail."

"If you don't come out, I'm coming in there," Miss Cranky fairly shouted.

One by one, we began slinking out sheepishly.

"Line up against that wall," Miss Cranky commanded.

She was tall and thin with hair so wild that anybody might have thought that she'd just stuck her finger into a wall socket. Her face held a perpetual scowl, and a sour disposition was her normal state. Now she added irateness to that condition. Her dark, print, mid-calf-length dress was drenched from the waist down. Water oozed from her flat-healed teacher shoes into a puddle on the floor.

About a dozen of us had pressed our backs as closely to the wall as we could get them. The Intimidator was attempting to appear the picture of innocence without much success.

Miss Cranky walked along the line, her lip snarled, looking menacingly into every anxious face.

"Who threw that water?" she demanded.

Total silence.

"Nobody saw who threw that water?" Her voice rang with incredulousness.

More silence.

"Okay," she said, "we're going to the principal's office."

This was not good news. T.H. Smith was the principal, and that was his real name. He was called The Bear for the simple reason that he resembled one. A bulky, fullback kind of guy. A strong disciplinarian. Some of the biggest, most belligerent country boys who ever passed through Trinity High had been reduced to whimpering children in his presence.

He had a paddle, and it was no little FLI-BACK pretender like the one my second grade teacher wielded to such little success. This paddle was a hardwood board two feet long with a handle carved at one end. It was an inch thick and eight inches wide. It had holes drilled into it, which were supposed to increase its pain-producing capacity, although I never understood exactly how, and as strong as my curiosity was it never had been stirred to try to find out.

I was scared to death of The Bear. I wanted no personal acquaintance with him—and especially none with his paddle.

Yet, here I was, a total innocent, in a line of hapless boys' restroom renegades, heading straight for The Bear's office, an indignant Miss Cranky marching resolutely beside us like a Marine platoon sergeant, her sodden shoes sloshing with every step. I had seen movies in which soldiers were marched before firing squads, and now I had a far clearer idea of just how those poor guys felt.

I thought I detected a slight flicker of amusement in The Bear's eyes when he saw Miss Cranky's soaked condition and learned the situation, but that could have been just optimistic observation. Whatever the case, he quickly assumed his authoritative stance. He went down the line, asking every boy, "Did you see what happened?" One after another shook his head no. I dreaded the question.

Snitches were not highly regarded, and I didn't relish becoming one, but as in the past, my Quaker upbringing and my promise to my parents to acknowledge wrongdoing and always tell the truth kicked into automatic gear. I couldn't help myself. I nodded yes.

"You come with me," The Bear said, leading me toward the inner office, where, I was well aware, the fearsome paddle supposedly resided. On the way, I caught a glimpse of The Intimidator shooting poisonous darts from his eyes my way, clear warning that if I told on him, whatever punishment The Bear might inflict on him would seem minor compared to what I surely would suffer at The Intimidator's hands.

My eyes were searching frantically for the paddle as The Bear closed his office door behind us. "Okay, Jerry," he said in a kindly manner, "tell me everything you saw."

My heart was racing, my stomach churning, my face reddening, but I blurted it all out. The Bear thanked me for my forthrightness and took me back to rejoin the group.

"I want to see you in here," he said to the glaring Intimidator as I attempted to shrink as small as possible.

The Intimidator was inside much longer than I had been, and he returned with a look on his face that I couldn't translate.

"All right," said The Bear, "I've not been able to determine exactly what happened here, but I want each one of you back here in my office first thing in the morning. I'm going to have a question for all of you, and I expect an answer from each one."

We had no idea what the question might be and a whole night to worry about the answer we should provide.

"Okay, here's the question I want each one of you to answer," he said, when our group reformed the following morning. "Would you rather tear up or build up?"

I sensed a great wave of relief among my fellow renegades, as if they all immediately knew the right response. I could see it in their faces. But I found myself in a bit of a dilemma. I wanted to respond truthfully, but I had found a great deal of pleasure in tearing up some things.

"I'd rather build up, sir," said the first boy from whom The Bear asked a response. Every other boy quickly offered the same answer, but I was still weighing what mine might be.

I was at the end of the line, and when The Bear asked the question of me, there was an unexpected pause. "It's a hard question," I said, hesitating as I attempted to form a truthful answer, "but I think I'd rather build up."

The Bear's face erupted in a big smile.

"Well, you've all come up with exactly the right answer," he said, "and now I'm going to give all of you a chance to build up."

Over the next five days, we would have to devote thirty minutes every day to cleaning the school grounds, building up its image as a neat and sanitary place, snatching up every gum and candy wrapper, every butt tossed aside by illicit smokers.

It's funny how some things take root in your mind, while others don't, but The Bear's question stuck in mine, and I came to realize that I was one of those who indeed wanted to "build up," to create and contribute, and that all of my interests were leading me in that direction.

Five

Throughout my childhood, I was much closer to my mother than to my dad. This may be true of most children. The bond between mother and child was created tight by nature. My dad worked so hard and put in so many hours to make sure that we had the necessities of life that we saw little of him, and when he got home, he usually was exhausted.

My sisters and I spent much more time with our mother. Except for the couple of years when she took the hosiery mill job after we moved into our new house, we usually were with her when we were not in school.

My mother was quieter and more reserved than my dad. The things that meant most to her were close to heart and hand—her faith; her family, both personal and religious; and her community. Whatever problems my sisters and I had, we always turned first to our mother for help and reassurance.

Neither of my parents was very emotional, but my mother seemed to have a calming talent, if there is such a thing. She had a special sense for people who were disturbed, upset, or hurting in some way, and she was drawn to them, as they were to her. Family, friends, and community members came to her for advice, help, and comfort, and she always gave it willingly, no matter her own distress or needs. Some who thought themselves in desperate, even hopeless, situations often would be calmed and gain the strength to go on after talking with my mother. This went on for many years, and it was a phenomenon to witness.

Our community was not restricted to our own Quaker congregation. It included several nearby churches, mostly Methodist and Baptist, and even a few scoffers and nonbelievers. If there was sickness, an accident, a death in the community, my mother was among the first to know and the first to offer her support, no matter their beliefs, their financial situations, or their contrariness.

I couldn't begin to count the number of meals she cooked to take to families in distress, or the number of times she answered calls for help. Yet she always was there to guide and care for us.

Part of this was due just to my mother's loving and giving nature, but the major factor was her faith in God, her deep commitment to Poplar Ridge Friends Meeting, and her devotion to its teachings.

It's not easy to separate the role that religious faith played in our lives because it was so intricately interwoven, so deeply imbedded in our very being. This goes back to my grandmother Myrtle, of course, who set the pattern. Her daughters carried it forth to their families. No part of our lives was unaffected by faith. We said grace at every meal. We prayed before going to sleep every night. My parents frequently read and discussed the Bible. We attended every function at the meeting house. Sunday school, Sunday services, Saturday night prayer meeting, revival services, summertime Bible school, homecoming. Whatever was happening in that white frame country meeting house, we were present unless sickness, or unforeseen circumstance, prevented us.

We were basically a fundamentalist congregation. We believed the Bible to be truth. We accepted that a person must be saved by the grace of God to have eternal life in heaven. I was only six or seven when I felt the need to be saved and answered the call.

Poplar Ridge Friends Meeting was not given to emotional displays. We had a minister, and in many ways our services were not unlike those of other churches in our area. We tended to be sedate and circumspect, and we always had a period for open worship. Sometimes this period was mainly meditative, but members of the congregation could speak whatever they were moved to say and often did. My dad spoke with much more frequency than my mother.

My dad and I usually became a little anxious if Saturday night prayer meeting dragged out, because we were eager to get home to our small-screen, black-and-white TV to watch our favorite show, *Gunsmoke*, with Jim Arness as Marshal Dillon, Dennis Weaver as Chester, and Amanda Blake as Miss Kitty. We were not happy if we missed *Gunsmoke*, or any part of it.

Religion was such a natural and unquestioned part of my childhood that I didn't realize it was forming my future as well. My parents and the people in our congregation truly lived their faith. They were honest, straight-

My family rarely missed any activities that went on at Poplar Ridge Friends Meeting, which my great-grandmother Charity began attending. My great-grandfather Edd helped to build the structure, although he didn't choose to attend its meetings.

forward, hardworking, and generous. They believed in simplicity and in depth of character. They were people of their word, people who could be trusted under any circumstance, people who always sought to do the right thing, people who cared more for others than for themselves. I thought that was the normal way for people to behave, and not until much later in life would I discover how great a role faith played in creating such people and in bringing peace and grace to their lives.

My mother's faith was complete. One illustration of that was the great polio epidemic that struck much of the nation in 1948 and continued into the 1950s. It hit our area hard. A big polio hospital opened in east Greensboro, and there were others around the state. Children were dying, being crippled, forced to live out their lives in massive iron lungs that gave them precious breath. There was immense fear every summer, the season when polio usually hit. Restrictions were put on public functions. Places where children might normally gather, such as public swimming pools, were closed.

My mother prayed fervently that my sisters and I would be spared from polio, and she finally came to be at peace about it. She felt that she had the Lord's assurance that we would not come down with the disease, and we didn't.

After the Salk vaccine was approved in 1955, it was made available through the public schools, first in elementary grades. Students brought home forms that had to be signed by a parent or guardian before the vaccine could be administered. My sister Diane brought home a form, but my mother refused to sign it. Diane got upset. Every other child in her class was getting the vaccine, and she didn't understand why she couldn't.

My dad asked my mother why she wouldn't sign the form.

"If I did, it would be a violation of my faith," she said. "When I was praying so hard that these children wouldn't get polio, I got assurance that they wouldn't. If I sign this, I'll be admitting that I really didn't believe that."

My dad always had an easy and loving way with my mother.

"You know, Bertie," he said, "God expects us to use our brains. He wouldn't ever be disappointed in us for doing the smart thing. Maybe the assurance you got was God's knowledge that this vaccine would be coming. You should think about that."

My mother thought about it and signed the form. I don't bring this up to reflect on her judgment in any way, but to show the depth of her faith and her willingness to accept reason lovingly offered.

I have wished that I'd had my mother's total faith, but my nature was to question, due perhaps to the influence of science, which also became so much a part of my life in childhood. I questioned most things, and at some points in my life, I would come to question the religion of my parents and of my childhood. But after hard thought and struggle, I determined that the path my parents set for me was the right one. I have remained a faithful and active member of Poplar Ridge Friends Meeting. I pray every day.

One of my favorite prayers comes from Mark, Chapter Nine, in which a man brings his demented son to Jesus, hoping to have him healed. Jesus tells him, "If thou canst believe, all things *are* possible to him that believeth."

In tears, the man cries out, "Lord, I believe; help thou mine unbelief."

I think that's the most honest prayer that can be prayed. I've prayed it many times.

At fourteen, as I was starting ninth grade, science dominated my interests and my hours much more than religion. Once I had gone as far as I could with Marconi's original experiments with the electromagnet spark-gap transmitter, I turned my attentions to my new dream of creating my own radio station.

It probably would be fair to say that this became an obsession, so much so that it no doubt could claim some credit for my flunking algebra in the ninth grade, much to my parents' consternation. Still they were supportive of my wild dreams and excesses, just as they always had been.

The signal generator that my dad got for his radio repair course became the focus of my new effort. It could create a signal at any frequency on the AM broadcast band, but it was weak and useful for very little other than testing. I got the idea that I might be able to go into that signal generator, seize a particular frequency, and if I could somehow modulate it to carry voice and sound, amplify it enough, and connect it to a substantial antenna, I could send that signal out to the world. I would have my own radio station.

I had read about a book called *White's Radio Log*, which listed the frequencies of every radio station in the country. I asked my parents to buy it for me, and they did. I used it to search out the frequencies of every AM radio station in our area. I wanted to find a clear, open channel that I could claim as my own. That turned out to be 1200 kilohertz on the radio dial, a frequency now claimed by WSJS talk radio in Winston-Salem, on which I have appeared as a talk-show guest. But once, that frequency was briefly mine, even if the Federal Communications Commission was unaware of it.

The signal generator had a one-tube oscillator, which created a signal that could be tuned to a particular frequency, but it had no amplifier, no way to power that signal enough to send it out very far. From my reading, I discovered that without an amplifier I was going to need a really big antenna to get any range at all.

This led me into an in-depth study of antennas and how they worked, and how I might be able to create one. I decided that it wouldn't be all that big a problem. I already had the main thing that I needed—the precious wire I had been collecting. I had several thousand feet of twenty-two gauge copper wire that I had salvaged, and that would do just fine.

I searched the woods for another tall slender dead tree that I could use as a pole. I found one about twenty-five feet long after the limbs were trimmed away and dragged it through a small valley in a pasture adjoining our land that was owned by Uncle Howard, my dad's brother. I struggled to get it to the top of a hill at the other side of the valley. Once there, I attached a glass insulator and hooked one end of a roll of wire to it. After I had erected the pole, I unrolled my reel of wire all the way back across that valley pasture and up the opposite hillside to a persimmon tree about forty feet tall. I climbed as high as I could get in that tree, nailed another insulator to it, brought my wire through it, and pulled it tight. That thin copper strand stretched for nearly five hundred feet, glinting promisingly in the sunlight.

The persimmon tree was a couple of hundred feet from the shop, and I had to run the wire through some other trees to get it into one of the shop windows so that I could hook it into the signal generator.

I felt certain that this antenna would work, but I still was a long way from having a radio station. I had to figure out how to modulate a signal so that I could send music and voice over that antenna.

I had a portable record player on which I could stack eight or ten forty-five-rpm records so that they would play in automatic succession. I tore into the record player to study its workings and try to figure out how I could harness it to my purposes. I ended up using a wire to connect the amplifier to the signal generator. This caused the amplifier to become a modulator, making it possible to send the music from my record player through the signal generator to the antenna and out into the air.

By this point, I had my own portable radio, my first one, a six-transistor Motorola. I fired up the signal generator and took my radio outside to see if I actually was broadcasting. I was, but it was splatter, a signal over a wide band of frequencies, not a lot different from what I was accomplishing with my electromagnet spark-gap transmitter. Splatter comes from over-modulation, which creates side bands that make it impossible to tune in on a radio. The amplifier on the record player was driving the signal generator too hard, creating the splatter.

It took a lot of work to get the right balance and fidelity so that I actually could transmit a signal and tune it in on my radio, but I finally accomplished it. I walked through the woods a mile or more listening on my radio as my record player spewed out Conway Twitty, Brenda Lee, and the Everly Brothers. It was a thrill unlike any I'd ever experienced.

Later, I got my dad to drive me around the country roads to see how far my signal was reaching. I knew that every antenna had a pattern. An antenna may dispatch signals much farther in one direction than in others. I wanted to know the pattern of mine, and I took notes for my careful records. We went in every direction from the house that we could take on those country roads until my signal faded away, and I made a map of my broadcast pattern. I was happy to discover that my signal was reaching out several miles.

Having your own radio station gives you a sense of power—especially if you can talk on it. That was my next step. I got a microphone and put a switch at the input of the record player's amplifier. This allowed me to run a wire to a microphone so that I could alternate between the record player and the mike.

Now I could speak on the air, say whatever I wanted, and people who tuned in could hear me for several miles around. I didn't say a lot. I still was in the depths of my shy and inward period, but I did give some consideration to the possibilities. It didn't fail to cross my mind, for example, that my radio presence might allow me to gain the attention of attractive young ladies to whom I was drawn but too shy to approach. I could dedicate songs to them. "Here's Conway Twitty, and this one's going out to…"

Unfortunately, my musical repertoire was somewhat limited. I didn't have all that many forty-fives, and the clear failure of my programming to serve as an allure to desirable young ladies convinced me that I probably should have had a lot more Elvis tunes. But I did begin spreading the word at school that I would be on air for an hour or so, say, starting at 5 p.m., and some people told me that they listened. A few actually even asked me to dedicate songs to their sweethearts, or would-be sweethearts.

It was about this time that my dad noticed a brief article in the *High Point Enterprise*. Local amateur radio operators were going to offer a free, ten-week course in Morse code at the YMCA. The course could lead to an amateur radio license. It would meet one night a week. My dad suggested that we take it together, and I jumped at the opportunity.

Amateur radio operators are called hams. The term actually began as a pejorative during the days of telegraphy. Slower and less accurate telegraph key operators were referred to as hams, for reasons unknown. After Marconi introduced wireless telegraphy, amateurs were quick to take it up, and they often produced signals so strong that they blocked out all others, frequently interfering with communication with ships at sea. Legitimate telegraphers referred to them as those blankety-blank "hams," causing the amateurs to take up the term with pride.

After the Federal Communications Commission was created in 1934, it recognized the value of amateur radio as an emergency, back-up communications system and granted licenses to hams, giving them legitimacy.

My dad and I were about halfway through the course, and I was enjoying it immensely, when my mother became seriously ill, and we had to drop out. My mother's illness was difficult to diagnose. Weeks passed before it was traced to her thyroid and she underwent successful surgery at

Baptist Hospital in Winston-Salem.

My dad realized my disappointment at having to drop out of the class and bought me some records that offered instructions in Morse code. I had my own telegraph key, and I spent many hours listening to my records and practicing until I had mastered Morse code almost well enough to have had a future as a wireless operator—if I had been living in 1912.

My dad had no doubt that I would go on to get my ham license. While I was practicing with those records, he ordered a kit so that I could build my first amateur radio. It was a T-50, a high frequency rig, from 1.8 to thirty megahertz, restricted to code only, no voice. But I was awfully excited to get it, assemble it, and put it to use.

Four classes of amateur radio licenses were available then: novice, technician, general, and advanced. You had to be able to send and receive at least five words per minute by Morse code to get a novice license. For a technician license, you had to pass a much more advanced written test. General and advanced licenses required greater transmission skills with Morse code.

After I became confident in my abilities at Morse code and had read everything that I could get my hands on about ham radio, I called one of the instructors of the YMCA course, and he offered to give me the licensing tests for the novice and technician licenses. I passed both and got both licenses. I was awarded the call sign WA4CWB. I wish that I still had it, but during a lapse in my ham activities brought on by life and work, I allowed it to expire. I later had to get a new license and a new call sign: KC4CQR.

From that point on, gifts from my parents for Christmas and birthdays always had to do with my amateur radio needs and desires. For Christmas, they bought me a Lafayette six-meter band transceiver so that I could talk on the air with other hams. This radio could be operated as a base station or as a mobile unit. Later, after I got my driver's license, I took it with me when my dad let me use the car. A couple of other guys at Trinity High got into amateur radio and also had mobile units. We would cruise the drive-in restaurants and the skating rinks in High Point and Thomasville talking back and forth on the radio, frequently about carloads of girls that we hoped might be desirous of our attentions. But for whatever reasons, ham radio didn't seem to hold the appeal for them that it did for us.

My dad found out that an engineer at the radio station in Asheboro had a Long John amateur radio antenna for sale. It sort of resembled a TV antenna. It was about fifteen feet long and had to be mounted in a horizontal position. We went to see it, and my dad bought it. We erected it atop a thirty-five-foot iron pipe at the back of the house, next to the heating oil tank, and ran the lines into my bedroom.

This antenna allowed me to talk to people in a thirty- to fifty-mile range, but when the ionization in the atmosphere was right, usually in summer, the band would open up, and I could converse with people 1,500 miles away. I frequently talked to ham operators in such exotic spots as Cuba, Florida, Washington, and New York.

Unfortunately, that impressive antenna also proved to be a tempting target. A bad thunderstorm approached one summer night after my dad had gone to bed. I was on my radio as usual, and he got up to warn me that I'd better shut it down and disconnect all the equipment. He went back to bed, but I went into the living room so that I could look out and see the lightning. Electrical storms always fascinated me.

This one was spectacular indeed. Lightning came in such a fury of close-by strikes that my dad got up again to see what was going on. He opened the bedroom door, and I turned to see him standing there in his underwear peering out apprehensively.

Just at that moment the lightning hit again, this time with an explosive blast—a direct strike on my Long John antenna. It jumped off the antenna onto the kerosene tank, leaving a big burned spot in the green paint, but amazingly resulting in no fire. Some of the charge surged through our electrical system. The plastic control knobs on my mother's electric range suddenly exploded, spreading shrapnel in every direction.

I had just turned to look at my dad when the lightning hit, and I'll never forget the expression on his face. He leapt into the air in a way I'd never seen a person jump before. He looked as if he were about to attempt a backward somersault. My mother jumped from bed to find my dad startled but all right, her range and hot water heater in ruins, and her son convulsing in the living room.

At first, she thought that maybe the lightning had scrambled the wiring in my brain, but I was convulsed with laughter that I couldn't control. The expression on my dad's face and his Olympic-gymnastics-quality leap in his underwear was the funniest sight I'd ever seen. Although my dad didn't quite see the humor in the situation at the time, he later claimed it as one of his favorite stories and told it frequently.

This incident did lead us to have a conference about my Long John antenna after all the damage was assessed. We concluded that perhaps we had been a little over aggressive in tempting fate, and considerably reduced its elevation.

Forty-six years have passed since I got my ham radio license, and I have kept my love of the hobby. It has given me much pleasure over the years and allowed me to meet many fascinating people whom I never would have been able to know otherwise. Lengthy periods have passed when I was far too busy to indulge the hobby, but I always have come back to it and I still enjoy everything about it.

In May 2005, on a whim, I suddenly left work and drove alone for eleven hours to Dayton, Ohio, to attend the big "Hamvention," which is held there every year and attracts about thirty thousand amateur radio operators. I had attended it several times before, but not in recent years. I had a wonderful time. I browsed through all the displays at the show, seeing all of the items I had read about in magazines and dreamed of possessing when I was fifteen and sixteen, although I couldn't afford them.

When high school finally delivered me to college, a job, a family of my own, I left behind my first little ham radio, the T-50 that my dad ordered for me. Not until years later did I begin to wonder what had become of it. By then nobody remembered. I regretted letting that little radio get away from me and often wished that I still had it.

At the Hamvention, I happened onto a dealer who had a T-50 exactly like mine. Not many were made, so they're fairly rare now. I bought it as a keepsake, a reminder of my boyhood experiences with radio. I won't let this one get away.

Six

As unlikely as it might once have seemed, high school would turn out to be a happy time for me.

My sophomore year brought me an especially revealing and beneficial experience. I can't recall now how I happened to end up in a public speaking class, which was anathema to my withdrawn and shy nature, other than that it would fulfill one of my English requirements for graduation, but somehow I did. And it had a drastic effect on me.

One of the methods used by the teacher in this class was to write different topics on little slips of paper, fold them, and put them into a bowl. Then each student would come forward in turn, pick a slip of paper, read off the topic, and give a brief, spontaneous speech on that subject. I panicked at the prospect. But I noticed that quite a few others did, too.

Some simply were unable to say a word beyond reading the topic. When my turn came, I'm sure that I already must have begun turning my normal anxious shade of crimson, sweat beading on my forehead, as I reached into the bowl. I pulled out a slip, opened it, and read the topic aloud. I wish that I could remember what it was, but, alas, I can't. I do remember standing there, pondering the possibilities, including, no doubt, fleeing, but instead suddenly realizing that there were a few things I could say on this matter.

I recall doing fairly well, but in retrospect I just may have muttered a few quick thoughts and sat down, the way I did on the rare occasions when I got called upon for a prayer in meeting. The important thing, though, was that I felt that I did okay. For the first time, I recognized that lots of other people were as scared of public speaking as I was, but, more importantly, I realized that I actually could think on my feet, that I didn't have to worry something to death beforehand. I could get up and say what came to my mind—and amazingly, people would accept it, respond to it, and sometimes even compliment me on it. I can't describe the level of confidence that would instill in me over time.

Looking back at this experience is a little strange because public speaking is such a big part of my life now. I often speak to audiences of varying sizes, sometimes several times a week. I speak to engineers, executives, politicians, news people, and others much smarter than I. And not only does it seem completely natural, but I enjoy it.

There is something deeply satisfying in connecting with an audience as if it were an individual. I love seeing and hearing people respond, sensing that they are with me and eager for the next thing I have to say, even when I don't know at the moment what it's going to be. Ironically, the thing that I once most feared about being called on to speak—that people might laugh—became what I deeply wanted. Hearing people laugh because you want them to is one of life's great experiences, no matter if it's one person or a thousand.

One of the aspects of speaking that I like most is the period for questions and answers at the end. That's when you really can connect. Sometimes the question-and-answer sessions go on longer than my talks, and the best way to have one end is with you and the audience feeling that you have formed a personal bond and regretting that the conversation has to stop.

I'm not sure that this speech class was solely responsible for bringing me out of my long, awkward, and timid period. My radio station experience no doubt played a part, too. You can't just sit saying nothing on the radio, whether anybody's listening or not. But the combination couldn't have come at a better time. High school offers too many opportunities for fun to go through it silent and withdrawn.

If I were going to gain any attention or popularity in high school, I knew that it was not going to be through sports. I enjoyed baseball and was not bad at it. We had a field not far from our house where country boys gathered to play on summer weekends and often drew an audience. But at Trinity High, football and basketball were the primary sports.

Although I was tall enough for basketball, I was worse than awkward at it. I was utterly inept and far beyond ungraceful. Attempting to go out for the team only would have brought derision from fans, misery for the coach and other players, and humiliation for me.

I actually considered going out for junior varsity football, however. I was big enough, and I liked the game. But my dad reminded me of an acquaintance who'd gotten his nose broken playing football. That was something with which I definitely could identify.

Only a year or two after we moved into our new house, the creek down the road froze solid one winter, and I attempted to demonstrate my skills at Olympic figure skating there, minus skates. Medals aren't offered for the kind of performance I put on—falling flat on my face and busting my nose. I well knew how painful a broken nose could be, not to mention how much blood it could cost you, and I didn't want to risk another one.

Instead, I became a great supporter of the Trinity Bulldogs football team. If I missed a Friday night football game during high school, I don't remember it. It seemed that the entire community turned out for the games, and there was great excitement. The lights were bright. Hot dogs and popcorn never were better. The band marched and played, stirring pride and stimulating the crowd. Cheerleaders leapt and swirled in skirts that exposed especially appealing aspects of their personalities. And it didn't hurt that we had a good team.

I loved everything about Trinity High football games, and I wanted to be as close to the field as I could get, right in the middle of all the action. I also discovered that this wasn't a bad place to meet girls, even if you weren't a star quarterback and had gotten your broken nose from athletic attempts that you wouldn't be inclined to brag about.

Farming still was a major part of life in Randolph County when I was in high school. Even people who worked at jobs in town still had big vegetable gardens, perhaps kept a few pigs and chickens. Some raised cattle along with the corn and hay necessary to feed them.

Trinity High had a Future Farmers of America program along with courses that were coordinated with it. I signed up for FFA in my sophomore year and would continue in it throughout high school, even though I had no more intention of becoming a farmer, as my grandfathers had been, than I did of working in a furniture factory, as my dad did.

I was not, however, without some farming experience. I labored in our own garden and plowed gardens for neighbors. I also worked in late summer for a family who raised tobacco, North Carolina's biggest producer of agricultural cash, although a crop not as common in Randolph as it was in other Piedmont counties. I helped them at harvest time, gathering the huge, sticky leaves from the bottom of the six-foot plants—a process called priming—and piling them onto a sled to be taken to the barn where they were tied on sticks and hung to be cured to a golden color by wood fires. It was hot, miserable, exhausting work, but it got me spending money all through high school.

FFA members had a project every year, and mine for my first year was to raise a steer for market. Our teacher was named Davis, and I'm not sure I ever knew his first name. Everybody called him Mr. Davis. He was an interesting guy who had been at Trinity High forever. He had a big pickup truck in which we FFA students rode on field trips sitting in the open bed, sometimes so raucously and recklessly that Mr. Davis would have to stop the truck to reprimand us. I don't recall any of us thinking that this could have been dangerous.

Mr. Davis also had sideboards that he could put on the bed of the truck so that he could haul livestock: pigs, cows, sheep, and goats. This made me watch where I sat on our field trips to dehorn calves, castrate sheep, and attach milking machines to the proper apparatuses at local dairy farms.

Early in the fall of my sophomore year, Mr. Davis put the sideboards on the truck bed and drove me to a farm in the mountains of Virginia to pick up the castrated Angus calf that I was to raise. We got it cheap. It had been rejected by other buyers, possibly because it had a pot belly and looked a little funny. Its genetic lines were sound, however, and as we were leading it up a ramp onto the back of the truck, Mr. Davis said, "I believe this steer can be a champion." I wasn't sure whether he was saying it to make me, or the steer, feel better about our prospects.

My dad and I had put up a shelter for the steer not far from the house. We built it of creosoted posts and roofing tin. We filled it with straw so the steer would have a comfortable place to rest. Around it we had created a lot fifty feet by thirty feet with a barbed wire fence so the steer could move

The Angus steer I raised as a Future Farmers of America project, was named grand champion at a stock show in High Point.

around without wandering away. We didn't want him moving around a lot, because my primary purpose was to increase his weight at an extraordinary pace.

I did this by serving the steer huge amounts of a special feed made of corn, wheat, molasses, shucks, cobs, and heaven only knows what else. The steer loved it. The only times I saw him moving fast were when I came toward him with another sack of this stuff. It smelled so good that my childhood fondness for molasses enticed me to bite into a handful of it one day. One of the great lessons that I truly can say I learned from my FFA experience is that aroma doesn't always equal taste.

When I got my steer, it weighed about 250 pounds. As the end of my sophomore year neared it was about one thousand. Believe me, that kind of growth entails a lot of toting of fifty-pound sacks of feed, and nearly as much cleaning up afterwards.

My test came at the Fat Stock Show in High Point that spring. My steer was named grand champion. It brought $1,000 at the sale. The FFA program had put up the money to buy the steer and the feed, and it had first dibs on the cash, but I got all that was left after the costs were deducted. That came to more than $200, big money for a fifteen-year-old at that time.

I should have felt excited and proud, and I tried to pretend that I did. But I had spent a lot of time with that steer. I had fed it, cleaned up after it, cared for it, checked on it regularly, talked to it, petted it. I had become close to it, and I had to say good-bye and watch it being led away to slaughter. The steer couldn't know what was awaiting it, or that I was complicit in its fate, but I surely did. I knew that I never could do anything like that again.

Getting a driver's license was a big thing for boys in our part of the world, and nobody wanted to wait a day past his sixteenth birthday to do it. More than anything else, a driver's license marked the end of childhood. Every boy I knew couldn't wait for that day to come. I got mine just as my sophomore year began. My dad had taught me to drive on our isolated country roads, and I took to it immediately. After all, I'd had plenty of early experience in those old junked Model Ts behind my grandparents' house. I loved the mechanics of driving, but that wasn't my primary motivation for getting my license. I wanted the mobility and freedom that it offered, among other possibilities. I had no trouble with the tests.

At that time, school buses in Randolph County were driven by students. And almost every student, except those who had cars of their own—and they were few—rode the buses. I had to spend more than an hour each day riding back and forth to school on the bus, and I figured that I'd rather be driving it than just sitting there gazing out the window. I signed up for the bus driving program at the beginning of my junior year, took the tests, passed them, and underwent a stringent training program.

Lots of other boys wanted to be bus drivers, too, and no slots were open when I finished my training. I was put on a waiting list.

Strict rules applied to bus drivers. If you got a ticket or had a mishap of any kind, no matter how minor, your bus driving days were over. A couple of months after I went on the waiting list, one of the drivers got a ticket, and I was assigned to his bus. I made a vow that I would be especially watchful and never get a ticket. My route took about an hour each way every day, and every evening I parked the big yellow bus in the yard beside our house.

I loved driving the school bus, partly because I just loved driving, and partly because I loved controlling such a big vehicle that not everybody could easily handle.

I was a safe and responsible driver from the beginning. My dad had drilled that into me. The only problem I ever had on the bus was with rowdy students. I had a simple solution for that. I pulled off the road, stopped, and announced that we wouldn't continue until everybody settled down. Peer pressure soon quieted the miscreants.

An extra benefit from driving a bus was that I got paid. I think it was about twenty dollars a week for ten hours of easy and mostly enjoyable work. Guys I knew who had part-time jobs bagging groceries, pumping gas, and hopping curb at drive-in restaurants had to work a lot longer and harder for that kind of money.

Driving a school bus even would bring me public recognition. At the end of my senior year, I would be named School Bus Driver of the Year, my only high school honor.

Although I had abandoned my little self-made radio station with its greatly restricted reach after I got into ham radio, I hadn't given up my dream of becoming a commercial radio star. I listened regularly to a disc jockey named Jesse Hill on High Point radio station WHPE, an AM station broadcasting from sunrise until sunset. Jesse was a country boy, too, maybe five years older than I. He lived near Thomasville, just a few miles from where I lived. I figured if he could get on the radio, I might be able to as well.

It seemed unlikely that Jesse would be willing to step aside to allow an unproven talent such as myself take his job, but I discovered that radio stations would sell air time to almost anybody under certain conditions.

I figured that if I could scrape together enough money to buy half an hour of time to start the Jerry Neal Show, maybe in an after-school spot, that listeners would be overwhelmed by it immediately, and that advertisers would come in such a rush that I'd have to pick among them to determine those who would be allowed to finance my quick rise to fame and fortune.

I called WHPE to find out the rates and what I would need to do to get my show on the air. I discovered that I would need to put together a demo tape to prove that my show would meet the station's standards.

What I needed for that was a reel-to-reel tape recorder, which I didn't have. But I did know a couple of guys who had them, Tommy Hill and Jimmy Johnson. One of them—I'm not sure which, but I think it was Tommy—loaned me his recorder to put together my show. I worked at it a long time. I taped and retaped. I got friends at school to give me requests and dedications for songs, and I played them on my record player and announced them in mellifluous voice just the way Jesse Hill did. I was really proud of my show when I finished. Clearly, it was just a matter of time until I became a radio star.

WHPE's transmitter and studio were in an isolated spot in Randolph

County, not far from High Point, and I drove my daddy's '55 green-and-white Chevy Bel-Air there to offer up my tape. The person I talked to was very nice. He invited me in to look at the studio, where, no doubt, I soon would be producing my own show. He promised that he would get the tape into the right hands and that I would be hearing from somebody about it.

Within a few days, I indeed got a call. The tape I had submitted, I was told, was unusable. The person explained that my tape had two tracks and that radio stations used single-track players and recorders. My tape, which I had borrowed from my friend, had previous material on both tracks. I had taped over the material on one of those tracks, but the previous material remained on the other.

When the tape was played at the radio station, whoever was listening heard my show on one track and the previously taped material playing backward on the other, all jumbled into incomprehensible garble.

I wasn't just embarrassed at this news. I was humiliated. I had failed because of a technical oversight. And mastering the technology was what I prided myself on. I would be so long overcoming this shame that it would effectively end my dreams of radio fame.

But that didn't cause me to give up the idea of working in radio, which had been a part of my being for nearly as long as I could remember.

I had a first cousin, Douglas Hyatt, whose sight was so severely impaired that he attended the state school for the blind, where he met a fellow student who later became a broadcast engineer, the person who attends the equipment that keeps a radio station on the air. Doug was interested in radio, too. His friend got a job at WLXN, the AM station in nearby Lexington, the county seat of Davidson County. It was only about fifteen miles away, and I would drive Doug over there to visit his friend.

I loved hanging out in the transmitter room seeing those huge amplifier tubes glowing red hot, and I loved talking with my cousin and his friend about radio technology. My cousin would go on to take broadcast engineering classes himself and land a job at a radio station in Cheraw, South Carolina. Hanging out with him and his friend in the transmitter room convinced me that I wanted to be a broadcast engineer, too. I might not become a radio star, but I could assure that the stars continued to shine.

Word about my radio activities and expertise in electronics spread throughout Trinity High, bringing me a degree of recognition. I was considered to be something of a guru when it came to matters electrical. I could troubleshoot almost any problem and had the gear to do it. That gave me far more appeal than I ever could have hoped to obtain from my looks, my charm, or my athletic or academic abilities.

If the drama club wanted complicated lighting for a school play, I was the one they turned to for the wiring and switches and the instruction in their uses. If a speaker system needed to be set up and adjusted, I got the call.

Many of my fellow students, not to mention teachers, seemed greatly impressed by, and even a little in awe of, my abilities. They were immensely grateful for my willingness to serve without fee. My dad had long told me that it was far better to be a problem solver than a problem creator, and that a problem solver always would be popular and in demand. The reaction that my electrical abilities and my willingness to serve brought me in high school forever convinced me of his wisdom.

I think our principal, The Bear, also was impressed that his lesson in "building up" actually had been taken to heart by at least one of the boys' restroom renegades.

Every fall, the senior class at Trinity High got to take a three-day bus trip to Washington to soak up our national heritage by touring the Capitol building, the White House, the U.S. Mint, the FBI, and the monuments. That, at least, was the ostensible purpose of the trip. Actually, it was a three-day blast in which none of the boys, and probably not many of the girls, got any sleep at all. It clearly was the highlight of our high school experience. I'm convinced that some students who might otherwise have dropped out of school stayed in just to make the senior class trip.

Many Trinity High seniors never had been out of North Carolina or in a city larger than Greensboro, so the trip was more than an enlightening experience. It wreathed all of us in an aura of sophistication that we never could have achieved in Randolph County.

Its allure was even greater than that, however. It also offered the possibility of romance. I'd had some dates in high school, but nothing serious. I'd never had a girlfriend. Overcoming my shyness hadn't yet led me that far.

But I did have my eye on a certain cheerleader. She was short and slim and far more outgoing than I was. Her name was Judy Lamar. She lived in Trinity. Her dad was an upholsterer in a furniture factory, and her mother was a secretary at the biggest hardware store in High Point. We sat near each other in a couple of classes and had talked frequently, but I never had been able to build up the nerve to ask her out.

One of the scheduled activities of our trip was a two-hour moonlight cruise on the Potomac River. I expected to be enjoying it along the rail with the other dateless guys, but as we stood on the dock waiting to board the boat, Judy walked up to me with a little grin and said, "You're with me, right?"

I couldn't believe my ears.

"Uh," I said. "Yeah, now that you mention it, I am."

From that night on, we were going steady.

•　　　•　　　•

Walter and Ruby Ward were friends of my parents and members of Poplar Ridge Friends Meeting. They ran a grocery on Archdale Road, and we often shopped there. They had a son, Kenneth, who was about ten years older than I. He was married and still a member at Poplar Ridge. I looked up to him because he was in the electronics business as a salesman. My dad had told Kenneth about all of my radio activities and other interests, and Kenneth and I sometimes talked about these matters after services.

In the fall of my senior year, Kenneth asked me what I planned to do when I got out of high school. I told him that I wanted to become a broadcast engineer at a radio station.

"You don't want to do that," he said. "Those guys don't make any money. You'll never be happy at that."

Beyond that, he pointed out, it was pretty mundane work. What I needed, he said, was to get a wider background that would offer more possibilities. That meant a degree in electronic engineering.

I wasn't sure that I could do that. My grades were okay, but I had devoted too much energy to my radio activities and to having a good time to be an academic standout. I thought that I was far too weak in math to qualify for engineering school. After all, I had flunked algebra and never had really applied myself to any of my math courses, unaware of how important they would be to my future.

I was well aware, however, that my parents expected me to go to college. They knew that my interests demanded more education than I could get in high school. That surely was the reason my mother had pressed me so hard over the years to do my homework and keep up my grades. When I entered tenth grade, she had taken a job in the cafeteria at Trindale Elementary School to save money to pay for my future education. I would have felt that I was letting my parents down if I didn't go to college.

Yet, I worried that I wouldn't be qualified and would fail to be accepted. I expressed my concerns to Kenneth one Sunday, and he told me that there were alternatives to four-year engineering programs. He already had talked about this with my dad.

Kenneth knew of two schools in the South that offered associate degrees in engineering. One was Southern Technical Institute in Atlanta, affiliated with Georgia Tech, and the other was Gaston Technical Institute in Gastonia, a cotton mill town west of Charlotte, not far from the South Carolina line. Gaston Tech was affiliated with the engineering school at N.C. State University, and Kenneth had gone there himself. He felt certain that I would be accepted, and he offered to take my dad and me to tour the place.

We went on a Saturday just before Christmas. Gaston Tech occupied an old brick textile plant in the center of town, and I was immensely impressed

My senior year photo for the Trinity High annual. I was named best school bus driver at graduation, but I was headed off to learn about electronic engineering.

by its laboratories, its electronic equipment, and the people I met there.

On the way home, my dad, Kenneth, and I discussed the advantages that the school offered. It wasn't far from home, less than a two-hour drive. The tuition was a lot lower than at a four-year college, and I knew that would be easier on my parents. It was a small place with a good staff, Kenneth pointed out, and all of the students got a lot of individual attention. Even better, Kenneth said, big technology companies recruited at Gaston Tech, and students often got job offers before they graduated, and at far higher salaries than a radio station engineer might make.

I got excited about the possibility of becoming a student there and put in an application. A few months later, I got a letter saying that I had been accepted.

By the end of our senior year, Judy and I were talking about marriage, but we recognized that would have to wait until we were better prepared to make a living for ourselves. I had told her all about Gaston Tech, and she was pleased that it would make it possible for me to follow my electronic dreams, although my attendance there wouldn't allow us to see as much of each other over the next couple of years. She had been accepted at High Point College, planned to live at home while studying there, and hoped to become a teacher.

Graduation was early in June, and it turned out to be a hot, stuffy, and boring affair in Trinity High's auditorium. While other students were lauded for academic achievements and scholarships won, I was recognized only as best school bus driver, hardly an auspicious indicator of future success, unless you planned to work for Greyhound.

I was happy to put high school behind me and was looking forward to a summer of fun before I had to knuckle down to the hard challenges that lay ahead. Judy's parents had a place at Carolina Beach, and after graduation, we went there with another couple and her mother to celebrate. The beach would offer a simile for that summer, which seemed to slip away as fast as a receding wave. Suddenly it was September, and I was faced with my future.

Part II

Building Blocks

Seven

On a Sunday afternoon at the beginning of September 1962, my dad and I loaded the Chevy with most of my clothes and ham radio equipment—with the exception of my Long John antenna, which was hardly mobile—and headed for Gastonia and my new life.

I'm not sure what the total enrollment was at Gaston Tech, perhaps 150-200 students, all male. Some lived in Gastonia or nearby towns and commuted to class. Others who lived farther away found lodging in private dwellings in town or the school's single dormitory, which was a big, two-story white house at 210 Dalton Street, across from the old mill that housed the classrooms and laboratories. It provided lodging for sixteen or eighteen students overseen by a matronly dorm mother who patiently maintained order. I was one of the lucky students chosen to live in the dorm.

My dad helped me carry in all of my stuff and get situated. Then we bade one another farewell. As I watched him climb into the car and drive off toward home, I was overwhelmed by a feeling of loneliness and uncertainty.

My roommate seemed to sense this. His name was Stanley Brothers, and he was from Winston-Salem. He was a second-year student, loved Gaston Tech, and took on the role of older brother. He knew all the ropes, as well as all of the instructors, and was a great font of information. He tried to make me feel at home, told me exactly what to expect when classes began on Monday, introduced me to other students, and assured me that I really would like the place. I would learn much and make a lot of friends there, he said.

He was right about all of that, of course, although it would take time for me to realize it. What I hadn't expected, and what he could do little to relieve at the moment, was the overwhelming homesickness that immediately engulfed me.

Perhaps I should have expected that. After all, I'd never been away from home for more than a week, which was when I attended a youth camp, and I was set in my place, my comforts, and my activities. To make matters worse, I also was in the clutches of first love, and the thought that I wouldn't be able to see Judy frequently, or talk to her every day, was almost unbearable.

Stanley did offer me a modicum of comfort for this distress. He had a car, and on most weekends, he went home to Winston-Salem. I was welcome to ride with him, and I never turned down an opportunity. My parents would drive to Winston-Salem to pick me up on Friday night and take me back on Sunday afternoon.

On a couple of weekends when Stanley didn't go home, I hitchhiked back to Randolph County, much to the consternation of my own family, as well as Judy's. They thought that hitchhiking was a certain recipe for disaster and feared that I would become a victim of kidnapping, robbery, murder, or some other form of highway mayhem. On both occasions, my dad made me take a Trailways bus back to Gastonia. It was a local. It stopped in every town, and even at passengers' houses along the way, turning a two-hour trip into a four-hour ordeal.

One of those trips was almost my undoing. Rain was falling hard, and the temperature was dropping fast when I got on the bus in High Point. Before we got to Thomasville, I could see ice collecting on tree limbs and passing cars. By the time we arrived in Lexington, the streets were sheets of ice, and I knew we wouldn't be able to continue. We were inching down a hill when the rear end of the bus started sliding around like a slow motion scene in a movie. I saw the driver struggling to regain control, but my experience as a school bus driver told me he wouldn't be able to do it. I braced myself. We made almost a complete circle before the bus slammed into a power pole and came to a halt. Nobody was hurt, but all of the passengers had to slip and slide to the nearby depot to take shelter. Five inches of snow fell during the night, and no buses were moving. The next morning, my dad took off from work, put chains on the car's rear tires, picked me up, and drove me the rest of the way to Gastonia.

Those weekend trips home, along with the strenuous classes and hard study that was required to keep up with them, helped to overcome my homesickness with time. But my anxiety about my math skills proved to be a self-fulfilling prophecy. Just as in high school, I flunked algebra first semester.

The instructor called me in for a conference. He had pulled my records and had all of my grades. I was doing well in everything else, particularly well in physics. Considering my interests and my other grades, he told me, there was no reason why I shouldn't be doing equally as well in math. He wanted me to repeat the class, and under his close guidance, I finally was able to grasp the role of math to theory and to all that I wanted to be able to achieve. This time, I passed, and I would go on to do well in trigonometry, and exceptionally well in calculus. By my second year, I would be on the dean's list.

Drafting was one of the many required subjects, and one for which I found a special affinity. We studied both electrical and mechanical drafting. For my mechanical drafting class, I created a complete set of drawings for building a governor for a gasoline engine. I still have those drawings, along with my drafting tools, although I never built the governor. I often would go back to the drafting room at night to work on projects that had nothing to do with my classes. I even designed a house for Judy and me; it was a typical ranch-style house with a carport on one end. I drew every single brick in that house and, of course, added my Long John ham radio antenna at the back, but not high enough to make it such an obvious target for lightning.

I remained active with my ham radio hobby throughout my two years at Gaston Tech. I got a couple of other guys in the dorm interested in it as well. One of them had a car, and we often drove to the peak of nearby Crowders Mountain, which sported several radio repeater towers. From there we had a clear line of sight in every direction for my high frequency mobile radio, and we could talk with hams for many miles around.

As the end of my time at Gaston Tech neared, I felt fully grounded in electronics—pun intended—and satisfied with all that I had learned. It had been an intensive two years. We had covered the full spectrum of electronics, studying AC and DC circuits, communications circuits, and radio theory. I actually had learned to use math to calculate solutions to electronic problems instead of using the hit-and-miss—mostly miss—experimentation I'd conducted in my childhood.

My new knowledge made experimentation all the more appealing. I spent a lot of time in the labs working on projects of my own just for fun.

Kenneth Ward's prediction proved true. Early in the spring of my second year, recruiters from big companies began showing up to talk to graduating students. Some of my instructors told me that I should consider going on to North Carolina State, or some other college, and getting a full degree in electrical engineering. As appealing as that might have seemed, I wasn't inclined toward it. I wanted to put my new knowledge to use in a practical way. I was intent on getting married, and I needed a job for that. I wanted to go to work and get on with life.

Sandia National Laboratories in Albuquerque, New Mexico, which did technological research and development for the U.S. Department of Defense, hired a lot of Gaston Tech graduates. Several of my friends would go to work there. I talked to the Sandia recruiter, but I had a deep, instinctive commitment to home—Albuquerque was too far from North Carolina, its desert landscape too alien to our lush hills, for me to give any serious consideration to working there.

I almost immediately connected on a personal level with one recruiter. His name was John Humphries. He was the superintendent of Carolina Power and Light Company's W.B. Robinson steam generating plant in Darlington County, South Carolina, near Hartsville. He probably was three times my age, but we started chatting and discovered that we had much in common. We both loved designing and building our own electronic components and could spend untold hours locked in a room in total seclusion doing just that. Mr. Humphries, as I always would call him, had a special room in his house jammed with electronic equipment. We had a great time talking about our projects and experiments.

Only a week after I met Mr. Humphries, I got a letter from him offering me a job at the power plant. The pay would be $425 a month. That sounded like a lot of money to me at the time. I called Judy to tell her about it, and she seemed pleased. Hartsville was only a couple of hours drive from Randolph County, so we both would be within easy range of home and family. My dad thought that the offer was a good one as well, and after considering it for a few days, I wrote to Mr. Humphries accepting the job.

That decision settled another matter. Judy and I now could set our wedding date, and we did: August 23. The ceremony would take place at Judy's church, Allen Jay Baptist, near High Point. She decided that she would drop out of High Point College and give up her plan to teach. We both wanted to start a family.

My graduation was on a Saturday in late May 1964. Judy and her parents came, as did my mom and dad. Afterward, we all went for a picnic at the state park adjoining Kings Mountain National Military Park, where a key battle of the Revolutionary War was fought in 1780.

As it turned out, I was among the last students to graduate from Gaston Tech. The following January, the school merged with newly organized Gaston College, which was operated by the North Carolina Board of Public Education, and the association with the school of engineering at North Carolina State University ended. In 1981, Gaston College became part of North Carolina's new community college system. It now occupies a sprawling campus of impressive buildings on U.S. 321 near the small town of Dallas,

My first job after college was at the W.B. Robinson power plant near Hartsville, South Carolina.

north of Gastonia. Gaston Tech is just a memory for those of us who were privileged to learn there.

Hartsville, South Carolina, was named for Thomas Hart, who carved a tobacco and cotton farm out of two hundred wild acres adjoining Black Creek in the 1820s, but the town itself would be built, and long dominated, by another family, the Cokers. Major James Lide Coker came to the county to farm, but he went on to create not only a town but a business empire that included the biggest department store between Richmond and Atlanta, a cotton gin, a bank, and other ventures in addition to his farms.

Coker's son, David, took a keen interest in science while he was at the University of South Carolina, and after he joined the family businesses, he began applying that knowledge to agriculture, hoping to help struggling nearby farmers. The result was the Coker Pedigreed Seed Company, which created new strains of cotton, tobacco, grains, and fruits that changed the way farming was done throughout the South and affected agriculture worldwide. In October 1965, while I was living in Hartsville, Coker's original experimental farm was named a national historic landmark.

Judy and I made our first visit to Hartsville soon after my graduation. We wanted to see what the town was like and take a first look at the big power plant where I would be working.

Hartsville offered the impression of a pleasant little Southern town. It had a thriving downtown business district and stately old houses on tree-lined streets. It was distinguished by its artesian wells; by the lovely campus of Coker College, a small but prestigious school, then for women only; and by Kalmia Gardens, built by David Coker's second wife, May, at the site of Thomas Hart's house on the sixty-foot bluff overlooking Black Creek outside of town. Kalmia Gardens was open free to the public year-round.

The huge power plant where I would be working was about five miles northwest of town on beautiful Robinson Lake off Highway 151. Its furnace and smokestack could be seen for many miles. We thought Hartsville would be a nice place to live and start a family.

I had to begin work immediately, and I needed to find a place to live temporarily until Judy and I were married. That turned out to be in one of those stately old houses near downtown. It was a two-story white house with porches all around and a beautifully landscaped yard in a nice neighborhood. It had been the home of a top state official, but he was long dead, and his elderly widow now rented out the upstairs rooms. I had the good fortune to discover that she had a room available on that one-day trip to look over the town.

Only a few days later, I came back alone on Sunday afternoon to move into the room and start my new job the next day. My dad had bought a new car, and he let me borrow the nine-year-old Chevy that summer until I could save up enough money to make a down payment on a car of my own.

I was a bit apprehensive about what lay ahead when I drove to the power plant early Monday morning to start my new job.

The coal burning furnace that created the steam to power the plant's huge generator was twenty stories high, surrounded by steel beams with elevators and open grated walkways that provided access to every level. Fear of heights or vertigo would be disabling conditions for the job I was about to undertake.

The steam created by the furnace was two thousand degrees Fahrenheit and under so much pressure that it could cut like a torch. If a steam pipe developed a leak, it would slice through everything around it, including human beings, and the plant would have to be shut down. There are a thousand ways for a person to get killed or seriously injured at a power plant, and safety is a primary issue. I had to undergo lengthy safety training before I could start work. Everybody had to attend safety meetings weekly, and we talked about it constantly.

Electronic instrumentation was used to monitor every aspect of the plant's operation, and keeping those instruments calibrated and working was to be my job. I was assigned to a unit with three other guys, all of them much older than I and with long experience. They took me quickly under their wing, grateful for the additional help. The work was routine to them, but my long fascination with everything mechanical and electronic made it exciting to me.

We had to go inside the big generator while it was running. It produced 180 million watts of power, and I got a close-up look at how electricity was created in a big way.

Our unit also had a lab where we spent a lot of time, and I discovered that it would be okay to come back after hours and work on my own projects, which I did frequently. I also would go back some nights and hang around the plant's control room, talking with the guys who worked there and learning how everything operated.

Cooking wasn't allowed in my room, so I took most of my meals at a downtown cafe called Blake's, only a short walk away, where I got to know the entire staff. I still have fond memories of the Delmonico steak at Blake's.

I got off at four each day, which left some time for exploring. I drove over to Darlington, eight miles away, to see the speedway where the Southern 500 was held, the race that my dad and I had listened to on the radio every Labor Day while we were cleaning up the shop. If I wanted to go to a city to shop or to have an exotic meal, say from McDonald's, Florence was only seven or eight miles beyond Darlington.

After work on Friday, I drove straight back to Randolph County to spend the weekend with Judy and my family, returning each Sunday night, much as I had during my two years at Gaston Tech.

As our wedding date neared, I began looking for a place where the two of us could live. I found that the choices were few due to restrictions on our part. We couldn't afford to pay a lot of rent, and we had no furniture, or money to buy any. We needed a furnished place temporarily.

The best I could find was a tiny duplex hidden away off a side street about five blocks from downtown. And I do mean hidden. It was behind a much bigger, older house. To get to it, you had to pass down a weedy dirt driveway through ancient, overgrown shrubs twelve feet high. The duplex, shaded by big trees, once had been white but had taken on a grayish shade. The entrance doors for the two apartments were at opposite ends, and there was no lawn, only a spot to park by the door.

The house in front of the duplex had a concrete swimming pool, long abandoned. But it remained full of water, dark and murky, thick with slimy algae, leaves, and other debris, ripe with the odor of decay. Mosquitoes swarmed from it, and I later would discover that a small alligator resided there, presumably rent free.

The apartment itself was tiny, probably no more than four hundred square feet. Drab might be a little overly kind in describing it. The furnishings weren't elaborate or lavish, or chosen with any particular decorating theme in mind. Cheap and worn might be a better description. Still, I thought it would do until we could find something better. The rent, after all, was only seventy-five dollars a month.

Judy didn't seem particularly impressed when she came to see it. But she didn't object. She didn't know about the alligator at that point. And not until we moved in would we discover that at night the apartment was considered free range by palmetto bugs, fearless and aggressive cockroaches big enough not to be intimidated by a shoe of any size less than one worn by Wilt the Stilt Chamberlain. I decided I might need a gun after my first encounter with one.

On the day before the wedding, I went to Southern Motors in High Point and bought my first car, a spanking new 1964 Plymouth Valiant with a slant-six engine. It cost $1,950, and my new job allowed me to finance it with easy monthly payments. I was really proud when I drove that car away from the showroom.

I was less than two weeks from turning twenty on the day of the wedding. Judy was ten days younger. After the Sunday afternoon ceremony and reception, we accepted all the good wishes, stashed away the presents, and drove off in that shiny new Valiant for a brief honeymoon in Cherokee and Maggie Valley, where we took the tram up a steep mountain to Ghost Town. Because I was new on the job, I only had a couple of days off. We hurried back to Randolph County to load up the car and head for Hartsville, our cozy apartment, and our new life together.

A couple of weeks later, Judy's mother came to visit. She took one look at our apartment and left little doubt that she was aghast at the situation into which her daughter had been delivered. She burst into tears, and she hadn't even seen the palmetto bugs yet. I took that as a sign that I should hasten my search for another abode.

A couple of months later, I found a small house for rent four miles outside of town, only a mile from the power plant. It had been damaged by fire and rebuilt. The interior was all new. It wasn't furnished, and we had to go into debt to buy essential furniture.

I liked my job at the power plant, but after a while the excitement faded. It was routine work, mundane and hardly challenging. I began to feel that I was no longer learning from it. Carolina Power and Light was planning to build a nuclear reactor at the plant, but that was several years in the future and likely would offer me no greater prospects. As strange as it may sound, the job didn't offer enough of the pure electronics that intrigued me. I got more satisfaction from the personal projects that I worked on at night, building equipment that would enhance my abilities and allow me to do all sorts of electronic work.

My private projects allowed me to develop a close friendship with Mr. Humphries, the plant superintendent. He and his wife often invited Judy and me for supper, and after we ate, the women would talk and Mr. Humphries and I would go into his personal lab and work out electronics problems.

After a year on the job, I knew that I didn't want to stay at Carolina Power and Light, but my fondness for Mr. Humphries made a decision to leave difficult for me. About six months later, my supervisor called me in for a chat, and I told him that I had something that I needed to say.

I liked my job, I said, and I appreciated the opportunity that CP&L had given me. The company had been good to me, and I enjoyed working with all of my colleagues, who always had been friendly and helpful. But the job wasn't providing me with the new knowledge or opportunity that I wanted. I didn't have any job prospects, I told him, hadn't begun a search, but I intended to. Eventually, I'd be leaving. I just didn't know when. The supervisor thanked me, said he understood, and the discussion ended.

Later I learned from Mr. Humphries that the supervisor had called me in to tell me that I was getting a merit raise, but after my disclosure, he didn't know whether to give it to me or not. He met with Mr. Humphries to discuss the situation.

"Were you planning to give him the raise for what he's done, or for what he's going to do?" Mr. Humphries asked.

"What he's done," said my supervisor.

"There's your answer. Go ahead and give it to him."

I always admired Mr. Humphries for that.

I needed six months to do it, but I did find a far more promising job that would take Judy and me back home. And I had an old friend to thank for that.

Eight

The person who directed me to my new job was Kenneth Ward, my friend from Poplar Ridge Friends Meeting who had convinced me to attend Gaston Tech. Once again, he set me on the right path.

Ken was an independent sales representative for several technology companies. Before that he had worked for a company called Bivens and Caldwell, which had offices in Atlanta, Orlando, and High Point. Bivens and Caldwell represented several technology companies for which it sold and installed equipment. It also maintained the equipment and trained customers to use it.

One of the companies it represented was Hewlett-Packard of Palo Alto, California. Hewlett-Packard had been formed in 1939 by Bill Hewlett and Dave Packard, longtime friends and electrical engineering graduates of Stanford University. They started the company with $538 in assets, including a Sears-Roebuck drill press, in a tiny rented garage behind the house in Palo Alto where Packard and his wife, Lucille, had a first-floor apartment. Their first product was an oscillator, a device that produces variations in electrical currents or radio frequencies. This one was for testing audio equipment. They called it the 200A to make it appear that they had created a lot of earlier oscillators.

This oscillator, however, was designed differently from others, so much so that it could be produced and sold far cheaper. Walt Disney bought twelve of a refined version, the 200B, to use for testing the special audio equipment required for the twelve theaters chosen to premiere his animated musical film *Fantasia* in 1940, and Hewlett-Packard was on its way.

Originally, the company planned to make only electronic gear for testing, measuring, and monitoring, but World War II brought special needs and caused it to move into microwave equipment as well, building signal generators and radar-jamming devices for the military. Its incredible growth continued through the '50s and into the '60s. When I joined Hewlett-Packard in the fall of 1966, it was expanding into other areas that would completely change the company's focus: medical monitoring equipment and, most importantly, computers.

I was hired by John Bivens and Dave Caldwell, who simply had switched over from managing their own company to becoming managers for Hewlett-Packard. Everybody who worked in electronics knew that Hewlett-Packard was one of the most forward-thinking and fastest growing technology companies in the world. In 1965, it had 9,033 employees and revenue of $165 million. By the end of 1966, it would have $203 million in revenue with 11,309 employees, and I was excited about being one of them.

Bill Hewlett and Dave Packard were icons in the business, and John Bivens and Dave Caldwell knew them personally. I couldn't believe that I had shaken the hands of men who had shaken the hands of Bill Hewlett and Dave Packard.

Hewlett-Packard's High Point office was on North Main Street, not far from Borden Dairy with its big Elsie the Cow sign. It had about seventy-five employees, of which I, who just had turned twenty-two, was the youngest.

When I took the job, Judy and I were living in our third residence in South Carolina, this one far nicer and more spacious than the previous two. It was a fully furnished and well-appointed brick house on a hill overlooking a private lake not far from the power plant. We had rented it from an elderly couple who were moving into a smaller place to simplify their lives. I really liked that house and hated to give it up, but my future was calling.

I was to leave Carolina Power and Light on Friday and start work at Hewlett-Packard on Monday. But too much had been going on to allow me time for dealing with such incidentals as finding a place to live in High Point.

Rash action is not uncommon to youth, but sometimes, amazingly, it actually works out. Hewlett-Packard was paying for our move. Most of the furniture we bought after leaving the palmetto-bug palace in Hartsville for a rental house outside town was in storage because the bigger house we later moved into was furnished. When the movers showed up early on Saturday morning to haul our belongings to High Point, we had no delivery address for them.

As the movers began packing, I struck out for High Point, two and a half hours away, and left Judy to oversee the moving. I told her if I hadn't found a house by the time she and the movers got there, I would arrange for the furniture to be stored. In that event, we would move in with her parents until we found a house or apartment to rent, preferably a house. I planned to report my progress to her mother by telephone. Judy was to check in with her mother regularly to find out where the movers should take the furniture.

I arrived in High Point about ten, bought a previous day's newspaper from a rack, and began going through the want ads for rentals. The first place that caught my attention was a house on Lawndale Street, just off Kivett Drive. I called the owner, and he agreed to show me the place that morning. I met him there shortly afterward. It was a neat little white house, just four rooms, on an unpaved street, but in a pleasant enough neighborhood. It would be a big step down from our house on the lake but good enough for now. I figured we could find a better place later. By noon, I was able to call Judy's mother and give her an address. By nightfall, all of our earthly belongings were piled in that forlorn little white house.

But we were happy to be back near home and family, and I was especially pleased about my new job. Despite my youth and inexperience, I fit in quickly at Hewlett-Packard. I was assigned to a workshop with three older technicians, who, like my coworkers at Carolina Power and Light, took me under their wing. Our group worked on instruments—signal generators, oscilloscopes, volt meters, and the like—sent in by customers to be repaired, calibrated, or set to standards. It was more interesting work than my job at the power plant had offered, and the pay and benefits were considerably better. I still wasn't able to put any money into savings for the future, but I figured that time and hard work would change that.

Not long before I got the job offer from Hewlett-Packard, we had discovered that Judy was pregnant. As joyful as these two developments were, they also left no doubt that we were facing dramatic and important changes over the coming months.

The greater of these began on the evening of December 10, when Judy thought that she was feeling labor pains. I was new at this business, and I rushed her to High Point Hospital, where I had been born. She was whisked away to the maternity ward, and I was directed to the waiting room for nervous fathers-to-be, where I spent the next several anxious hours. In those days, fathers didn't take part in deliveries and had no role other than sitting, waiting, and thumbing through old magazines.

Finally, Judy's doctor, Kay Williams, a well-known local obstetrician, came out to tell me that labor had indeed begun. But with first children, she said, these things often took a long time, and she expected that to be the case for Judy. There was no point in me sitting up all night waiting, she said. A nearby patient room was empty, and she suggested that I go to bed there. A nurse would wake me if anything happened. I knew that I had to work the next day, and that's what I did.

Early in the morning, several hours later, a nurse woke me to tell me that Judy was in the throes of delivery, and I got up and went back to the waiting room. Dr. Williams soon came to tell me that I was the father of a daughter, and that both mother and daughter were fine, even if the new mom was a little worse for wear. That was an immense relief, and I said a short prayer of gratitude.

I checked in on Judy after she was taken to a room, then went to the nursery, where an attendant brought my daughter, swaddled in a white hospital blanket, to the window so that I could gaze upon her face for the first time. I'm sure that every father thinks his newly born daughter is beautiful, but I was in awe of mine. We named her Annette.

• • •

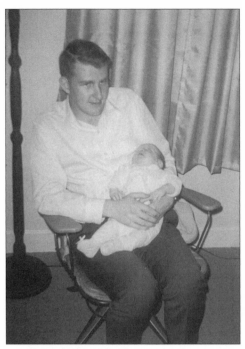
My daughter Annette was born shortly after I went to work for Hewlett-Packard in High Point.

Annette's birth gave us new incentive to get out of the small house we'd moved into temporarily and into a bigger and nicer place. But I didn't want to keep paying rent, which never accrued any equity. And I couldn't muster the money for a down payment on a house of our own.

I was talking about this with a coworker one day several months after Annette was born. He told me that the company might advance me money for a down payment.

Moreover, he knew of a house that soon would be coming on the market. It was in the subdivision where he lived in Randolph County, Caraway Hills, named for nearby Caraway Mountain. That was near Hillsville, only a few miles from where I grew up, where my parents still lived and my roots were deep. Most of the houses in this subdivision were on five-acre tracts, the same size tract my dad had bought when he built his first and only house. It allowed plenty of room for a garden and for children and animals to play, as well as providing a sense of country living, my coworker said.

Judy and I went to look at the house. It was a typical brick rancher (and almost a perfect match for the house I had designed for us on lonely nights in the drafting room at Gaston Tech). It was about four years old, and only one family had lived in it. It sat atop a bare ridge, the highest point in the sub-division, and even offered a view of sorts.

We both knew that we wanted at least one other child and possibly a third. This house provided three bedrooms, a big selling point. But the thing that appealed to me most about it was the full, unfinished basement, which was above ground at the back of the house and had garage doors in one end. Annette could play there—and so could I. I'd have plenty of room for all of my electronic gizmos and my ham radio gear.

Once I found out what the down payment would be, I went to Dave Caldwell to tell him about the situation and ask if the company might consider lending me that amount. No problem, he said. Indeed, the company would just take the payments out of future bonuses so that my salary wouldn't be affected.

Not long afterward, we moved into our own house, and to make my joy even greater, my job was about to become even more interesting.

One of the many things that I really liked about Hewlett-Packard was that it was fully committed to training. The company had a big training and education center in Cupertino, California, in what is now known as Silicon Valley, and training was conducted at other company facilities around the world as well. The instructors were first rate, and there was no limit to what a committed employee could learn. Most sessions were for a week or two with eight hours of classes a day, but some were longer. I eagerly sought all of the training I could get.

Oddly enough, much of my early training with the company turned out to be medical in nature. In 1961, Hewlett-Packard had bought the Sanborn Company in Waltham, Massachusetts; Sanborn made medical diagnostic and monitoring equipment. That equipment was growing increasingly complex and sophisticated as technology evolved, and every hospital needed it. Much of it had to do with the heart—EKG machines, defibrillators, and eventually computer-controlled catheterization units and complete coronary care systems with central stations and bedside units. I was sent to Waltham to learn the equipment's purposes, how it was designed, how it worked, how to install and maintain it, and how to train people to use it.

Later, I put this equipment in hospitals all across North Carolina, ranging from the large Duke University Medical Center to hospitals in smaller towns such as Thomasville, Siler City, and Mount Airy. I installed the first heart catheterization unit at High Point Hospital. I found it hard to believe that I was instructing doctors and nurses, but I was. They had hundreds of questions, and I had to be able to answer them quickly and correctly. That made me work hard to ensure that I could answer every one. The gravity of the power held by the technology in these machines—lives lost or saved—didn't escape me.

I spent a lot of time in hospital coronary care units. I was present when people went into cardiac arrest. I heard nurses cry, "We're losing him! We're losing him!" I watched as doctors tried to shock silent hearts back to action. I saw them succeed—and fail.

All of this did not go without effect on me.

The heart is a marvelous organ. It works great as long as you aren't aware of it. My experience in coronary units made me all too keenly aware of the functioning of my own heart. Once you start paying attention to it, listening to it, checking frequently for a pulse, it begins acting erratically. It slows to a snail's pace. It pounds like a jackhammer. It rumbles like thunder. It streaks pain like lightning. It grabs you by the throat and chokes off your breath.

After I had gone to doctors with imaginary heart attacks two or three times, they assured me that my heart was sound and that what I was experiencing was common to medical students when they first begin working around heart patients.

The medical equipment kept me constantly on the road, and I didn't spend a lot of time at the office. One day, I checked in and discovered something different in one of the workshops.

It was unlike any electronic device I yet had encountered, a big, cumbersome thing, with all manner of flashing lights, dials, and switches. This was Hewlett-Packard's first computer, the 2116A. It was designed to automatically control many of the electronic instruments produced by the company, including the medical devices. It was the biggest piece of equipment Hewlett-Packard ever had built, and it was the first to use integrated circuits, the semiconductor chips that eventually would make computers smaller and smaller, more and more powerful, and less and less expensive, until they became considered essential to life as we know it. I couldn't have imagined then how quickly computers would begin to play such a vital role in our lives.

Despite its size, this behometh would come to be described as a mini-computer. At that time, other computers were much larger. They later would be described as mainframe computers to distinguish them from interlopers such as the 2116A. Mainframe computers employed vacuum tubes and magnetic tapes and were so sensitive and temperamental that they could operate only on spring-loaded floors in controlled environments. Nobody could afford them other than governments and the biggest corporations and institutions.

The 2116A was a rugged thing, designed to work anywhere without any pampering. It would make the advantages of rapid electronic computing available to far more businesses and organizations, but it wasn't easy to convince people that they needed it. The price was part of the problem. It ranged from $25,000 to $50,000, depending on its options and uses, a lot of money at the time.

The 2116A had been introduced in 1966 about the time I joined the company, but it had taken nearly two years for the first one to reach us. I saw it as a curiosity at first. Just another piece of equipment. It interested me, but I don't recall thinking of it as any big deal at the time. I was too deeply engrossed in medical matters, and Hewlett-Packard was coming out with so much new stuff that it was hard to keep up with all of it. I had no idea what this machine actually could do, or how dramatically it soon would affect my own life.

This particular machine was a demonstrator. Some of our salesmen had received preliminary training on it and soon would be taking it out to show it to potential customers. That wasn't a simple matter. The contraption must have weighed four hundred pounds. It barely would fit in the back of a station wagon that the company had outfitted with anchors so it could be securely strapped in place. It had to be moved on a gurney, and it took a swarm of people to get it in and out of the station wagon.

The straps that were supposed to hold this monster in place turned out to be not so reliable. About six months after we got that demonstrator, a salesman who was transporting it was involved in a traffic accident. The computer broke free, crushed the driver's seat, and pinned him beneath the dashboard. Part of the computer was sticking through the roof when emergency crews arrived. Both computer and station wagon were destroyed, and the salesman was critically injured.

Only a few months after I first laid eyes on the 2116A, my supervisor, Robert Moore, approached me one day.

"You want to go to California and learn about computers?" he asked.

Of course, I did. I never turned down a chance to learn.

This time I spent a full month at the company's education center in Cupertino, and it turned out to be a true revelation. I came away not only with a full grounding in early computer science, but with a new realization and excitement about the role this machine likely would play in the future. Still, I didn't picture it as changing the entire direction of this huge corporation, which was exactly what was about to happen, just another example of the never-ending marvels that new technology can bring.

My month in Cupertino learning about computers also gave me an important lesson in life. My daughter, Annette, was only two, but when I returned home I could see dramatic changes in her. I got the slightest glimmer of what my dad's experience must have been like as he went away to war when I was not a month old and returned to find me running from him like a turkey. I vowed that I never would stay away from my child for that long again.

Compared to computers today, the 2116A was truly primitive. Think of a caveman's stone club compared to, say, a fully armed Black Hawk helicopter. It came with a few ultra-simple programs that it could run, but it was designed to be tailored to fit a customer's particular needs.

Programs for those needs had to be created and punched on paper tape to be installed into the computer. But to make that happen, an operator had to follow a set of sixty-four instructions, using switches and lights on the front of the computer. Some guys I knew could hold all sixty-four instructions in their heads; I couldn't. I kept them on a card in my shirt pocket at all times. This process was anything but quick and easy.

Information put into the machine was stored on tiny, magnetized steel doughnuts, about 5/100ths of an inch in diameter. There were 64,000 of them, any one of which could fail at any given time.

When this machine was running perfectly, as it often did, it was a beautiful sight to behold with its big display of flashing lights. People were dazzled by its capabilities, too. We put one in a North Carolina tire plant to control the equipment that molded the tires. We installed one in the library at the University of Virginia in Charlottesville to catalog its resources, and another in the accounting department at Wake Forest University in Winston-Salem.

But as effective as the 2116A was, it didn't always run perfectly. It had a lot of bugs. It would stop suddenly, and nobody would know why. I was one of those who had to figure that out. Armed with simple diagnostic tools, my coworkers and I would set out on hunting expeditions inside this monster. Sometimes we found that one of the memory doughnuts in the seemingly endless chain of doughnuts had failed, or that a connection had broken, or a hole had been improperly punched into the paper tape feeding the information. We were well acquainted with hanging chads long before the 2000 presidential election.

Often we had to probe to the elemental level of digital ones and zeros, on-and-off switches, tracing a single binary bit to the source of the problem. Not surprisingly, we came to be known as the Bit Chasers.

Time and new technology eliminated many of the bugs we had to deal with in those first computers. Later models were greatly improved and less expensive, and we were installing and maintaining more and more every year. The memory doughnuts that held so little information soon disappeared, taking the punched paper tapes and hanging chads with them.

They were replaced by aluminum disks eighteen inches in diameter with magnetic material infused into them. The disk rotated at high speed, and just above it, floating on a cushion of air, was a head with an electro-magnet in it. The head put information into the magnetic material, or removed it, at the operator's command. If the head ever actually touched the disk, the magnetic material was scraped away and all the information stored there was lost.

I'd get a call from some frantic person at a business saying their computer had stopped working. I'd ask a few questions and realize immediately what had happened. I'd go out and find a crashed disk.

"Where's your backup disk?" I'd ask the operator and immediately see that deer-in-the-headlights look. Nobody had been making a backup. All of their valuable information was gone. Sad story, oft told.

As time went on, my life was much as I had hoped it would be. I had a great job at a great company with interesting work, good pay, and opportunity to learn and advance. Judy and I had two more children, both born at High Point Hospital: a son, Jerry, on February 12, 1969, and a daughter, Margaret, nearly four years later on January 12, 1973. Judy, the children, and I regularly attended services at Poplar Ridge Friends Meeting, just as I had done throughout childhood. We had family close by and often had big get-togethers.

My great granddaddy, Edd Hoover, who had instilled his love of the Randolph County countryside in me, had died just before I turned fourteen and was buried in the Poplar Ridge cemetery. My granddaddy, Jeff Dorsett, had joined him there in 1966 while I still was living in South Carolina. He had fallen dead of a stroke while working in his garden. But my grandmother Myrtle was still living in her house with her unmarried daughter, my Aunt Gracie, and we still had Sunday dinners there.

Our house at Caraway Hills was exposed to the wind, and I constantly had to replace shingles that blew off the roof. The yard had a few little trees planted by the previous owner, but they weren't big enough to offer shade, and in summer the house and yard were in the sun's full glare. I started thinking about building a house somewhere out of the wind with some trees to shade us, a house that we could fit to our own needs.

We built it on an acre lot in Windemere Heights, another new subdivision north of Hillsville, only a few miles away. This house was bigger and much nicer. We had a fireplace in the living room, a narrow inset front porch with small white columns, and a double carport. I bought five adjoining acres, mostly wooded, so we would have plenty of room, a supply of firewood, and a buffer against crowding.

While we were at Caraway Hills, I had a lot of grass to mow, and I had bought my first lawn tractor, an Allis-Chalmers B110. I had loved tractors from the time I was eleven and my dad bought his first one, an Allis-Chalmers Model G. The Model G was an odd-looking machine, a bare frame painted bright orange with tall, narrow rear wheels. The engine was in the back, and implements had to be mounted on the front. I begged my dad to let me drive it, and he taught me to use it safely. He sold the tractor after I left home, and I was sorry that he had let it go.

Soon after we moved into the new house at Windemere Heights I was promoted to customer engineering manager at Hewlett-Packard, and I bought a second tractor, a Kubota, bigger than the Allis–Chalmers but still not a full-size tractor. I built a shed among the trees near the house to harbor both.

By this time, my friend Kenneth Ward had moved to Williamsburg, Virginia. We went there for a visit one weekend and toured the restored colonial village. I loved Williamsburg and was intrigued by its history and its restoration as a major historical site and tourist destination under the direction of John D. Rockefeller. We made several trips there, sometimes taking friends. I was especially taken by the colonial architecture and read

The shed I built for my tractors when we moved to Windemere Heights.

a lot about it. I decided that I'd like to live in a two-story colonial-style house myself.

I mentioned this to my grandmother Myrtle one weekend, and not long afterward, she told me that she had spoken with my mother and they had reached a decision. My mother was supposed to inherit a third of the family farm. My grandmother loved having family close by, and she had asked my mother if it would be okay to carve out five acres of her share and deed them to me so that I could build a house there. My mother was pleased with the idea. Both knew how much I treasured the heritage of that land.

My tract would be right across from my grandmother's house. It included the garden spot where my grandfather had died and the barn where as a child I often had gone with him to feed hay and corn to the mules and the cow.

I started planning another house, a two-story white colonial, just down the hill from the barn. I thought my life was set when we moved into this house in 1974. I was living exactly where I wanted to live. We had three children and didn't intend to have more. Everything was going just as I had dreamed, and I was happy and content. I even had bought a bigger tractor, a new full-size Ford Model 2000 with a diesel engine so that I actually could farm the land my ancestors had farmed.

But the curiosity that had infected me from earliest childhood was unrelenting. I was constantly experimenting and tinkering with my own electronic gear, my head always swimming with new ideas. And that was about to lead to consequences so drastic that they would become almost unbearable.

Nine

Sometimes it's the littlest, most innocent things that pull you into the deepest, most desperate crises. In my case, it was a small chunk of ceramic with a few simple electronic components that didn't work.

One of the clients I visited regularly for Hewlett-Packard was the Coastal Plains Soil, Water, and Plant Research Center operated by the U.S. Department of Agriculture just outside Florence, South Carolina, on the Darlington Highway. We had installed a lot of equipment there to monitor instruments used by the center's researchers. One of the researchers I got to know was Dr. Claude Phene, a soil scientist.

Dr. Phene was trying to come up with a way to monitor the amount of moisture in soil so that irrigation could be supplied when it was needed in the required amounts and controlled automatically. He had been trying to create an electronic sensor that could be buried in the ground to detect the amount of moisture and relay the information to a monitor and control system. He had thought out the principle of such a device, indeed had written his PhD dissertation about it. But making one that functioned well enough was eluding him.

By the time I met Dr. Phene, he had made dozens of prototypes. I got to talking to him about it, and he showed me his most recent one. It was a ceramic cylinder about three inches long and an inch in diameter. You couldn't tell by looking at it, but this ceramic was porous, filled with tiny capillaries, like a sponge. If you put your tongue to it, you actually could feel it pulling in the moisture. Place it in a small amount of water and you could see the water disappearing into it.

Once buried, this chunk of ceramic would pull water into it much the way that a plant does. If a small electronic heater and heat sensor could be installed in the ceramic and periodically turned on for brief defined periods, the amount of moisture it was pulling in could be determined by variations in the temperature inside the cylinder.

If no water was present, the temperature would be higher than if the heat was dissipating through water. Using the temperature variations, formulas could determine the amount of moisture available for plants.

But many variables had to be figured into the equations, and creating this device, as simple as it seemed, actually was an immensely complicated project.

Naturally, it fascinated me immediately.

One of Dr. Phene's problems was that the electrical components he had been using were obsolete. They were based in germanium, which was less effective than silicon for this purpose. I thought that I probably could figure out the electronics and make this thing work. Dr. Phene welcomed any help I could provide. His interest was in soil much more than sensors. He just wanted something that would help in his work.

To me, of course, this was a challenge, and it affected me just as the electronic challenges of my childhood did. Once it took hold of me, I couldn't let it go. I had to see it through. I was determined to make it work.

Beginning in 1971, I devoted much of my spare time to this project. After moving to the new house at Windemere Heights, I had closed in the carport and divided it into two rooms, a playroom for the children and an office and workshop for all of my electronic equipment. I usually was in that shop for at least a couple of hours most nights, and often on weekends, working on this sensor. It never was far from my thoughts.

The electronics were fairly simple. I needed a few wires, a battery for power, a resistor that would produce a small amount of heat when current was applied, a silicon diode to detect the heat, and a meter to display the temperature. The electronics would be installed in a hole drilled in the center of the ceramic cylinder.

But these electronics would short out if exposed to water and had to be protected from it. I spent far more time experimenting with polymers to insulate the components from water than I did on the electronics. One problem was that the polymer had to be able to conduct heat.

After about eight months, I thought I had everything figured out. I assembled a sensor that I was convinced would work and took it to Florence to show it to Dr. Phene. He, too, thought it might be the solution to all of his past problems. Now all we had to do was get enough made to run some trials.

Dr. Phene had no interest in retaining any rights to this device, and the research center didn't want to produce it. But Dr. Phene said that if I could get enough made to start testing, the center would buy them from me.

I now had the two essential ingredients for a business—a product and a customer. All along I had thought that this thing had commercial potential. Now I knew it was at least viable as a sideline business with the possibility of becoming something much bigger.

I wasn't sure that I'd have time to handle a sideline business by myself. I had a friend at Hewlett-Packard, Tom McCuene, who worked with me on medical equipment. I had been talking to him about the sensor, and I offered him the chance to join me in this venture. We both put up $1,400 as capital to buy a typewriter, a drill press, heat guns, a tape machine, and

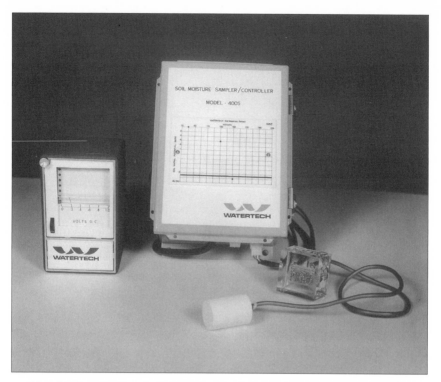

The soil-moisture sensor and control system I designed became the basis of my first business.

other necessary equipment, and began assembling sensors in the basement of his home in Wallburg, a small community south of Winston-Salem, about twenty-five miles from my house.

By the fall of 1972, we had begun selling them to the research center, and I was trying to line up other potential customers. Over the next three and a half years, we would build several hundred of these sensors, all prototypes. And all of them had flaws. I was constantly reconfiguring this thing, trying to get it to do what it was supposed to do. I'd fix one thing and another would fail.

By the end of 1975, Tom and I had taken in a grand total of about $19,000 from our venture. We weren't getting rich for sure, but we had a margin of about 44 percent. By this time it had become clear to me that the market for this sensor and equipment related to it could be worldwide and very big. A lot of money could be made. But it would take more than two guys working part-time to do it.

When I suggested to Tom that we consider giving up our jobs and turning this into a full-time business, he balked. He didn't want to leave Hewlett-Packard. We both realized we'd reached a turning point, however, and he was willing to sell out his share of the business if I wanted to attempt to make a go of it on my own.

I wasn't certain that I did. I wrestled with this decision for a long time. I loved Hewlett-Packard. I loved my job. Until this came along, I had thought that I would retire from the company after a long and satisfying career. Hewlett-Packard had given me many opportunities and allowed me to acquire knowledge beyond my imaginings, not only about electronics and technology but about business and management and the way a company should treat the people who worked for it.

Employees didn't easily walk away from jobs at Hewlett-Packard. They were paid well and granted the independence and latitude that were allowed at few other companies. They were made to feel appreciated and an integral part of the business and its success. Understandably, Hewlett-Packard had low employee turnover.

Beyond that was the frightening reality of the risk I'd be taking. I had a new house and a new tractor and many monthly payments. I had three children to rear and put through school. I would be giving up a good paycheck and all the benefits that came with it with no assurance of income to meet my obligations.

My other big worry was the capital that would be necessary to expand the business and allow it to grow. I didn't have any on hand, and little prospect of borrowing any. But I did have some Hewlett-Packard stock that all employees were allowed to buy at a reduced rate. I could sell that. And when I reached my tenth anniversary with the company, which would come in a matter of months, in May 1976, I could take my retirement money, about $10,000, in cash. That would give me about $25,000.

It would be a meager start for a company, but I had enough potential customers lined up that I felt certain I could build and sustain a big enough flow of revenue to meet expenses.

Realistically, the odds of making a quick success weren't with me. But I had been committed to this project for so long, believed in its prospects so fully, that I knew I'd never be able to live with myself if I didn't take the chance. If it didn't work out, I figured I always could find another job.

I worked out a deal with Tom to buy his share of the company for $7,500, which I could pay in yearly installments. And at the appropriate time, I took one of the most difficult steps I'd ever taken and gave my notice at Hewlett-Packard. Everybody there understood. They all wished me well.

When I had moved from Windemere Heights to the new house on my grandparents' farm, I had jacked up the shed I'd built for my tractors, loaded it onto a Low Boy trailer, and hauled it to the new house, snapping telephone lines all along the way. My granddaddy's barn provided shelter for my tractors, so I put this structure to new use. I built a foundation for it and later installed a floor, a drop ceiling, insulation, walls, lights, and

103

electrical outlets. I transformed the shed into a small office and electronics lab. It became world headquarters for my new, soon-to-be-global company WaterTech. I decided not to include photos of it in advertising mailings out of concern that it might be less than impressive.

Brenda Monroe was a former neighbor in Windemere Heights, a fellow member of Poplar Ridge Friends Meeting, a good friend, and a good person. I'd known her all of my life. She agreed to come to work with me. A couple of other women at Poplar Ridge were willing to do piece work at home, assembling some of the electronic components on their kitchen tables. Brenda and I would do the actual manufacturing, along with the selling, marketing, boxing, packaging, shipping, billing, accounting, floor sweeping, and whatever else had to be done.

Despite the normal anxiety that accompanies the beginning of any new enterprise, there also is a feeling of excitement, almost giddiness, especially when things are going well, and they seemed to be at first. In addition to the sensors, Brenda and I were making read-out boxes, using parts that I was buying from Hewlett-Packard. And I was beginning work on designing a compatible irrigation controller so we could expand our product line even more.

I went to a trade show to spread the word about our new company, and we began getting orders. They came from other research facilities, from landscape architects, even from a highway department in Australia that planned to use the sensors under a road bed. We also had attracted attention that could bring fast and tremendous growth.

Dr. James Fouss had been director of the Coastal Plains Research Center, and he was familiar with the sensors Tom and I had built and the ongoing experiments with them at the center. Dr. Fouss had left the research center in 1975 to become vice president of research and development for Hancor, a company that made products for drainage and water conservation, in Findlay, Ohio.

Dr. Fouss called to tell me that Hancor was interested in the sensor and might consider backing it financially and marketing it in a big way. He arranged for me to come to Findlay and make a presentation to the company's top officers and directors. I went on July 11, only about six weeks after Brenda and I had set up operations in my former tractor shed.

I had kept careful notebooks on every step of developing this sensor. I used them to prepare a full report, replete with technical details, drawings, and results of experiments to date. I took sales reports and financial records, lists of customers and potential customers, plans for new products, a prospectus as complete as I could make it

I thought the presentation went well. I got lots of questions, and everybody seemed to see the potential for our products. I was told I'd be hearing something soon, and I returned home feeling good about the visit.

But weeks passed and I heard nothing. Meanwhile, I had attracted another suitor. A landscape company in Alabama had ordered some of the sensors, and I got a call from the company owner. He was overflowing with excitement. He thought I was onto something really big, and he wanted to be part of it. He offered to buy WaterTech outright, and I went around and around with him for a while, until I discovered he was a con artist and broke off further contact. He never paid for the sensors we shipped to him.

Four months after I went to Findlay, a letter arrived from the vice president of finance at Hancor. The board had decided that WaterTech wasn't for them, he said, and they had no further interest. The letter came with a packet of materials I had left with the company. I had stamped many of the documents "Confidential. Do Not Copy." Every document I got back was a copy.

My disappointment was deep, to say the least. I'd really gotten my hopes up, had seen this as our one big opportunity, and now it was gone.

To add to my dismay, I began getting calls about erratic readings from the most recent sensors. It usually took months for problems to show up after these things were put into the ground. It sounded as if water was getting to the electrical components again. I'd have to come up with a new formula to prevent that from happening.

I was working on that when I began getting even more distressing news. Some sensors also were splitting apart, indicating a serious defect in the ceramic. I was going to have to start all over again.

Clearly, we would have to stop making and shipping sensors until I could figure out what the problems were and come up with a new design. That meant we would have no more revenue. But that was just part of the problem. Although our customers understood the situation and were sympathetic, they fully expected us to make good the faulty products we'd sent them. Just when we most needed money, most needed to be moving forward, we were going to be without revenue, spending more money, and heading backward. I couldn't recall ever being quite so discouraged.

To make matters even worse, we were almost broke. In an attempt to raise new capital, I ran classified ads in *The High Point Enterprise* offering my tractors for sale. They sold quickly, but watching the new owners hauling them away on trailers were sad moments for me. Brenda, meanwhile, volunteered to work without pay until we could get money coming in again.

I was deep in the midst of dealing with these problems when in February 1977, only four months after Hancor had told me it had no interest, I got an unexpected call from Dr. Fouss. Hancor was reconsidering, he said, and he wondered if I'd be willing to come up and talk about it again. This was a lifeline tossed into a stormy sea, and I grabbed it. I went in March.

I was completely forthright. I told the company officers and directors everything that had happened since I had spoken to them in July, all of the problems that had developed. I told them, too, about the progress I had made in solving those problems. I had no doubt that I could correct the waterproofing problem, despite past failures. The ceramics situation was more complicated. I was researching all the experts in the field and was confident that I would be able to come up with a new design. Finding a reliable supplier was another difficulty, but I had solid leads on that as well.

This time I didn't have to wait so long to hear back from Hancor. To my immense relief, they wanted to acquire WaterTech and were willing to put a million dollars into getting this sensor ready for market. Throughout April, I was negotiating the terms with Hancor lawyers. A lawyer in High Point, Perry Keziah, was assisting me. By May, we had an agreement.

I would get 20 percent of WaterTech's stock and receive 25 percent of pre-tax profits. I would remain president of the company; have an employment contract with a guaranteed salary, although it wouldn't be as much as I had been making at Hewlett-Packard; and get a company car. The faith I had in our products made me certain that my share of the profits and the growing value of the stock would pay big dividends. Hancor would get all of WaterTech's assets, including full rights to the products under development.

We had agreed that the company would remain in North Carolina. I would rent a building in High Point, hire a staff, and begin production as soon as I worked out the technical problems with the sensor. I had never incorporated WaterTech, and Hancor's lawyers did a search and discovered that name might infringe on another company. So Hancor changed the name to Moisture Control Systems and incorporated it.

Hancor had started in 1886 as a family business making bricks and later turned to ceramic water tiles, which came to dominate their products. When plastics came along, Hancor converted and became a major manufacturer of plastic drainage pipes and associated equipment. The company still was run by family. Jim Childs, who was getting on in years, was chairman of the board. His son, Jim W. Childs, was president. Various other relatives held top positions.

I was to answer to a cousin who ran a division of the company. I'll call him the Hulk. He was a lawyer with little technology background, but he was enthusiastic about the sensor and eager to get it into production. Too, eager, I soon would discover. He had no patience, and his lack of knowledge about technical problems caused him to constantly press for things to be done faster than it was possible to do them. He also had a tendency to explode in anger when things didn't go to suit him.

Only a few weeks after I sealed the deal with Hancor, Jim Childs, the elder, arrived to begin an evaluation of the new acquisition. This went on for several weeks, with others also involved, while I struggled to fix the problems with the sensor, making good progress, I felt. Once again, I laid out everything, hiding nothing, as I had done twice before. Late in July, Childs circulated a memo of his assessment to top officers and directors. When the Hulk got it, he flew into what we in the South call a conniption fit. I was summoned to Findlay for a meeting.

The Hulk never minced words. I stood accused of deceiving Hancor about how soon we would be ready for production. I was stunned. I hadn't misled the company or kept anything from its officers.

Jim W. Childs, the company president, was present. His nature was more moderate than the Hulk's. He told me that his inclination was to terminate me, but he had decided to give me a chance to prove myself. He presented me with a laundry list of almost insurmountable tasks that had to be achieved. Foremost among them was the completion of a trouble-free, fully functioning sensor ready for production.

I had eight weeks to get all of this done, starting August 19. If I didn't meet every expectation, I'd be declared in violation of my contracts, and I'd be dismissed, left with nothing.

I was hurt, angry, and disillusioned. But I'd been working at this too long to give up now, especially since I believed I was so close to success. I returned to Randolph County and began a marathon of fifteen-hour workdays and seven-day weeks.

Working with the engineering school at Clemson University, which had a ceramics program, I had come up with a completely new design. The sensor element would be flat now, instead of a cylinder. A company in Greensboro, Computer Labs, was getting into hybrid semiconductor technology, and I began working with an engineer there, Bob Johnson. We designed a completely new electrical system, fusing pure gold, the best electrical conductor, into ceramic, onto which the electrical components were attached. This made the electronics package far smaller and much easier to protect against moisture. With the technical problems worked out, Brenda and I hurried to assemble and test twenty of these new sensors before the deadline. They worked fine.

I had been sending regular reports on our progress to the corporate offices, and the response was good. In October, I was summoned again to Findlay and congratulated on my work. Jim W. Childs told me he knew I'd been under a great strain and that the company had been tough on me, but all of that was past now, and I'd never have to worry about such treatment again.

• • •

My relief was immense. We now could start production and make this company work. I was sure it was going to be a big success. In November, Hancor gave the go-ahead for me to find a building, set up a production line, and start hiring people. I found an industrial building on Textile Drive in High Point. It had 2,500 square feet of floor space, plenty of room to get us started. It also had a loading dock. I hired carpenters to build a reception area and offices in the front of the building, bought furniture and business machines, and ordered equipment to begin setting set up a production line and a packaging and shipping department.

All of this took time, of course, but we were making good progress. By the beginning of 1978, only six weeks after I had rented the building and begun renovating it, I was advertising for help and interviewing people. By spring, we had five employees other than myself and Brenda, who now was working part-time. We had begun production. We were making, shipping, and selling sensors.

In addition to overseeing the operation, I was completing the design of a system that would employ the information relayed by the new sensors to automatically control irrigation equipment, which would make our sensors an even more appealing product. We were well on our way to success. Or so I thought.

On the morning of April 22, 1978, I arrived at the office and was greeted with a surprise visit from the Hulk. It was so unexpected that it was almost startling to see him there. He was accompanied by another person, a consultant, I later was to learn.

This did not seem to be a friendly visit. He wanted to see the facility, and I showed it to him. He wanted to see all the books, and we went over those. He asked lots of questions.

Two hours into this inspection and interrogation, a third person arrived, a human resources official from Hancor. The Hulk suggested that we all go into my office to talk.

I had no idea what this was about, but I was almost certain that it wasn't good news.

The Hulk wasted no time in making that clear.

"We're shutting this place down today," he said. "I want you to terminate all of these people now. We're moving this operation to Findlay."

I was dumbstruck. This came out of nowhere. I'd had no hint that anything was wrong.

Production had been entirely too slow in getting underway, the Hulk went on. I was being removed as president of the company, and he was assuming that position. The facilities people would move all the equipment to Ohio and have a new production line set up and functioning within four weeks. A general manager and a new staff would be hired. I would have to move to Ohio, train the staff, and become director of research and development.

Anger welled in me from depths I didn't know existed. I'd never felt such anger, and I struggled to control it.

"I will not terminate these people," I said.

"If you don't, then *you* will be terminated," the Hulk said, going on to tell me that if I disobeyed an order I also would be in violation of my contracts and they would be declared invalid.

"I have to think this over," I said, and without another word, I got up and walked out of my office, and out of the building. I got in the '77 Pontiac Hancor had provided me and started driving toward Randolph County.

I was in shock. I was devastated. I'd never been blindsided like that before. I'd come to work that morning filled with vigor and confidence, ready to face a new day, only to be struck by disaster that came out of nowhere. I now had an understanding of how victims of tornadoes must feel as they crawl from the wreckage. I couldn't think. I didn't know what to do.

Instinctively, I drove to my parents' house. My mother was there. She only had to see my face to know that something awful had happened. She did her best to comfort me and assure me that as long as we had faith in God, everything would work out. I wasn't so sure at this moment.

I dreaded going home. A strain had come into my marriage well before this. Judy and I had been staying together for the sake of the children and appearances. We were not hostile to one another, but the deep, abiding love that binds a marriage was no longer present, and we both knew it. Tossing this news into the mix might be the breaking point.

After I got home, Brenda called to tell me that she and the other employees had been fired and ordered out of the building. She had boxed

Hard at work in my High Point office just before the facility was unexpectedly shut down.

up my personal belongings before leaving and had them for me. The Hulk, she said, had called in a locksmith to change the locks on the building.

For the first time in my life, I dissolved into despondency. My anger turned to grief, and it was overwhelming. I sought relief in sleep, but it wouldn't come. After a fitful night, I got up the next morning, drove to High Point, and hired a lawyer.

Over the next two weeks, all of my contacts with Hancor would be through my attorney. He was trying to arrange a meeting for me to make a presentation to Hancor officials. I wanted to try to convince them that the move was a terrible mistake that would significantly set back everything.

I planned a presentation that would be filled with enough facts and figures to be convincing, but I no longer had access to the books and much of the material I needed. Brenda agreed to work with me to try to reconstruct as much as we could. But we didn't have a place to work. My former tractor shed was empty. Everything in it had been moved to the building in High Point that no longer was accessible to us.

But a close friend of Brenda's, a former neighbor of mine in Windemere Heights, offered to let us use her house, which was unoccupied.

Barbara Terry Ford and her husband Larry were fellow members of Poplar Ridge Friends Meeting. They had two young sons. They always sat in the pew directly in front of my family at Sunday services. Two months earlier, the congregation had been shocked to learn that Larry Ford had been shot to death in his bed in the middle of the night. Brenda had gone to the house at one in the morning to comfort Barbara and later cleaned up the bloody mess in the bedroom. The shooting was thought to have been an accident.

But a week before the shutdown of Moisture Control Systems, Larry Ford's body was exhumed from the Poplar Ridge cemetery. Three days after the shutdown, a brief newspaper article reported that Larry's death had been ruled homicide, but in the midst of our upheaval, Brenda and I missed that article and didn't learn about it until much later.

Barbara didn't want to stay in the house where her husband had died. She planned to move back to her hometown of Durham, but she wanted her sons to finish out the school year in the school they were attending. Brenda offered to let Barbara and the boys move in with her family until school was out. She mentioned to Barbara that we had no place to work, and Barbara offered her house. We worked several days at the kitchen table unaware that we were at a murder scene.

Nobody was charged with Larry Ford's murder, but ten years later, Barbara's second husband, Russ Stager, died under uncannily similar circumstances. This time she was convicted of murder and sentenced to death, although the sentence later was reduced to life in prison. Her story became the subject of a best-selling book, *Before He Wakes*, as well as a TV movie starring Jaclyn Smith. Believe me, Barbara did not look like Jaclyn Smith.

The lawyer I'd hired was a private pilot, and he rented a small plane to fly us to Findlay for my presentation. Everybody was cordial and listened politely. Three days later, my lawyer called to say he'd heard from Hancor. The move had been affirmed. I could remain with the company under the conditions previously outlined with no disruption in pay, but I'd have to move to Findlay, report to work immediately, and sign a document stating that I wouldn't sue the company over the move.

Despite this setback, I still thought the company would make it, and under the circumstances, I had no choice but to stay with it. Judy told me she had no intention of moving to Findlay, and we both knew this was the end of our marriage.

I explained things as best I could to Annette, who was eleven, Jerry, who was nine; and Margaret, who was five. I promised that I would be back to see them at least every three weeks. I wouldn't stay away for as long as a month. They didn't cry, but I could tell that they were deeply upset about this sudden cataclysm in their lives.

On the following morning, I loaded my clothing and personal items into the '77 Pontiac, hugged and kissed my children, and set out for Ohio on the saddest and loneliest drive of my life.

Findlay was a pleasant town, not quite a city, smaller than High Point. It was about forty-five miles south of Toledo in an area of oil fields, and Marathon Oil had headquarters there. There also was a college bearing the same name as the town and a big plant where RCA made washers and dryers. In the center of town was a street lined with magnificent Victorian mansions. The Hancock County Courthouse also was there, an impressive, ornate structure filled with walnut, marble, and beautiful stained glass.

I moved into a furnished, second-floor apartment in a big complex, and reported to work to discover that I had been exiled to an old house in the middle of a field on a company research farm outside of town. I worked alone designing training procedures for the people who would be hired to produce the sensors.

All of the furniture and equipment I had bought for the building in High Point was spread out in a warehouse next to the company's machine shop in town. James Leedy, an engineer who was the company's facilities manager, had overseen the closing of the High Point building and the movement of the equipment to Findlay. He was a nice guy, the first to befriend me at Hancor. He invited me to his church and introduced me to people there. He believed that I had gotten a raw deal and assured me that production of the sensor would not begin any time soon.

This turned out to be the loneliest period of my life. I was alone at work, alone in my apartment at night, far away from everybody I loved and everything I cherished. Nothing was happening with the company I had conceived. I fought despondency and lived for the weekends when I would depart Findlay early on Friday morning, drive all day, get to Randolph County that evening, pick up my kids, take them to my parents' house and have two nights and one whole day with them before I had to leave on Sunday for the long drive back.

Three months after I left for Findlay, Judy and the children moved out of the farmhouse and into a house in Trinity provided by her mother. She took the children out of Poplar Ridge Friends Meeting, and they began attending her family's church, Allen Jay Baptist. I later rented the house, and to reinforce the way my luck was running, my tenant turned out to be a drug dealer.

Summer dissolved into fall, and still nothing was happening with Moisture Control Systems. All of the equipment was still sitting in the warehouse. The company had a research building next to the headquarters and sometimes I would elude my exile and visit there.

On one such trip, I discovered the researchers were having problems with a big water valve they were designing. They showed me the valve and told me about the problem. That night—and I am not making this up—I dreamed the solution to the problem. The next morning, I went to a hardware store, bought some magnets, returned to the research lab, mounted them on the valve, and it worked perfectly. I made some friends that day.

Early in November, I was summoned to a meeting with the Hulk. Little still had been done to begin production of the sensors, and I thought that might be the topic of the discussion. Not so.

The company had decided that since I no longer was president of Moisture Control Systems, I would have to forgo my percentage of the profits that might result from it. The Hulk wanted me to sign a paper agreeing to that. If I didn't sign it, he said, he was prepared to shut down the operation, and there would be no further need for my services. I was furious, but I maintained control. I'd have to think about it, I said.

I went to my apartment, got out my contracts, read all the fine print, and discovered that if Hancor shut down the company prematurely, I had the option to buy it at market value. The next day I went back to see the Hulk. I told him that I would not sign the paper, and if the company moved forward with shutting down the operation, I was giving notice that I wanted to exercise my option to buy it back at market value, which, considering the circumstances, couldn't be much. The Hulk's face turned vividly red as he shouted and stormed around, but he finally calmed enough to say he'd have to get back to me.

A few weeks later, I got word that the company was withdrawing its request for me to relinquish my share of profits and would move forward to production. My one little victory.

By this time, the company had hired a general manager for the operation. He was twenty-two years old, attending technical school part-time, and seemed to me to have little comprehension of the workings of the products he was about to begin manufacturing. At about the same time, I was relieved of my exile in the country and given a lab in the research department, where I began working on improving the sensor and creating other products.

Christmas was a happy break for me. I took a week off, went home, and was able to spend much of that time with my children. I was determined to make this a special Christmas for them. Back in the summer I had started work on a huge dollhouse for Annette and Margaret. I wanted them to have something they could cherish for a long time. This was a mansion, four stories tall with many rooms. It had a hinged roof so furniture could be arranged easily. I wired it with miniature lights and used individual boards for the front porch. I put a brass plaque in the back with Annette's and Margaret's names on it. Working on that toy filled my nights and many weekends for months, and I was proud of it. It took up the whole back seat of the Pontiac when I drove home with it. Annette has it on display in her home to this day.

By the end of January, a production line for the moisture sensors finally had been set up in one of Hancor's plants. Workers had been hired and were being trained. But we still weren't to the point we had been in High Point when that facility had been shut down nine months earlier.

Working on the dollhouse I built for my daughters during my miserable days in Findlay, Ohio.

113

By spring, however, production had begun and things seemed to be going fairly well. I was working on improving the ceramic for the sensor, and I just had learned that Computer Labs, which recently had been bought out by a much bigger company, Analog Devices, had come up with a new component to sense temperature that would be far more reliable than the one we were using. I wanted to incorporate it into the new design.

Although my work situation had improved, nothing could overcome my homesickness. I'd been in Findlay for more than a year now, and I longed to be close to my children. I wanted to be back on Randolph County soil.

Late in the summer, after my divorce had become final, I went to the Hulk with a proposition. Nothing about my job now required my presence in Findlay, I told him. I could do it just as well in North Carolina. I wanted to go home. It was a plea for mercy. He said he'd think about it.

Not long afterward, the Hulk called me in.

"Here's what we'll do," he said. "You sign over your stock, and we'll give you $30,000 and a new employment contract and let you work in North Carolina."

That sounded great to me. I'd still have my share of the profits, still be able to make some money.

Lawyers got involved and it took about a month to hash out the details, but both sides finally agreed. At the beginning of 1980, I would start working in North Carolina.

On October 1, before the documents were signed, I drove to Detroit to attend a seminar on microprocessors. I was sitting in class the next day when somebody came to the door and called me out. I had an urgent phone call. The Hulk's secretary was on the line.

"I have a message for you," she said. "The offer agreement has been rescinded."

I was expected to be at a meeting with the Hulk and company lawyers the following morning.

I thanked her, went back to the classroom, gathered up my stuff, walked to my company car, and drove to the Detroit airport. At the Eastern Airlines counter, I bought a one-way ticket to Greensboro. I sealed the car keys inside an envelope, gave it to the ticket agent, and told her that somebody from Hancor would come for it. I called the Hulk's secretary and told her where the car and the keys were.

"What am I supposed to tell Mister...?" she asked.

I was too polite to answer.

What I was doing was utterly uncharacteristic. I never before had been a person to give up, or to make rash moves, nor have I since. I always seek a conciliatory path.

Sometimes I see people on TV court shows say, "I don't know why I did it. Something just snapped." I have some understanding of that.

Something just snapped. I had been pushed as far as I could be pushed, and I flew away.

My parents picked me up at the airport. A couple of weeks later, I received notice from Hancor's lawyers that I was in breach of my contracts. They later would sue me, seeking my stock and percentage of profits. I would countersue, and the case would drag out over a couple of years before a settlement was reached. I agreed to give up my stock and profits, and the company agreed to pay me $12,000. By that time it didn't matter. The Hulk had long before shut down Moisture Control Systems.

The '64 Plymouth Valiant that I had bought the day before my wedding nearly fourteen years earlier was parked at my dad's house. Its paint was faded now, and it had a big dent in one fender. Its speedometer had registered far more than 100,000 miles. I got it running again. The floorboard had rusted through near the control pedals; I covered the hole with an old license tag. I drove that faithful car on one final visit to Findlay, Ohio. I rented a U-Haul trailer, loaded up my belongings, and headed toward home.

I had no money, no job, and no prospects. Far worse, my dreams had failed. I'd reached the lowest point of my life.

On that long trip back, I couldn't help but think about my granddaddy Neal, who had lost his job, his house, and his farm to the Great Depression. With a sick wife and a passel of children, he had come to Randolph County seeking to build a new life. I had some idea now of what my dad must have felt as he and his brother made their way to an uncertain future in a loaded wagon pulled by a mule and followed by a reluctant and balky cow. He had no way of knowing then that the difficult period he was going through was a necessary prelude to the happy life that he and my mother had found together.

My parents were deeply worried about me. Both prayed daily about my situation, my mother fervently so. Before I left on this trip, she told me that she had received divine assurance that everything was going to be all right for me. The faith that she and my dad had instilled in me allowed me to believe that.

Ten

My mother hadn't been just praying for happiness to return to my life. She also had been acting to give it a chance to happen.

Linda Stewart began working with my dad at Alma Desk Company right out of high school. He came to have a high opinion of her and frequently talked about what a good, caring, and hardworking person she was, and how lively and funny she could be. My mother got to know her, too, and both came to love her as if she were their daughter.

My parents kept up with Linda after she married a Green Beret and moved away to Okinawa, where she had a son. They offered moral support when her marriage failed and she returned to High Point to rear her son alone, working two jobs to do it, one of them back in the office at Alma Desk.

I had known about Linda for many years, but I never had met her. After Judy and I started our divorce proceedings, my mother knew how lonely and miserable I was in Findlay. She wanted me to meet Linda.

"She's the cutest thing," my mother said.

I'd seen photos of her over many years and knew that she was attractive.

"If I ask her if it's okay for me to give you her number and she says yes, will you call her?" my mother asked.

I'd consider it, I told her.

My mother later called to tell me that she'd talked with Linda, and Linda said it was okay for her to give me the number. What else would Linda say to somebody who loved her as much as my mom did?

I did call her, though. We talked about my folks and chatted about things in general. I really enjoyed the conversation. Linda was another connection to home, and when I asked if it would be okay if I called again, she said sure. So I waited for what I thought would be an appropriate time and did just that.

After several telephone chats, I told Linda that I'd like to meet her and suggested that we have a meal together on my next trip home to see my children. She said that would be nice.

My mother was thrilled when I told her that Linda and I were going out to dinner.

Linda lived in a small house next door to her parents off Skeet Club Road in High Point. I was a little taken aback when she answered my knock.

She was far more than cute. She had the most gorgeous long, dark hair. Her blue eyes sparkled with flecks of yellow and were instantly unforgettable. Her smile was simply radiant. She was tiny. I doubt that she weighed much more than eighty pounds. Her outgoing nature was immediately apparent. She invited me in and introduced me to her son, James, who was five, and to her sister Becky and Becky's husband Eddie.

We drove to Greensboro to a popular Italian restaurant called Anton's, where we ate in the romantic cellar. I don't remember our conversation that night, but I did come away with a deep impression of this woman whom my parents loved and admired so much. She was strong-willed and never hesitant to speak her mind. That appealed to me.

I began calling her a couple of times a week from Findlay, and I really looked forward to those conversations. I found that I could talk about anything with Linda, and she never would allow me to feel sorry for myself. She even enjoyed my low-keyed but ever persistent sense of humor. We laughed a lot in a time when I had little to laugh about.

I saw Linda on every trip back home. We'd go out to eat or to see a movie. She came to Findlay on a visit with my parents. After several months, I found myself in a dilemma. I was thinking about Linda a lot. And I realized that my feelings for her had grown deep.

From the second or third time we had gone out, Linda had made one thing very clear to me. She liked me and enjoyed our friendship. But she had no interest in a romantic relationship. If I had any thoughts in that direction, she told me, I'd better pack them away right now. She never intended to marry again. She had only one goal and that was to rear her son

to be a good and honorable person and to give him the best chance she could provide to have a full education and a joyful and successful life.

I understood, I told her. I was happy just to have a good friend.

How could I get out of that? And did I have any realistic chance of persuading such a strong-willed woman to move in a different direction?

I decided on a strategy— okay, a ploy—to see if I could make that happen. I called and

Linda shortly after I met her, a gorgeous and strong-willed woman.

117

told her I had something I needed to talk about, and it involved her. I was having stronger feelings about her than I had intended to allow, I said. I knew that wasn't what she wanted, and I certainly had no desire to put any pressure or strain on her because of my own emotions. So I thought the best thing for us to do was just to break off our relationship and not talk to each other anymore.

She understood, she said, and she thought that I had reached exactly the right decision. That wasn't what I wanted to hear. Next thing I knew, we had wished each other well, said good-bye, and I hung up the phone with a queasy feeling in my stomach. Had I outfoxed myself? Did she really mean that?

One anxious day turned into two. My phone didn't ring, and I didn't call her. Two days became three, and then a miserable week had passed, but the impasse hadn't. By the end of the second week, I began to think that I might have really messed up.

And then a phone rang. I won't reveal whose. And we both were saying how much we had missed the other. And everything changed.

We recognized that our futures were one. We began talking about marriage after my divorce was final. That was one of the reasons I had gone to ask the Hulk to let me return to North Carolina to work. I wanted to be close to Linda, and neither of us wanted to live in Ohio.

After I left Findlay and came home to live with my parents and begin a job search, Linda and I decided that there was no need to put off the wedding. We set the date for November 16. We didn't plan to make a big deal of it. We both loved the area around Boone and Blowing Rock in the North Carolina mountains, and we had made several one-day trips there on my visits from Findlay. We decided to get married in Boone. We got our license and the required blood tests and drove to the Watauga County Courthouse without prior arrangements.

Linda was a picture of grace and beauty, wearing a lovely lavender dress and carrying a white Bible and a small bouquet. I couldn't believe my good fortune as we strolled into the courthouse. I'm sure that everybody who saw us knew why we were there.

Inside, we searched out the small office of the justice of the peace. An older man in a wheel-chair sat behind a desk. I asked

Linda on our wedding day.

if he could marry us, and he said that we'd come to the right place. He quickly rounded up a couple of witnesses, and we began the short ceremony.

The door of the small office was open, and in the hallway a group of young men had gathered, talking and laughing. About halfway through the ceremony, they started roughhousing, whooping, and hollering.

The justice of the peace suddenly put down the book from which he was reading aloud. "Excuse me," he said. He whirled his chair around and rolled to the doorway.

"Hold it down!" he shouted. "We're trying to marry these people in here."

Linda laid down her Bible and bouquet and shot me a hard look of sheer disgust.

Muffled mutterings issued from the hallway as the justice of the peace rolled his chair back toward us.

"Okay now, where were we?" he said, resuming the ceremony.

"Whoo-hooo!" came a loud call from the hallway as he pronounced us husband and wife.

"I'm sorry about all of that," the justice of the peace said, "but at least you're married."

We signed the required documents. I paid up. And we beat a hasty retreat to the car.

Linda burst into tears the moment we got inside. "This is the worst day of my life," she cried.

I began to get the feeling that I probably should have put a little more thought into planning. But there was one thing I could count on for sure. I knew that Linda wasn't marrying me for my money or my success.

Despite its infelicitous beginning, our marriage was my salvation. We didn't have money for much of a honeymoon, but we spent a few days in the mountains and had a wonderful time. When we returned, I moved into Linda's small house with her and James. We explained everything to James, and he was accepting. He became my son, and my children became Linda's.

A few weeks after our wedding, I started a job with a major company to sell computer systems to businesses. I'd never tried sales before and didn't know how I might do at it. I suspected that my personality wasn't suited for it. I thought I was too low-keyed, not outgoing enough.

Before I could begin work, I had to attend three weeks of training in Pennsylvania that was tantamount to boot camp. All the others at the session were in their twenties. At thirty-five, I was the old guy. Much of the training was devoted to the hardware and software that we'd be selling and would have to teach customers to use. But big chunks were set aside for learning sales techniques.

We video-taped role-playing sessions that went on for four hours at a time during which instructors played reluctant customers and we had to overcome their objections. I loved that and turned out to be good at it, the top student. A lot that I learned in these sessions would prove to be of great help to me later in life. A good salesperson, I realized, is one who instills confidence in customers, never deceives or misleads, builds relationships, and makes certain that customers are satisfied no matter how difficult it may be.

I was enthusiastic about starting to work early in 1980 after my training. But real sales turned out to be a lot different than those in role-playing exercises. I had a big territory in the western part of the state that previously had not been served by the company. Computers still were a novel idea to many business owners, and they were extremely wary of them. My job was to make cold calls, at least eight a day. Statistics predicted that with any luck I might sell one system in sixty-four calls. I spent most of my time driving and being turned away by people far too busy to talk with me and completely unwilling to be overcome by the techniques that had won me accolades in training.

Within six months, I knew that this wasn't for me and began keeping an eye out for other jobs, something that would get me back to my passion for hands-on electronics, but little was available in our area. I could have gone to work immediately if I'd been willing to relocate to California, but I wasn't. By this time, Linda, James, and I had moved into an apartment in north High Point. I still had my house on my grandparents' farm. It was rented, and the rent was making the mortgage payments. Months passed without prospects of a job that would deliver me from selling. Early on Sunday mornings, I would go out and buy the High Point, Greensboro, and Winston-Salem newspapers, return to the apartment, and spend the next hour or so poring through the help wanted ads before we headed to Poplar Ridge Friends Meeting for Sunday services.

Meanwhile, I had begun seeing fellow salespeople for the company who would say anything, do anything to get business. Then I discovered that the company was refurbishing equipment that had been leased and selling it as new. This was a failure of ethics at the top levels of the company in my view, and I refused to have anything to do with it. I had to leave whether I had another job or not.

On a Sunday morning soon afterward, I spotted an ad that caused my heart to leap. The Computer Labs Division of Analog Devices wanted a quality engineer in microelectronics. This was the company I had turned to for help in redesigning my soil moisture sensor.

I called as soon as the offices opened on Monday morning and spoke to the personnel director, George McKeets. He invited me over for an interview. He was a big guy, quite a character, and I liked him immediately. He set up an interview for me with the manager of the quality control department. There was no question that I could do the job, which required testing circuits and setting up procedures for assuring quality. I had big hopes.

But when George called it was to tell me that the quality control manager had decided that my experience wouldn't allow me to be satisfied in that job. My heart sank.

"Have you ever thought about marketing?" George asked.

In my preliminary interview, I had told him that I wanted nothing else to do with sales.

Marketing had a sales element, he said. I would be working closely with salesmen but my technical knowledge would be more important to the position, which could prove to be quite challenging. Would I like for him to set me up an interview with the marketing manager?

In only a minute or so, I had gone from hope to desperation and unexpectedly back to hope. I had no idea whether I'd be interested in marketing, but I wasn't about to turn down an opportunity.

Lynn Cummings was the marketing director, and he and I seemed to hit it off from the beginning. He explained what a marketing position would entail, and it was a dream job for me. Everything I had done and learned had prepared me for it. I left thinking that there was a good chance I'd be hired and that I finally had stumbled onto my career.

Not until years later would I learn how close to being wrong I was about that.

Bill Pratt was the general manager for the Computer Labs Division. When Lynn went to him to say he wanted to hire me, Bill looked over my résumé and said, "That guy won't stay with us. He's had his own business. He'll want to do it again." Hiring me would be a horrible idea, he said, and he opposed it. Lynn had to do a lot of talking to get him to change his mind. Bill would turn out to be exactly right, although it would be he who enticed me into another entrepreneurial business venture. But that would be years down the road.

Everything was going my way, and I had no doubt that it all had begun when my mom decided she wanted me to meet Linda. Linda was the key to everything, my happiness and whatever success I might have at a career.

At about the time that I was waiting to hear from Analog Devices, Linda and I decided to take a brief vacation trip to the Amish country in Pennsylvania. I was intrigued by Amish devotion to tradition and the past and long had wanted to go there. It was beautiful country. We toured several farms, saw the men and horses at work in the fields, encountered the buggies on the roads, and talked with some of the friendly and circumspect people.

Our visit to
Amish country
in Pennsylvania
made me long to
return to rural life.

My mother posed
on my first
John Deere tractor
outside our
farmhouse.

Mom and Dad with Linda and our children.
Left to right on sofa, Mom, Linda, Annette, Jerry, Dad.
On the floor, James and Margaret.

Those few days stirred powerful feelings in me. I wanted to be back in a rural setting again. I yearned for the chorus of peep frogs, katydids, and hoot owls on summer nights; the sight of fields and forest; the smell of freshly turned earth and newly mown hay. I yearned for the same kind of tradition I saw in the Amish but with the luxury of electricity and gas-powered engines. I wanted to be back on the land on which my family had lived and farmed for generations. I wanted to have a tractor again.

Linda never had lived in a rural setting and didn't like the idea. Before we married I had told her that she wouldn't have to live in the house in Randolph County. But on this trip, I confessed to her that I really would like to move back there. My need to be back on the land of my ancestors was something too deeply set even for me to comprehend. I didn't expect her to understand it.

She didn't like the idea, she told me, but if it would make me happy, she would agree to the move. I can't describe my happiness at that moment, or the depth of my love for this woman who had changed my life so dramatically for the better.

I became a regional marketing manager at the Computer Labs Division of Analog Devices. Vast is entirely too small a word to describe my territory. It began at Chicago and included all of the Midwest and the West. It continued on from there across the Pacific to include Japan, Korea, Taiwan, Hong Kong, and China before venturing on to Australia.

Our division of Analog Devices made hybrid microcircuits, amplifiers for high frequency radio signals, and the world's fastest converters for changing data from analog to digital. A lot of what we produced was used by either the military or companies making medical equipment, including x-ray machines and other devices.

My job was to offer technical support to these companies and to our sales team. I spoke to groups of engineers describing our technology and trying to convince them to design our parts into their systems. I wrote technical articles. I worked on pricing strategies. If some part that we sold didn't produce the speed or performance expected from it, I would look into it and try to figure out what was going wrong. I dealt with a great blend of technical and business matters, and I loved every minute of it. I was learning more every day.

I was assigned my first big project soon after I joined the company. Two defense companies, General Dynamics and Ford Aerospace, were vying for a battlefield missile contract. General Dynamics was a customer of ours, and I made many trips to Pomona, California, to convince engineers and executives to design in a converter that would receive a radar signal and digitize it so that it could be fed into a computer controlling the missile.

We got the part into the prototype, and then there was a shoot-off between the two companies to see whose system performed best. General Dynamics won hands down. I was overjoyed. This would mean millions for our company and a big boost for me. But when the contracts were announced, they went to Ford Aerospace. Bureaucrats theorized that if Ford didn't get the job, the company might not survive.

This was a big disappointment and a setback for me and the company, but I was assured that these things happened, and there was nothing to do but put it behind us and move on. I took on two more military projects that never got much past the design phase before they were dropped, one of them with Motorola. People in the marketing department started referring to me jocularly as "the albatross."

Then the M-1 tank clanked into my life. Hughes Aircraft had developed a laser-controlled range finder for the big gun on the tank. We supplied an amplifier for it, a multi-transistor module, not with integrated circuits. This system had to be fully tested against radiation, and every part had to be qualified as radioactive resistant. Radiation from a battlefield atomic explosion could change the characteristics of some transistors and make the whole system inoperable.

We had qualified our module, but when manufacturing began, one particular transistor was hard to obtain. A procurement manager found another transistor that would work just as well and substituted it without realizing that it had to be resistant to radioactivity. This one wasn't. A simple mistake, but a huge one.

After these systems were installed in M-1 tanks all around the world, the Army did some tests and discovered the transistor would fail when subjected to radiation. The systems had to be pulled from every tank so the faulty module could be replaced. The Army was not happy with Hughes Aircraft, and Hughes wasn't happy with us. Hughes was one of the companies I handled, and this incident would provide me with one of the great learning experiences of my career, one I would put to good use many times in the future.

My first instinct was to fly to Hughes, find out the dimensions of this embarrassing and costly problem, and work out a plan to solve it, an instinct that made my problem-solving dad proud. We eventually replaced all the modules. I negotiated a settlement for the extensive costs, and we were able to keep Hughes as a customer and do a lot more business with the defense contractor.

"Jerry, the thing I like about you is that you always run toward problems, never away from them," Bill Pratt, the Computer Labs general manager, told me after this, and we began to form a friendship.

Japan was a hotbed of technology during my early years at Analog Devices, but our division did little business there, only about 5 percent of our revenue. I wanted to change that.

Analog Devices had an office in Tokyo, which employed one hundred people or more, and another in Osaka. I started making regular trips to Japan to pitch the advantages of our products to engineers and executives of major electronics companies. At the time, Japan was ahead of the rest of the world in electronics, and many people thought that the Japanese would end up dominating the field of semiconductors, the tiny integrated circuits that power computers and many other electronic devices.

I took instructions in Japanese business protocol and got passing grades on the tea drinking ceremony, the ritual business card exchange, and the proper time to bow. That was the easy part. Convincing Japanese engineers that American-made electronic components weren't inferior was the hard part. I'd go to Toshiba, Mitsubishi, and Hitachi and hear the same thing over and over. I was a long time overcoming it, but eventually I began presenting seminars and demonstrations of our parts that made an impression, and we began getting more orders.

I made several trips to Japan every year, usually for two or three weeks at a time, and I came to love the country—in climate and terrain it's much like North Carolina—as well as the people I met. On one of my early trips, I was working at the Tokyo office when a young female employee came to my door and asked if I'd like anything.

"Maybe a Diet Coke," I said.

She bowed and hurried away. After a while she returned looking a little breathless and carrying a Coke. Several times a day she would reappear at my door and ask if I'd like a Coke. "Oh, that'd be nice," I'd say, trying to be agreeable.

This happened every time I went to Japan, and it was not until a couple of years later that I discovered what this young woman had been going through to please me. Whenever I said I'd like a Coke, she rushed to the petty cash keeper; got the required coins; ran down five flights of stairs, out of the building, and down the street to a vending machine where she got the Coke; and ran all the way back. I have no

I visited the Golden Pavilion in Kyoto.

idea how many miles that young woman ran to please the visiting American, but it had to be a lot.

The first few times that the building I was working in began shaking, I became more than a little concerned about the possibility of being swallowed up in a big earthquake and never heard from again. But my Japanese friends paid so little attention to this phenomenon that I began accepting it as just a normal part of life in Japan. Even when I got shaken awake in bed, I'd just wait a minute to see if this was the big one, then roll over and go back to sleep.

Ask any visitor to Japan about favorite spots and you are apt to hear about the Imperial Palace, any number of ancient shrines and temples, Mount Fuji, or many other beautiful sights. Mine was a district in Tokyo that was jammed with stores filled with electronics of every imaginable kind. I spent much of my free time there. A dollar bought many yen at that time, and I got some real bargains.

I first went to this district because I wasn't fluent in the language. All that I could understand on Japanese TV was sumo wrestling, and I wanted to hear the news. I went in search of a good shortwave radio so that I could pick up the *BBC World News*. I had gotten away from ham radio in recent years, but these shops were loaded with ham equipment. I ended up buying some and returning to that hobby of my youth.

Within a few years, I was able to double our division's business in Japan, and I turned my attentions to establishing a foothold in an even bigger potential market where we had no customers: China.

We had an office in Hong Kong that I visited regularly. Salespeople there were working on opening the mainland for our products. I was called upon to make a three-city tour giving seminars to technology conferences. A marketing person from our headquarters near Boston accompanied me. We were to give separate presentations at every stop. The first conference was in Nanking.

We were a little hesitant when we walked onto the tarmac to board the plane to Nanking and saw what looked like a patchwork quilt. Mismatched panels in many colors and languages from numerous planes had been hobbled together to create this one. The engines didn't quite seem to match either. I took a window seat, and my partner had the aisle. When he leaned back, the whole seat flopped straight into the lap of the passenger behind him. When he called this to the attention of the flight attendant, she directed us to two other seats.

The same thing happened. I know that this sounds like an old joke, but when he summoned the attendant again, she said, "Oh, just don't lean back." We made it to Nanking with my partner sitting bolt upright the whole way, arriving after nightfall. Miraculously, we got through customs with five trunks filled with technical manuals. A driver with a van was supposed to be waiting for us. But as we set out through the terminal pushing these heavy trunks, everything went black. We were in total darkness.

We stopped and waited for several minutes, but the lights didn't come back on. We started calling for help, timidly at first, then a little louder. As we were reaching the shouting stage, somebody finally pulled a string on a single dim, dangling light bulb in a hallway about fifty yards away, and we headed for it as fast as we could go.

We eventually located the driver, who could speak English, loaded the heavy trunks into the van, and headed for the city, which was maybe ten miles away.

The driver appeared to have ambitions to be the Chinese Richard Petty. He drove with a heavy foot, rarely applying it to the brakes. But that wasn't my major concern.

"Shouldn't you turn on the headlights?" I asked him.

"We have law," he said. "Use lights only at intersections."

My concern wasn't so much for us as for others. We were in a sea of bicycles, and the riders seemed to swerve away only an instant before they would have been mangled beneath the van's wheels. At intersections, though, the driver dutifully switched on the lights as he harrowingly dodged and weaved between cars, trucks, and bicycles before shooting back into darkness. I've rarely been so grateful to get to a hotel.

The conference was at a big university. Thousands were attending it. My seminar was in a huge hall, and every seat was filled. It was unbearably hot, and there was no air conditioning. I took off my suit jacket as I started my lecture. I was going to explain digital converters, and I planned to use an overhead projector with lots of transparencies of diagrams and the like. I had been provided a translator, a polite, neatly dressed young man who stood a couple of feet away.

I put up my first diagram, described it for a minute or two, and turned to my translator so that he could convey what I had said. He just stood there staring at me with a blank look on his face. I waited. He said nothing. I nodded as if to give a signal to go ahead. He stepped forward and whispered in my ear.

"I don't understand."

"Oh," I said.

We whispered back and forth a little. Maybe if I used just a few words at a time, he said, he could do better.

I tried three or four words, and he smiled and spoke. We were getting somewhere. I tried three or four more. We kept going. Sometimes I would speak three or four and get that look again. He'd step over and whisper for clarification. I'd try different words. Sometimes that worked. Sometimes it didn't.

Sometimes I'd speak three or four words, and he'd talk for a minute

The locomotive that took me to Shanghai during a speaking tour in China.

or two. I couldn't fathom how he could have gotten all of that out of those few words. A few times the audience erupted in laughter, although there was nothing funny in the three or four words I'd spoken. Four hours later, sweat-soaked and exhausted, I finally finished my one-hour lecture. I got a huge round of applause. I expect it was out of gratitude that the audience no longer had to endure that grinding misery.

Our next stop was Shanghai, and it was an all-day journey on a train pulled by a steam-powered locomotive. I'd seen trains like that as a little kid in High Point. The car I was assigned was stuffy and uncomfortable and jammed with passengers carrying teapots, cooking gear, and all manner of other goods. They even brought their own chickens and ducks, but thankfully they were in cages in another car. The train seemed to stop every fifteen minutes, reminding me of my Trailways bus trips back to Gaston Tech.

We soon learned that when darkness descended, the train would stop and wouldn't proceed again until daylight. Everybody had to get off. If you hadn't reached your destination when darkness arrived, you had to make do until sunrise. Most passengers simply

I asked a passerby to snap this shot of me on the Great Wall.

camped out by the tracks, starting fires, simmering tea, and killing and cooking chickens and ducks.

Thankfully, we arrived in Shanghai before dark. We didn't have a chicken or duck between us, not to mention a pot to cook it in.

In Shanghai we had no problems. The seminar was again at a university, and my interpreter seemed to understand everything I said and conveyed it quickly and smoothly to an audience that seemed truly appreciative. Of course, word may have preceded us of the ordeal that the conference participants in Nanking had endured, and for all I knew the interpreter could have been citing Chinese proverbs just so everybody could get out on time. Whichever the case, I, at least, was grateful.

Next stop was the national capital, Beijing. There my partner and I split up. My seminar was at a military base. My taxi driver let me out about a hundred feet from the gate. I was about halfway to it when I saw a squadron of soldiers running toward me. I stopped, and they formed a circle around me, rifles aimed directly at my head. I could look straight into the bores. They looked awfully big. I kept thinking a hole that size in me could be painful.

I set down my fat briefcase, raised my hands high above my head, contorted my face into a smile big enough to hurt, and turning in a slow circle, put on the best imitation I could muster of Andy Griffith playing Sheriff Taylor in Mayberry. "Hey, how y'all?" I repeated over and over. "Good to see you. How you doin'?"

I heard a shout from the gate, and a civilian came running toward us. He spoke sharply to the soldiers, and they lowered their weapons, backed away, and started smiling back.

"Mr. Neal?" said the man. I nodded. "Welcome, welcome."

I picked up my briefcase, straightened my coat, gave a little wave to the soldiers, and we proceeded to the gate.

"What was that all about?" I asked my guide.

He laughed. "They were just practicing."

After my final, somewhat nervous performance, although not a single gun was aimed at my head, I had time for some sightseeing. I went to the Great Wall, the Ming Tombs, and the Forbidden City. I had my photo made standing in front of a huge poster of Mao in Tiananmen Square. Kids followed me wherever I went, and I shook their hands and photographed them.

But we got little business out of that trip, and it would be years before Analog Devices could overcome the governmental bureaucracy and the technology differences to get substantial sales in China.

On one of my trips to the far reaches of my territory, this time Australia, I returned to the Greensboro airport to find Linda waiting for me. As soon as I saw her face, I knew that something was wrong. She wouldn't tell me what it was until we got to the car.

"Your granddaddy's barn burned down," she said.

The charred rubble was a sad sight. Several family heirlooms had been lost in the fire, and nobody knew what had started it. All of the tools and farming equipment that had belonged to my granddaddy Jeff and my great-grandpa Edd were gone. So was my first little lawn tractor, the Allis-Chalmers, the one on which I mowed my big yard at Caraway Hills holding Annette in my arms when she was just a tiny baby.

That barn had given me a lot of wonderful childhood memories, playing in the hay loft, going there with both of my grandpas to check on

I had many great childhood memories of the barn built by my great-grandfather Edd.

The barn burned down while I was on a business trip to Australia.
My cousin Dwight Loflin and I rebuilt it to look the same.

the animals, slipping ears of corn to the cow and the mules. Whenever my granddaddy Dorsett led the mules to the well to draw buckets of water for them, he would let me climb onto the back of one of them and ride it back to the barn.

After I had hauled away the debris and cleared the site, my cousin Dwight Loflin, who had his own memories of the barn, and I started rebuilding it, using rough-sawn boards from a nearby sawmill. It would take us a year and a half but we finally finished it, and when the boards had time to weather, the new barn looked much like the original.

I thought my grandpa Edd would have approved.

Eleven

Just as I once had thought that Hewlett-Packard would be my career, I came to think the same about Analog Devices. But unexpected circumstances intervened. My friend Bill Pratt, the general manager, became seriously ill and had to undergo brain surgery. He was out of work for many weeks. He returned to find that he'd been eased out of his job.

Bill, a visionary engineer, created a new center in Greensboro to develop new products for the company. He opened it in an office complex near the airport. His friend and mine, Powell Seymour, a fellow Analog Devices employee, joined him to produce prototypes.

They worked at improving digital converters at first, but Bill had taken an interest in cellular phones, which then were in their infancy. He thought the company should get into that field. He began visiting phone manufacturers to find out their needs and designed the first radio frequency integrated circuits, the microchips that would make the cell phone phenomenon possible.

As the 1990s began, serious recession had settled over the technology industry, and early in 1991, Analog Devices began layoffs. Bill and Powell were among the first to go. The company had decided against the cell phone field, and as part of their settlement, Bill and Powell were allowed to keep rights to the handful of radio frequency chips Bill had designed.

They decided to start their own company, RF Micro Devices, and they invited me to join them as a partner. My job would be to raise the capital to get the company going and to handle marketing.

I found myself in the same position I'd been in fifteen years earlier when I had had to decide whether to leave Hewlett-Packard to start my own business. That had turned into disaster, and I wasn't sure I could face such a prospect again. Still I didn't like what Analog Devices had done to Bill. I didn't like the layoffs (my own sister Diane was among them), and I didn't like the sometimes ugly office politics. But I had a safe position, a good salary and benefits, and I liked my job. Analog Devices had made life far brighter for Linda and me.

I agonized long and hard about this decision, and in the end it was Linda who told me that if I didn't grab this opportunity, I wouldn't be able to live with myself. I knew that she was right. Besides, here was my chance to finally work in radio, my childhood passion.

For the second time in my life, I pushed headlong into the uncertain and risky world of technological entrepreneurship, where I'd vowed I'd never venture again. And I couldn't have been more excited about it.

At the beginning, Bill had thought that we would need $750,000 and a couple of years to reach a profit. We soon revised that to $1.5 million. It actually would take nearly six years, $28.5 million, and several close brushes with total failure before we would see the first nickel of profit.

I have told the story of the phenomenal success of RF Micro Devices in an earlier book, *Fire in the Belly: Building a World-leading High-tech Company from Scratch in Tumultuous Times.* I hope that you will read

Linda encouraged me to take the chance on another new business.

it if you haven't. The book details the spectacular rise of RF Micro during the dot-com boom and bust. Unlike many technology companies that disappeared after the bust, RF Micro remains a thriving and growing company with global reach.

But at the same time that our new company was bringing radical and happy changes to my professional life in the early 1990s, other profound events were taking a personal toll.

The first sign of the disease that would rip my parents' lives apart came on Christmas Eve 1984, although I wouldn't learn about it until months later. Mom and Dad were doing some last-minute Christmas shopping at the mall in High Point. A bitter cold snap was passing through, the temperature dropping radically in a short period. It had fallen into the teens when they emerged from the mall; the wind was blowing hard. They thought they might not make it to the car, so harsh was the wind and cold.

Once in the car, shivering, with the engine going and the heater beginning to blow warm air, Mom turned to Dad and said, "Albert, did you cover the pump house with leaves so the water won't freeze?"

When we moved into the house my dad had built thirty years earlier, our water came from a spring and my dad had built a small pump house there. Every winter he covered it in a big pile of leaves to insulate it.

"Bertie, you know we don't use that spring anymore," my dad said. "We've been on Davidson County water for years."

"Oh, that's right," she agreed.

133

But that remark was a red flag to my dad. He began watching, listening, and taking note of other things my mom said and did. He became concerned enough that after a few months he told my sisters and me about my mom's growing memory lapses. It could just be normal forgetfulness, we all thought. After all, she was turning sixty-five.

But time would prove that not to be the case. My mom always had been an immaculate housekeeper, but now she began letting ordinary chores go. Sometimes she rearranged things in ways that she never would have done before. My sisters would call and ask her what she had done that day, and she would turn to my dad and ask him before she answered.

My mom made the best chocolate pie in the entire world. Everybody raved about it. It was her pride and joy, and she made it for every special occasion. But we and others began noticing differences in the pie. She clearly was leaving out crucial ingredients. Sometimes it was almost inedible, but we had to pretend otherwise.

Mom always sweetened the iced tea—it's a Southern thing. But she would forget that she had sweetened it. She would sweeten it again and again until it almost was syrup and nobody could drink it. My dad told us that she was hiding bananas in drawers all around the house.

Clearly, something was drastically wrong. But when my dad suggested that maybe she should see a doctor, she wouldn't hear of it. There was nothing wrong with her, my mother adamantly maintained.

Dad conferred with my sisters and me, and we all agreed that something had to be done. Early in September 1986, we made an appointment with a gerontologist at Moses Cone Hospital in Greensboro and took her there. The diagnosis was what we feared: Alzheimer's disease.

Nothing could be done about it. The verdict was clear. It was a death sentence, but it would take years to play out. The doctor spelled out exactly what we could expect. It was a horrific picture, but my dad didn't flinch in the face of it. His devotion to my mother was as complete as his devotion to God. His future was set at that moment. He would care for her and protect her. He would do whatever it took to alleviate her suffering. That wasn't just his duty in his view. It was the ultimate level of love.

In her later years, my dad's mother, Ethel, had fallen into senility. He would go to see her, and she wouldn't recognize him. "I don't know who you are," she would tell him, "but you sure are a nice man."

He now would face that situation with the love of his life. "Who are you?" my mother would demand. "What are you doing in my house? You better get out of here!"

My sister Betty summed up the effect of that on my dad. "For Mama to do that, it was just like a knife through his heart."

My mom became afraid of water, even small amounts. She refused to take baths and wouldn't let my dad near her with water. My sisters would have to wet washcloths out of her sight to bathe her. She went into a long period of constant agitation, rarely sleeping, stalking the house throughout the day and night. She was strong and could walk for miles, and my dad lived in constant fear that she would get out of the house and become lost in the woods or step in front of a car on a nearby road.

He began taking all kinds of security precautions and at one time even had to nail the bedroom door shut with both of them inside so he could get a few hours sleep. He discovered that one thing would calm her—riding in the car. He would drive her for hours.

My sisters and I became deeply concerned about my dad's own health. The physical and emotional strain of caring for my mom was wearing him down, although he never complained. We began looking for a place that could care for her. But we found long waiting lists at Alzheimer's facilities. We did find a day care program in downtown Greensboro that would accept her and give my dad a break. We started taking her there in the fall of 1990.

I still was at Analog Devices then, and my sister Diane worked there in accounting. We alternated taking my mom to day care before going to work. My dad would pick her up, or sometimes we would return for her.

Old habits die hard. Greensboro was upgrading its cable system at that time. I saw the work going on all around town. I also noticed that some of the big wooden reels that this cable came on were being hauled away with small amounts of cable still on them. That cable was superb for handling high frequency signals, and I could use some of it with my ham radio gear and satellite receiver.

One day I stopped and asked a crew member what was happening to those reels that still had cable on them. All of them, he told me, empty or not, were being stashed on the grounds of an abandoned school. I went there, found a supervisor, told him I'd like to have some of that cable, and he said to help myself, take all I wanted. It was just waste.

Inveterate wire collector that I was, I started hauling these reels to my farm in the back of my Ford Ranger pickup truck. There was a hill in the schoolyard where I could back the truck up to it and easily roll these reels, which were about five feet high, into the bed. I usually hauled two at a time. I actually needed about one hundred feet of this cable, but eventually I would have a field full of these reels and about a mile of cable if all the pieces were spliced together.

I had to pick up my mom at day care one afternoon and went by the school first to load a couple of these reels. This time I became a little overly ambitious and managed to wedge three into the bed, although I had to leave the tailgate down to do it.

I hurried to get my mom, and we headed off into rush-hour traffic toward home. By this point, we never were certain whether Mom recognized us or even had any moments of cognizance. At the top of a steep hill, I encountered a red light and stopped. When the light changed and I pressed the accelerator, the truck jerked slightly and I sensed something was amiss. I looked into the rearview mirror to see one of the big reels exiting over the lip of the tail gate. I hit the brakes, but it was too late. The other two reels followed quickly.

Horns blared. Tires squalled. I turned to see cars darting hither and yon as the reels gathered speed heading downhill, all in different directions. A look of panic hit my mother, and she buried her face in both hands. I couldn't help but believe that she was having a moment of awareness and that what was flashing through her mind was an old fear: "I knew that all that messin' with wires would lead to something like this."

I told my mom to stay put, locked her in the truck, and ran down the hill to see what I had wrought. I expected to find some eighty-year-old guy, out for his afternoon stroll, hobbling on his cane, flattened by a huge cable reel, and I didn't know how I'd be able to live with myself.

Vehicles were scattered in disarray over the street. Traffic was beginning to back up, and some people were yelling unfriendly things out their windows at me. I discovered that all of the reels had miraculously avoided collisions with people, vehicles, or structures and had done no significant damage. One had jumped a curb and settled in somebody's yard, another had sprawled onto a sidewalk, and the third was far down the hill in the gutter.

I fetched them one by one but had no idea what to do with them. I couldn't load them onto the truck. They were far too heavy to lift. A gas station was nearby. The operator had seen what happened and had come out to watch the real-life version of carnival bumper cars that had ensued.

I asked him if I could stash the reels at the gas station until I could come back for them, and he agreed. The problem was that the reels all were down the hill from the gas station. I spent the next hour straining my back and legs rolling those reels up the hill. Not a soul offered to help. By the last one, the one farthest away, I began to feel like the mythical Sisyphus, doomed forever

Mom and Dad behind their house shortly after Mom began showing the first signs of Alzheimer's disease.

to roll a big wire reel up a steep hill only to get to the top and have it come crashing back down on me.

Mom's doctor told us about a new Alzheimer's facility near Moses Cone Hospital in Greensboro. To our great relief, she got accepted. My dad, my sister Diane, and I took her there. But my dad realized immediately that security wasn't sufficient enough to keep my mom from wandering away and perhaps into the traffic of one of Greensboro's busiest thoroughfares, which was only a short walk away. He wouldn't leave her there, and we had to start a frantic search for another facility.

On September 6, 1991, we finally got my mother into the Alzheimer's care unit at the Evergreens Center on Wendover Avenue in Greensboro. This was a trying time for our entire family but particularly so for my sister Betty. A week later, her son Dean died of pancreatic cancer. He was just thirty.

My dad drove the thirty-five miles to Greensboro every morning to spend the entire day with my mom. He fed her. He walked her. He sat beside her and held her hand while she dozed. Sometimes he would check her out and take her for a ride. At other times, they would just sit in the car and listen to the radio. He would put her to bed about seven, then drive back home.

We worried about my father driving back and forth, especially at night when he would be so tired and when the winter weather turned bad. We wanted to get Mom into a facility called GrayBrier near Archdale, not so far from my dad's house, as well as mine and my sisters. And in 1992, we finally got her accepted there.

My dad continued his routine of caring for her. In the three and a half years that my mom would be in nursing facilities, he would miss only three days and those would be days when he was too sick to go.

My mom's slow degeneration continued. And every step of it was a new heartbreak for my dad. She forgot how to talk. Then she forgot how to walk, and my dad pushed her through hallways in a wheelchair until she no longer could sit in a chair.

My dad still fed her every meal, and he began noticing that she was stashing food in her cheeks, like a chipmunk. She was forgetting how to swallow. My dad was afraid that she would choke. He knew that she no longer could be fed by mouth, and he couldn't stand the thought of watching her starve to death. He wanted to have a feeding tube inserted. She was scheduled to go to the hospital for that procedure on Monday, February 20, 1995.

But on Saturday night, February 18, as my dad was getting ready to leave for the night, he noticed a change in her breathing pattern. He fetched a nurse, and when they returned to the room, she asked him to step outside for a moment. He went to the telephone, called my sisters, and said that he didn't want to alarm them but that maybe they ought to come. Before he could call me, the nurse summoned him back to the room. My mom had forgotten how to breathe.

"Son, your mama's gone," he said when he called me. She was twelve days short of turning seventy-five.

My dad didn't show emotion. As always, he was as solid as a rock.

The investors and board of directors at RF Micro had been thinking of taking the company public even before our first profit in the fall of 1996. By early 1997, the time seemed right. And in June, RF Micro stock started trading on the Nasdaq Exchange.

As odd as it may sound, Bill, Powell, and I never had thought much about making money. We just wanted to build the company and have fun, and we had devoted endless hours and all of our energies to that. By the time we reached the public offering, the 40 percent of the company that the three of us had owned after receiving the first investments had fallen to less than 10 percent. The rest had been given up to gain additional investors.

Still, if the stock brought the price we expected, our original shares plus options we had been granted would have considerable value. It would be a while before we could sell any stock and realize our first profits, but that time would come.

All of us lived middle-class lives, nothing extravagant. We never had known wealth. Linda and I still lived in the farmhouse. I'd bought another tractor after the barn fire, a small John Deere 750 with a three-cylinder diesel engine. I still had it, although I'd had little chance to use it since we started the company.

Before the public offering, I sat down to have a talk with Linda about what was to come. It was likely that we would have more money than we'd ever dreamed, I told her. It could change our lives, and we needed to start thinking about that.

Tears suddenly welled in her eyes. "I don't want our lives to change," she said. "I love our lives."

It's a little awkward trying to console somebody about good news, but this time I knew exactly how to do it.

"You've always wanted to do something to help children," I told her. "Now we'll be able to do that."

Part III

A House for Giving

Twelve

As a Christmas present to Linda in 1997, I gave her a trip. Three days after Christmas, we got into my white Dodge diesel pickup truck and headed west on I-40 to Memphis, Tennessee.

Our destination was St. Jude Children's Research Hospital.

Thanks to television, many people are aware of the story of St. Jude Hospital—I'll call it St. Jude for short. It was the inspiration of Danny Thomas, one of America's most beloved entertainers, who was known for his popular TV shows in the '50s and '60s: *Make Room for Daddy* and *The Danny Thomas Show*. Later, he also produced hit programs such as *The Andy Griffith Show,* especially beloved by North Carolinians, and *The Dick Van Dyke Show*.

As a young man, uncertain of himself and his future, Danny Thomas, the son of Lebanese immigrants, knelt in a church dedicated to St. Jude Thaddeus, the patron saint of hopeless causes, and prayed for direction in his life. He later promised to do something to repay St. Jude for the good fortune that his faith, his talent, and hard work had brought to him.

What better way to deliver on that pledge than to tackle the least understandable examples of hopelessness—children stricken by deadly diseases and snatched away without a chance at life?

Thomas decided to build a hospital to research and fight the causes of these childhood illnesses, and he settled on Memphis as the mid-America site for it. He organized major show business stars to get behind the effort, and he and his wife, Rose Marie, roamed the country by car, going city to city, raising money to get the hospital built.

Once construction was assured, he and a group of friends from the Arab-American community formed the American Lebanese Syrian Associated Charities (ALSAC) to express their appreciation to the country that had welcomed them and their ancestors and allowed them to live in freedom and prosperity. ALSAC's job was to build support for the hospital and to raise funds to keep it operating.

St. Jude opened in 1962. It has grown dramatically since then, spreading miracles in spiraling dimensions and saving the lives of untold numbers of children around the world who, without the work that goes on at St. Jude, would have been hopeless and lost.

We were just vaguely aware of St. Jude's history at this time. We knew the Danny Thomas connection. We thought the hospital dealt mainly with children stricken by cancer. In 1994, Linda had sent a $25 check to the hospital after seeing an emotional appeal on TV. In 1996, shortly after RF Micro made its first profit, she sent a $1,000 donation by credit card. I knew well how she felt about children, especially children who meet misfortune or have little chance of living long and healthy lives. She had expressed a desire to do more.

Before Christmas, I called the hospital and reached a young woman named Leslie Bailey (later to be Davidson). I told her that I wanted to give my wife a trip to St. Jude for Christmas, and she thought that was wonderful. She would arrange a full-day tour, she told me. I didn't mention even the possibility of a donation.

That Christmas turned out to be one of the most memorable of our lives. Christmas is about love and faith and giving. That's exactly what we found at St. Jude in a big way. And the gift it offers is the most precious of all—life itself to the most innocent of all: children.

St. Jude fills a sprawling, fifty-acre campus in downtown Memphis. Any tour of the hospital begins with a visit to an unusual star-like, gold-domed building that sits in front of the hospital's entrance inside its walled compound. The building was designed to resemble the Dome of the Rock Church in Jerusalem. This is the Danny Thomas/ALSAC Pavilion, and it is open free to the public every day.

Inside, a visitor can learn the story of St. Jude's purpose and how it came to be, as well as the story of ALSAC and its work to keep the hospital growing and its mission expanding. Here, too, is a virtual museum of Danny Thomas' show business memorabilia, as well as his many honors, including his Emmys and the Congressional Medal he received for his vision in founding St. Jude.

Danny Thomas died on February 6, 1991, two days after he celebrated the twenty-ninth anniversary of St. Jude. He was interred in a crypt in the pavilion, and nine years later his wife, Rose Marie, would join him there. Adjacent to the pavilion is a garden named for Danny Thomas and Rose Marie, where patients, their families, staff, and visitors alike can find refuge from the stresses of their lives amid the comforting beauty of trees, shrubs, flowers, flowing water, and songbirds.

During our tour, we learned that St. Jude employs more than three thousand people, including some of the world's top medical scientists, and ALSAC has about five hundred full-time employees. St. Jude has treated patients from every state and more than seventy countries. It maintains an average of nearly 4,700 active patients and sees about two hundred daily. Patients with the most difficult diseases to cure are selected from physician referrals. They are not charged for treatments for which they have no insurance, and those without insurance aren't required to pay. Operating the hospital costs more than $1 million a day.

We visited research labs and treatment facilities and chatted briefly with physicians and scientists about the many diseases on which they were working. We also met some of the children being treated and their parents.

Surely nothing can be worse than losing a child, and when you look into the eyes of parents facing that prospect, you see fear and dread made physical, but at St. Jude it's countered by the hope that fills every heart there.

Near the end of our visit, Linda and I went into a tiny chapel at the hospital that was donated by a couple named Albert and Emeline Harris, both now deceased. The chapel had a stained-glass window of St. Jude surrounded by children. In that chapel were books containing hand-written prayers left by gravely ill children, their parents, and others over the years. These books were filled with heartbreak, but also with stirring hope and incredible faith. Reading these prayers was a deeply moving experience that made us acutely aware of our own blessings.

On our way back home the next day, we both realized that this trip had been a life-changing experience. Once you visit St. Jude it's not a place you can forget. We knew it would be part of us forever, and that we would do whatever we could to keep its work going. A day later, we signed over five hundred shares of RF Micro stock to the hospital. Our stock still held about the same value that it had at issue, and St. Jude, whose policy is to sell stock donations immediately, would net only about $6,000 from that donation. But this was just an initial gesture.

A year later, our stock had more than doubled in value, and at Christmas we made a bigger donation: one thousand shares netting $25,000. Linda and I had been talking a lot about St. Jude, and she was succinct in her position following this donation.

"We can do more," she said.

A few weeks later I called Leslie Bailey, whom we both love now as if she were family, and told her that we had decided that we wanted to become volunteers for the hospital in whatever ways we could be useful. We were setting up a trust so that upon our deaths a portion of our estate would go to St. Jude. We also planned to continue making annual donations with a goal of giving at least $1 million over our lifetimes.

We wanted to return to the hospital and spend more time learning as much about it as we could. Leslie said she would arrange that, but the logistics proved difficult. This turned out to be an extremely hectic period for our company, and every time we set a tentative date, I wouldn't be able to keep it, or something else would interfere. Finally, I decided that I'd just have to take the time, no matter what was going on, and we scheduled a three-day visit for Linda's birthday in mid-September 1999.

This visit turned out to be an eye-opener, a real education. We were able to get an up-close and vivid look at the hospital's mission and its work, and to learn of some of its many successes. When St. Jude opened, children with acute lymphoblastic leukemia had a 4 percent chance of survival. Now the survival rate is 85 percent. But nobody's resting on that good news. They want 100 percent, and they won't settle for less.

On the first day of our visit, Dr. Joseph Mirro, the chief medical officer, gave us a complete overview of the hospital's work and its future plans.

We had a truly special moment while touring one of the patient care units. We happened to be present when Samantha Watlington, five years old and a victim of acute lymphoblastic leukemia, had her Coming Off Chemo party after two and a half years of treatments. We joined in the applause when nurses sang the "Coming Off Chemo Song" and Samantha was showered with confetti. Her smile said more about the work at St. Jude than anybody could have told us. Incidentally, as this is written, Samantha is eleven and doing fine.

Afterward, we signed up as full volunteers and underwent orientation by Lisa Sulipeck, the volunteer services coordinator.

On our second day, we spent time playing with children who were patients at the hospital and talking with their parents. These parents are in the worst struggle anybody could endure, the outcome unknown. The strain of that affects every aspect of their lives—their marriages, their finances, their relationships with other children, their own health and sanity—and in them we saw strength and courage of the type that rarely is encountered.

We also met with Dr. Michael Kastan and Dr. Ed Horwitz to talk about the research underway and new treatments being developed to fight cancer and blood diseases. Afterward, we joined other volunteers in activities going on at the hospital that afternoon.

That night we had a delightful dinner with a brilliant and funny couple

Linda and I meet with Dr. Joseph Mirro, St. Jude's chief medical officer.

from the hospital, Drs. Bill Evans and Mary Relling, husband and wife, and both pharmaceutical scientists. Five years hence, Bill would become director and chief executive officer of St. Jude. Joining us that evening were Bobby and Ann Leatherman of Memphis, both enthusiastic supporters of St. Jude.

In 1992, the Leathermans had brought their two-year-old daughter, Eliza, to the hospital. A huge tumor filled the right side of her chest. It had collapsed her lung and was obstructing her breathing and threatening her heart. Doctors at the hos-

I'm demonstrating a parachute for some of the children who are patients at St. Jude.

pital had seen only one other tumor of its type. Ann told us that on the day surgeons removed the tumor, one of their friends arrived at the hospital.

"Good morning," she said as she walked past a guard who didn't know her.

"It will be a good day when we get little Eliza Leatherman through surgery," he responded.

That, she said, was a perfect example of the compassion found at St. Jude, where, she firmly believes, God's work is being done.

Eliza is now a thriving and active teenager.

Dr. Elaine Tuomanen is director of the hospital's Children's Infection Defense Center. We had breakfast with her on the third day of our visit. She told us that infectious diseases are the greatest killers of children, claiming more than twelve million annually, about a third of all childhood deaths, three times as many as cancer.

The single greatest killer of children is pneumonia and other respiratory diseases, followed by AIDS; intestinal diseases, particularly cholera; and tuberculosis. There are no vaccines to protect children from these diseases, and many of the bacteria that cause them have grown resistant to antibiotics.

Dr. Tuomanen's specialty is the bacterium that causes pneumonia, the deadliest of all bacteria that infect children. She is breaking down this killer genetically to determine how it works in the hopes of creating a vaccine or more powerful antibiotics to stop it. She brought up the possibility of a microchip that could be embedded in the lung of pneumonia patients so that researchers could gain information on how the disease develops from the

Linda with Dick Shadyac, then CEO of ALSAC,
St. Jude's fund-raising arm.

inside. We discussed it at length, and later I arranged for Dr. Tuomanen to come to Greensboro and talk to my partner Bill Pratt about the technical prospects of such a chip.

After breakfast, we met with Dr. Raul Ribeiro, who's in charge of the hospital's international outreach program. He told us about problems getting necessary drugs to patients in China because of governmental red tape, and I put him in touch with our company's top manager in China, who has governmental connections and could help him connect with the right people to work out the problems.

Our meeting later that morning with Dr. Julia Hurwitz in her laboratory was absolutely fascinating. Dr. Hurwitz and her research partner Dr. Karen Slobod have developed a vaccine for AIDS that is now being tested and has great potential for slowing or stopping the worldwide disaster that disease has wrought. Dr. Hurwitz drew pictures of the vaccine for us and showed us how the viruses are grown to make it.

We went to lunch this last day of our visit at Jim Neely's famous Interstate Bar-B-Que on South Third Street. Leslie and others from the hospital came with us. By this time Linda and I had reached a decision.

We hadn't made any extravagant purchases or any changes in our lifestyle since the success of RF Micro Devices. We had given blocks of stock to all of our children, and I had bought Linda a new car and myself a restored John Deere tractor that I spotted at the Old Threshers Convention held every Independence Day weekend at Denton Farm Park in adjoining Davidson County, not far from our home.

We had decided that the first major expenditure from our own good fortune should go to St. Jude. At lunch, Linda told Leslie that we had changed our mind about our pledge to give $1 million over our lifetimes. We intended to give it before year's end.

We would have given it then, but securities laws allow stock transactions for corporate officers to be made only during certain prescribed periods. We were having a phenomenal year at our company. We were in the midst of what would become known as the great dot-com boom. Our stock was rising so fast that we'd had two splits during the year, and the price was now fourteen times its issue price less than two and a half years earlier. The transfer of twenty-three thousand shares would take place on October 28. It would bring St. Jude $1,160,270. By that time we had decided that we wanted the money to be used for research in infectious diseases where the need is greatest and the most lives might be affected.

I was invited to serve on ALSAC's Professional Advisory Board, and we had the great pleasure of getting to know Richard Shadyac, ALSAC's chief executive officer. Dick was a close friend of Danny Thomas and had been involved with fund-raising for the hospital from the beginning. He became CEO of ALSAC in 1992 when raising money for the hospital became harder because the chief fund-raiser, his friend, Danny, had died the year before. Dick chose to focus on the children themselves, whom he loved deeply. He did a magnificent job, nearly quintupling annual donations before his retirement in June 2005. Dick was succeeded by our good friend John Moses, with whom I had served on the Professional Advisory Board.

Linda and I remain deeply committed to St. Jude. I have helped with recruiting and other activities at the hospital. Linda has known the sorrow of losing a patient with whom she became close as a volunteer. That's a sorrow that touches everybody at St. Jude. Every loss is a huge and deeply personal one, but the focus always stays on the lives that can and will be saved.

The interest in architecture that was stirred by my first visit to Williamsburg had grown over the years. I preferred classical styles and so did Linda. Whenever we traveled, whether for work or pleasure, we visited historic houses. We had made special trips to see Thomas Jefferson's Monticello, George Washington's Mt. Vernon, and numerous others.

I can't remember how many trips we've made to Charleston, but if there's a historic structure there that we haven't been in, it's not open to the public. Some of these we've visited several times. And, of course, it would be hard to overlook America's largest privately owned home, Biltmore, right here in North Carolina, in Asheville. A French Renaissance manor designed by Richard Morris Hunt, Biltmore was built by George Vanderbilt. Completed in 1895, it covers four acres and has 250 rooms, including a banquet hall with a seventy-foot ceiling. We visited it numerous times. I was fascinated by its construction, which took more than six years, and read a lot about it.

We also made trips to England to see castles, country estates, and other notable houses there. Whatever city we happened to be in, if it had historic houses that were open to the public, we went to see them.

If books had been written about these houses or their gardens, I bought and read them, gathering quite a collection in the process. I also bought and read books about the history of architecture. It became a fun and fascinating hobby.

Our own white colonial farmhouse was simple and not very big, only 2,200 square feet, vinyl-sided. Linda had come to love the house as much as

I did after a little remodeling. We knocked out an upstairs wall to make our bedroom bigger and add closet space. It was cozy for us, but we had grand-children now, and we began to think that we needed a little more room for family gatherings and overnight visitors.

Our house sat a couple of hundred feet off the road across from my grandparents' small house, where my Aunt Gracie lived, about halfway down a narrow hollow that once had been forested. I cleared most of the five acres before building the house, leaving only the bigger trees. The house faced the woods across the hollow to the east instead of the road, giving us a greater sense of privacy.

I began thinking about how we could increase the size of the house. The lay of the land would make it difficult, I realized. I thought we could at least double our space by adding a wing to one side, giving the house a T shape. That was the way most people in our area expanded. The front of the house then would face the road.

One feature that Linda and I liked in a lot of the old houses we had visited was a double spiral staircase leading from the second floor to a foyer at the entrance. We agreed that if we added on to the house, we wanted that. I took lots of measurements all around our house. I studied and pondered for a long time.

We wanted to keep the house simple. But despite my past skills at a drafting table, a new wing was beyond my ability to conceive and set down on paper so that somebody actually might be able to construct it. What we needed was an architect.

So late in 1998, I called one in Greensboro. He agreed to come and look over the situation. We told him vaguely what we had in mind: traditional, spiral staircase, a few other features that we thought would be nice. By this time RF Micro stock had begun to increase in value, and we had the wherewithal to make an even bigger addition than I first imagined. We also had decided that we needed space to be able to entertain for our business. We left it to the architect to decide the size, and he went to work drawing plans.

He came up with the first design in the spring of 1999. The addition actually dwarfed our little house. It was 10,000 square feet. As soon as we saw it, we knew that it wasn't what we had in mind and that it didn't really fit the picture we hadn't quite been able to describe. It seemed too much and too little at the same time.

We discussed it with the architect, and he went back to the drawing board. The second design didn't suit us either. The scale seemed off. The spiral staircase looked out of place in its setting. We began to think that the idea of expanding our house just wouldn't work.

When I was at Analog Devices, I had bought ten acres adjoining our land from my Aunt Gracie. Later, I bought another four and a half acres from her alongside the road. This was the field that my great-grandparents, like pioneers, had cleared of trees, brambles, and stumps using only hand tools and an old mule so that they would have a place to grow grain and vegetables. I had feasted on the harvest of that field throughout my young life.

Maybe we should just build a new house there, Linda and I thought. The architect went back and drew completely different plans for a free-standing house, considerably smaller than the addition he first had conceived. It was nice, but it still wasn't what we had in mind. And by that time, I had decided that putting a house on the field that my great-grandparents had cleared would be a desecration. It should continue producing crops in tribute to the spirit of my great-grandparents and grandparents who had farmed it for so many years.

We thanked the architect for his efforts, paid him, and were back where we had begun many months earlier.

Meanwhile a community matter had come to dominate my thoughts and efforts.

In the summer of 1998, my neighbor and good friend, Mark Peterson, told me that a tract of 159.4 acres adjoining his property, not far from mine, was on the market. Up until the late 1940s, this land had been owned for generations by a family named Kindley and once had been known as the Kindley place.

When my grandmother Myrtle married Jeff Dorsett, they first set up housekeeping in a tiny cabin on that land. They rented it from the Kindleys. The land later was bought by Jack and Virginia Jackson, and they began calling it by a different name—Stonehinge Farm.

Virginia was a Thayer before her marriage. The Thayers were a prominent and prosperous family in our community. One of our area roads is named for them. They had lived in the community, alongside my family, for six generations. The old Thayer Plantation, as it was called, was just down the road from my house. Don't be fooled by the word "plantation." The word had a different meaning in this part of North Carolina. It wasn't like the huge plantations of Charleston, Savannah, or other spots in the Deep South. This was just a farm, a little bigger and with a house that once had been some-what nicer than others in the area. Now it was just a decaying old farmstead.

Virginia went off to Greensboro College for Women, where she was graduated in 1936. A month later she took a job at the Southern Furniture Exposition Building in High Point, now known as the International Home Furnishings Center.

Our part of the state has long been the nation's furniture manufacturing hub, and each year High Point hosts two furniture markets that draw buyers from throughout the world. The Southern Furniture Exposition Building was the center of those markets, and Virginia worked there for fifty years, serving as administrative manager and secretary of the corporation. She was one of the pioneer female business executives in our area.

Before World War II, Virginia had met and married Henry T. Jackson, called Jack, a salesman for a lamp company. During the war, Jack was sent to India in the Quartermaster Corps. After the Japanese invasion of China in 1931, the Chinese lost all of their ports. To keep supplies coming from outside, they built the Burma Road from Lashio, Burma, to Kunming, China. When the Japanese occupied Burma in 1942, cutting off the road, U.S. Army engineers began building a new road through mountains and jungle—"over the hump"— from Ledo, India, to a spot near the China-Burma border. Jack moved supplies along the Ledo Road for two years and experienced much bloody fighting, death, and devastation.

After the war he wanted a place where he could live in peace and serenity. He and Virginia had bought the old Kindley place to fill that need.

The Jacksons were environmentalists and preservationists. So were just about everybody in our area, although most didn't use those terms to describe themselves. Jack and Virginia wanted to live in harmony with nature and do as little damage to the landscape as possible. They constructed a lake and two smaller ponds on their land. And they began building their home using materials available on the property.

The house was unlike any ever seen in our area, long and low, built of native stone. Wood for the roof and the interior was cut right on the land.

I was just a kid when it was being built. I remember walking over there on a Sunday after one of my grandmother's big dinners. I went with my Grandpa Jeff and my Uncle Eugene Loflin.

The house was set high on a hillside above the lake. The dam was part of the driveway that led up to it. The house was nearing completion then, and it was beautiful. We all marveled over it.

It looked like a house that you might see on TV, maybe in the hills above Hollywood, not in Randolph County. It had a triple-bay garage on one end. Rustic though the stone made the house seem, it was extravagant for these parts. It had lots of big windows so that a person could stand on one side, and look right through the house out to the other side. It had tile floors and two huge stone fireplaces, big enough for eight-foot logs. What on earth would anybody need a fire that big for, my grandpa wondered, much less two of them? The house was the talk of the area.

The Jacksons lived happily in their forested isolation for many years. Jack raised cattle. Virginia raised German shepherds. Every year they had a big party and a cookout for family and friends on the Fourth of July.

Jack died in June 1985, and at his request, family and friends gathered on the hillside in front of the rock house and formed a circle representing eternity. Each in turn scattered a small portion of his ashes on the land he had loved so deeply. Two months later a similar service was held in the same spot for Virginia's sister-in-law.

Jack and Virginia, both animal lovers, were strong supporters of the North Carolina Zoological Park, one of the world's great zoos, south of Asheboro in Randolph County. In his will, Jack expressed his desire for Stonehinge Farm to be left to the zoo following his death and Virginia's so that it might be protected in its natural state.

In addition to her other considerable abilities, Virginia also was an artist and an author. Her first book, *Aunt Mattie and the North Carolina Caveat Law*, was about a battle she successfully fought to get a state inheritance law changed. Virginia retired a year after Jack's death and took a trip retracing his travels to India and Burma during World War II. She later used photos from the trip to illustrate a book of her husband's wartime letters to her: *Henry Tull Jackson, 1909–1985, World War II Letters, 1943–1945*.

Virginia stayed on in the rock house, and three years after her retirement, she was diagnosed with non-Hodgkins lymphoma and began a long fight against the disease. Three years later, she married a neighbor, W.T. Harris. They lived in the house for nearly four years before it became too much for them to handle, and they moved to a retirement village near Thomasville.

Before Virginia's move to the retirement village, my friend Mark Peterson, a contractor who is always respectful of the land on which he builds homes, had spoken to Virginia expressing an interest in acquiring Stonehinge Farm. Virginia knew Mark—his house was only a short distance from hers—and knew how he felt about the land. She detested most of the development that was going on in the county, and according to her younger sister, Juanita Kennerly of Richmond, Virginia, she feared that something similar might happen to Stonehinge farm.

Although in her will Virginia had followed Jack's desire that the property be left to the zoo, she began to reconsider. After moving to the retirement village, she became seriously ill and was hospitalized. She knew that she wouldn't recover, and she instructed her sister to call Mark and tell him that she wanted to talk to him about purchasing the land. Mark, however, was on vacation, and by the time he returned and got the message, Virginia no longer was able to make decisions. She died on July 27, 1997.

Under the terms of her will, Stonehinge Farm became the property of the North Carolina Zoological Society, a private agency that supports the state-owned zoo. According to family and friends, Jack and Virginia had thought that the zoo society would preserve and use their land for nature programs and other such activities. Instead, the society announced that it would accept sealed bids for the sale of the property.

Mark and I were concerned that somebody might get it and develop it in a way that would change the whole nature of the area. We decided to go in together and submit a bid in an attempt to protect it.

Unfortunately, our greatest fear was realized. Stonehinge Farm went to a pair of developers notorious for stripping land and creating huge, densely packed developments of manufactured homes. In February 1999, we learned that the company intended to put 104 doublewides next door, although the number later would be dropped to eighty-six units.

The land was zoned agricultural and residential, and the new development required a zoning change. I was among many from our community who attended the zoning board hearing in Asheboro on March 2. I spoke against the change, pointing out the rural nature of the area and talking about my family's long history there and the effect this development would have on our community.

The board ruled in our favor, but the developers appealed to the county commissioners. This time, Mark and I helped to organize the entire community. We had a big turnout for a gathering at Poplar Ridge Friends Meeting to discuss strategy. We urged everybody to attend the commissioners' meeting on April 5, 1999, to oppose the development. The community turned out in force, packing the commissioners' room. Members of Virginia's family who lived out of state had written letters saying how appalled Virginia and Jack would be about what was happening to their land, and we presented those.

I had hired a lawyer in Asheboro, Jonathan Megerian, to take up the fight, and he was one of the key speakers. He condemned the zoo society for preaching about land conservancy in places such as Africa, while participating in irresponsible and damaging development in its own county. Barney Pierce, the former minister at Poplar Ridge Friends Meeting, spoke about the adverse effect the development would have on the community. So many residents wanted to speak that discussion had to be cut off because the meeting was going on so long.

The commissioners voted unanimously to deny the zoning change.

After the meeting, I spoke with one of the developers. I told him that I intended to keep fighting development on the land, but that I didn't want to hurt him and his partner financially. I would buy the land from him and see that he suffered no losses. I had cleared this with Mark in advance. He just wanted the land preserved.

Two days later, I made an offer to the developers. They didn't accept it.

Their lawyers filed an appeal, and I expected a long court fight.

Our company was going through an incredibly busy period, and I put the property battle out of my mind for months. In September, Linda and I went to St. Jude Hospital for our three-day visit. We returned on the 18th. Three days later, we drove to Charlotte to depart on a long-planned trip to London with all of our children.

I was parking in the long-term garage when my cell phone rang. It was the developer with whom I'd spoken after the commissioners' meeting. He and his partner had decided to let me buy Stonehinge Farm. I was overjoyed. I told him that we'd work out the details as soon as we returned.

We got back home on September 27, and on October 1, we took possession of the land that old-timers in our area still called the "old Kindley place," where my grandparents once had lived. I couldn't have envisioned then what eventually would evolve there. Neither could I have imagined that our experience at St. Jude would play a role in it.

Thirteen

We never gave any thought to making Jack and Virginia Jackson's rock house our own home. Jack and Virginia had designed it precisely for their needs, and theirs didn't fit ours. Although it offered great open spaces, it had only one small bedroom, for example.

Beyond that, it had fallen into a terrible state of disrepair. The roof was worn and leaked. Window sills had rotted. A colorful mosaic that Virginia had created of corn and other grains and seeds on an interior wall had attracted varmints that had no appreciation of art, particularly if it was edible. Those varmints had drawn snakes that fed on them, and they in turn had attracted bigger varmints. The Jacksons' dream home ironically had converted to a condition that only a pair of naturalists truly could appreciate.

The house had been built on a concrete slab. The plumbing was embedded beneath the tile floors, along with the heating and cooling ducts. Some of it had collapsed; much of it was filled with muck and debris. None of it was usable. Replacing it would be an immense chore.

My first instinct was practical: tear down the house. To begin with, it was too close to the property line to suit me. And the costs of repairing it likely would be more than the worth of the house when we finished. A new house of the same size and much more utility could be built quicker and cheaper.

But Linda loved the rock house. And she thought it would be shameful to destroy Jack and Virginia's dream, the place where they had lived out their lives. She thought that we should restore it. We could use it for family gatherings and overnight guests, she said. And groups from Poplar Ridge Friends Meeting could use it for special activities. I couldn't disagree. The Jacksons' unusual rock house and their great respect for the land were important parts of the community's heritage.

I hired a neighbor, Mike Willis, to put a new roof on the house and he brought crews to clean up and begin the more exasperating details of restoration. It would take us nearly a year and a half to complete it.

Even before we bought Stonehinge Farm, Linda and I still planned to build a new house, although we weren't sure where. We had bought my grandparents' house from my Aunt Gracie and gave her lifetime rights to stay there. It gave her money to live on, and she was happy for me to have it because she knew we would preserve and maintain it as a family treasure after she was gone.

The house was across the road from ours, and it came with ten acres of land. We had considered putting a new house somewhere on that property.

From the time we had begun thinking about an addition to our farmhouse, I had wanted my friend and neighbor Mark Peterson to be the builder. All of the homes he constructed were beautiful and of high quality.

After our earlier experience with an architect in which we hadn't been able to come up with a design to fit a vision we hadn't quite been able to articulate—perhaps because it wasn't fully formed—Linda and I had discussed what we should do next. Considering the type of house we wanted, we got the idea that maybe we should begin a new search for an architect in a city we loved, Charleston, where such houses were common and where we had visited so often.

I talked to Mark about this, and he thought it was a good plan. At the end of August, we invited Mark and his wife Joanna to go to Charleston with us to begin the search for an architect and have a fun weekend.

We arrived on Friday afternoon and checked into Charleston Place, a nice hotel in the historic district. As soon as Linda and I got to our room, I picked up the Yellow Pages and flipped to the architect section.

One ad quickly jumped out at me. It was for Bill Huey and Associates. His office was not far away on King Street. The ad said that he specialized in historical restoration and design.

"This sounds like just the guy we're looking for," I told Linda.

I dialed the number. A woman answered. I told her that I was planning to build a classical house, a fairly large one, and that I was looking for an architect. Mr. Huey wasn't available, she told me, but if I left my name and number, she would pass along the information. I asked if she knew of any new houses of this type that had been built in the area. She suggested a few as well as some developments we might want to check out. We didn't get a call back from Bill Huey that weekend, but we did see a lot of new houses, although none that caught our fancy.

It took a while for Bill and me to hook up by telephone, but we did a week or so after we returned home. He invited Linda and me to come back to Charleston and meet with him about the kind of house we wanted to build. But I was particularly busy at work then, our three-day trip to St. Jude was looming, and it would be followed by our family trip to London, so we couldn't return to Charleston anytime soon.

In fact, it was during that London trip that we learned we would be able to buy Stonehinge Farm. Linda and I immediately decided it should be the site for our new house. Three weeks after I purchased the property, I hired an aerial photographer to take photographs of it so we could study the lay of the land and decide on the best location for the house. Two days after receiving these digital photos Linda and I went to Charleston to meet Bill Huey, taking the photos with us.

Bill turned out to be a young man, only thirty-six. His wife Elizabeth was a CPA, and they had two small daughters. Bill had grown up in Greenville, South Carolina, where his father had been a cotton buyer. His dad didn't think there was much of a future in textiles and encouraged Bill to follow another path. He was a pre-med student at Clemson until he encountered organic chemistry. That trying subject and his love of drawing had propelled him into classes on architecture, where he found his calling. After graduation, he went to work for a large firm in Atlanta and spent a year designing fountains.

Bill had met Elizabeth in college. She was from Charleston and returned there to work after graduation. After their marriage, Bill got a job with a one-man architecture firm in Charleston. He had an affinity for classical architecture, and eventually, he started his own firm, devoting most of his efforts to restoration. He had designed the restoration of the old Riviera Theater, one of the country's outstanding examples of Art Deco architecture, turning it into a convention center for Charleston Place. He also had redesigned the original building of the Citadel, Charleston's proud military college, constructed in 1842, turning it into a hotel.

We were immediately impressed with Bill. There was no question of his love for classical architecture. Our thoughts on the subject melded. Equally as important, his personality was so engaging that we knew he was somebody with whom we could work.

We still didn't have in mind a lot of detail about the house we wanted to build, but we knew the basics. We thought the house should be in the range of 12,000–15,000 square feet. We wanted it to be of brick with some lime-stone features. A lasting roof, copper or slate was a requirement. A grand staircase, of course, was central to the house. And columns. I was fascinated with columns. A cupola was another necessity. I had put a small cupola on my house at Windemere Heights when I enclosed the carport and made it into two rooms. Most of the historic houses we visited had cupolas, and I had admired the cupola on Wentworth Mansion in Charleston, now a hotel, several times.

Beyond that, we wanted a formal dining room, formal parlor, a family area with a kitchen and casual dining space, fireplaces, an elevator, and a back staircase. We thought that five bedrooms with baths would be plenty. I remember mentioning a family theater, an exercise area, a radio room for my ham gear, and a sewing room for Linda where she might display her doll collection.

Bill said that he would come up with a proposal and get back to us shortly. A few days later, on October 27, I received the draft proposal.

A couple of weeks later, I asked Paul O'Connor, a landscape architect, to come out and take a look at the property. Paul had designed the landscaping at our new company headquarters in Greensboro. The property had frontage on two different roads, Snyder Country, where we lived, and Thayer, which intersected Snyder Country. So there were two possible accesses for a house, nearly a mile distant from each other. The Jacksons had used Thayer Road as their entrance.

Paul and I studied the aerial photos and walked the entire 159.4 acres. Whatever we did, I told him, I wanted to respect the Jacksons' wishes to keep the land in its natural state and do as little damage as possible. Paul pointed out that if we put an entrance on Snyder Country Road, we could have a mile-long driveway. It could follow the ridge, dipping into the hollows, and would require the removal of only a relatively small number of trees. Only two culverts to convey streams would be necessary, one of them quite large, and very little earth would have to be moved.

Although we considered two possible locations for a house, one in the woods not far from the rock house, the obvious site was apparent from the beginning. Deep into the property was a big grassy knoll where Jack had kept cattle. It rose from the bank of a fairly large creek and was the highest point on the property. It would allow for a sweeping circular drive.

Paul talked about the importance of presentation for a distinctive house such as the one we hoped to build. The long drive through the beautiful woods would deliver visitors down a hill around a curve and into the openness at the creek where the house would suddenly and impressively appear atop the open knoll. I almost could picture it as Paul talked about it.

Early in December, Bill drove up from Charleston to take his first look at the land, and he agreed that the spot was perfect.

We gave the go-ahead for Bill to begin planning the house blithely unaware that we were embarking upon the great adventure of our lives. I'm sure that Bill had no idea what he was getting himself into either, or how closely our lives, troubles, and frustrations would become over the next five years.

Many details were undecided when Bill began working on the design, partly because we still didn't know exactly what we wanted. Bill called every week with questions, sometimes more frequently. And I often didn't have the answers. I also regularly called Bill with suggestions and new ideas. Proportion came to dominate the design as it went along. Bill and I constantly talked about proportion. That had a big effect, causing the house to grow in size, but day by day I had no sense of just how much it was growing.

Linda and I continued our travels visiting old houses, taking note of features we liked and wanted to include in our house. Early in the spring of

2000, we flew to New Orleans, rented a car, and followed the Mississippi northwest toward Baton Rouge to visit a string of old plantation houses that had survived the Civil War. I was particularly impressed with Oak Alley at Vacherie, Louisiana, a Greek Revival mansion completed in 1839 and framed by a quarter-mile canopy of live oak trees thought to be nearly three hundred years old. I bought a print of a painting of the house.

On this trip, I learned that it was possible to rent one of these mansions for a night. That was Nottoway Plantation at White Castle, an eccentric house with Greek Revival elements completed in 1859. Nottoway had been fired on by a Union gunboat during the Civil War. A cannon ball had lodged in one of its square wood columns and remained there for more than twenty years before it dislodged.

I wanted Mark to see these houses, so I arranged to rent Nottoway, for Easter weekend in late April, and Linda and I returned to Louisiana with Mark and Joanna. After dinner on Saturday night, we returned to Nottoway and Mark and I set to work measuring every room with an ultrasonic device and drawing floor plans of the entire house. We took lots of photos.

Linda and I had been debating about ceiling height. We had told Bill that we wanted ceilings ten or twelve feet high. I'd seen eighteen-foot ceilings that were impressive. Nottoway's ceilings were fifteen feet high, and they struck me as perfect. Nottoway had another feature that Linda and I decided we wanted. Windows at the front of the house could be raised so that you could walk through them.

After we returned home, I called Bill and told him to go with fifteen-foot ceilings and to put walk-through windows at the front of the house. By this time, Bill was almost finished with his design. Only a couple of weeks later, he came to Randolph County to give us our first peek at his work. We met at the rock house, where we had invited him to stay. He had done a big color drawing of the front of the house, and it was displayed on an easel.

As soon as we saw it, I knew that we were on the same wavelength. Bill had captured the classical feeling that I wanted in the house. It was a Greek Revival house three stories high with a basement. The columns for the portico were impressive: there were a dozen front and back. The roof was copper, the windows big, the cupola a beauty.

The floor-by-floor drawings were stretched out on the dining room table, and we gathered around to go through them. It quickly became clear that Bill had not made the same mistake as our previous architect and gotten the rooms too small. All of our struggles with proportion had seen to that. Proportion had, in a word, made this house huge. Really huge. Easily twice the size that we originally indicated, although some of the basement and most of the third level would largely be unfinished space.

The house had everything we had requested plus some other wonderful features: a library, a solarium, a big garden room, potting room, a shop, a huge garage, and much more.

Bill also had brought along a revised proposal reflecting the growing size of the house.

Obviously, it was going to take a while for us to absorb all of this, and we told Bill that we needed to think about it and would get back to him.

At first, we wanted to believe that this was the house for us. But the size was overwhelming. This was a scale that we hadn't really considered and couldn't quite grasp. And the look of it didn't wear well with time.

After a week or so of really trying to like the house, Linda said, "Let's face it. It looks like a schoolhouse."

She was right, I thought. But part of that was due to a lack of perspective of the front view in the drawing.

We showed it to Mark and Joanna and to other friends. They all oohed and aahed about it. Then we would ask them, "Do you think it looks like a schoolhouse?"

They would pause, hesitate. "Well, you know—maybe—a little—yeah."

As we pondered this house plan, we had something more troubling to think about. RF Micro's stock price had increased dramatically in 1999, giving us confidence that we could build a house of the size we first had mentioned to Bill. When we authorized Bill to proceed at the end of October, the stock, after two splits, was selling at about $42. By year's end, it had risen to almost $70. But in 2000, it began a phenomenal rise that we watched in awe. It hit almost $195 on March 6.

Then on April 14 came Black Friday, the day the so-called dot-com bubble burst, a collapse of stock prices comparable to the crash of 1929 that set off the Great Depression. Our stock closed at $79 that day, still nearly double its price when we had authorized Bill to proceed. By the time we saw Bill's first design, the stock had climbed back a little, but many Internet companies clearly were going to go out of business and likely would take other technology companies with them, and there were predictions of a coming recession.

Although our company was healthy, we were well aware that stock prices could plummet as fast as they rose, and that provoked caution. We didn't want to commit to a house that might suddenly be beyond our means, and we were well aware that we had to keep a close eye on costs.

After a few weeks, we met with Bill, told him that the size of the house had to be trimmed considerably and that we thought it looked too much like a schoolhouse. He went back to the drawing board.

Meanwhile, in June we had core samples drilled on the knoll to find out what problems we might encounter beneath the soil. A house of the size we anticipated building would require the movement of a lot of earth, and we didn't want to hit solid rock or other problems. The samples indicated that the site would be fine.

One thing had changed for certain when we saw the scope of the house that Bill had designed. A house such as this, even significantly reduced, should be built with a frame of steel and concrete, not wood. Bill pointed out that we would need a contractor who constructed commercial buildings.

My friend Mark, who built houses with wood frames, had recognized this immediately. He agreed to take on the site preparation and to handle any construction external to the house, such as retaining walls, walkways, patios, steps, and a mechanical building, no small amount of work.

As Bill set about cutting the size of the house, we stayed in close consultation. The core of the house that we had expressed to Bill was in the original design, but he had added wings on two sides. Those wings disappeared as Bill worked defining the core.

I meanwhile had begun talking with contractors. One was a North Carolina company that had built RF Micro's new headquarters. Another was an area company, and the third was in New Jersey. The house was to be contracted in two phases. The first would include the foundations, the thick concrete basement walls, the steel framework and the concrete that would support the floors of the basement, the other three levels of the house, and the cupola.

By January 2001, the design was far enough along that Bill could provide figures for contractors to submit bids on the first phase of construction. And on February 1, Bill came back to the rock house with the new design. This one had a slate roof. Slate was beautiful, but it was heavy and would require much reinforcement to bear the weight. We would decide that we really liked the green patina that aged copper took on, even though we might never live to see it, and preferred that. Otherwise, we loved the new design.

There was just one problem. It was too small.

As the house had been evolving, our thinking about it had evolved as well. We had begun with the idea of adding on to our farmhouse to have more room for family functions and occasional guests. That had grown with the thought that we needed something more elaborate so that we could entertain business associates, customers, employees, maybe even board members. The acquisition of Jack and Virginia's Stonehinge Farm had provided a perfect setting for something special and spectacular, and Bill's first design, which had grown week by week, aided and abetted by us, reflected that.

Obviously, we had reached a point far from our original intention. We hadn't thought this out in advance. It just happened, one step leading to the next. We hadn't foreseen where it was taking us. Later, Bill would say it was as if the house had taken on a life of its own and was defining its own purpose. That appeared to be the case, because we now were thinking about it in an entirely different way.

As Linda and I toured historic houses, we had become aware that almost all of them had purposes other than to provide homes for their owners. They were used to attract people. They brought people together, became centers of community activity. And the bigger and grander they were, the more people they attracted, the more they impressed, no doubt the reason why religions build great temples and cathedrals, why seats of government are imposing structures. More than a million people a year now pay to visit George Vanderbilt's Biltmore Estate in Asheville.

Frequently, these big historic houses served as springboards into politics for their owners, or as means of entertaining and maintaining relationships for those with power and prestige. In almost every case, these houses were used to influence people in one way or another.

Linda and I had no political aspirations and sought no power over others. But our growing involvement with St. Jude Children's Hospital, and our wish to help other causes, particularly involving children, led us to begin thinking about the house in an entirely different way. We could use it to attract people to the causes that we thought worthy. It could be a place for fun fund-raising events of many types, for conferences on important topics, for weekend retreats where, say, researchers from St. Jude could revive spirits and ponder new possibilities. We could make it a house for giving.

Some people, no doubt, can separate charity from business, but I can't. Business success is vital to charity. Danny Thomas never would have been able to start St. Jude if he hadn't found success in his career. Look at all the great and inspirational institutions—universities, hospitals, museums—that originally were funded by philanthropists who made great fortunes in business.

We had no huge fortune, and this house would take up most of what we had made, but we could put the house to similar good purposes. I also wanted it to stand as an example of what is possible through entrepreneurship and to promote that as well, maybe through conferences or other educational activities. I wanted people to come to this house and realize that if they had ingenuity, resourcefulness, energy, and willingness to work hard, they could find success. And in the process they might be moved to give some of their returns to worthy causes such as St. Jude.

If this were to become a house for giving, Linda and I wanted it to keep on giving even after we were gone. We decided that after our deaths, if not before, we would leave it to a charitable organization, or form one to maintain it, with stipulations that it was to continue to be used for philanthropic purposes. We had seen what had happened to Jack and

Virginia's property after they had left it to the zoo society, and we didn't want to risk that being repeated.

All of this led us to decide that the house needed to be bigger again. Although Bill's redesign had included more finished space in the basement and on the third floor, we decided that if the house were to be used for the purposes we now wanted, it required more room. We considered the possibilities for expansion and came up with the idea for an adjoining guest house, something along the lines of an English country cottage.

In little more than a month, Bill produced a plan for a two-story guest house that would sit west of the main house, a wide patio separating the two. We liked the design. The guest house would have two large bedrooms with baths, a huge fireplace, a dining area, two small balconies that eventually would overlook a swimming pool, a big central area that could be used for meeting space open all the way to the cupola at the top, and a private area for work or contemplation. But we thought it would be inconvenient for guests to have to go out into the weather to get the main house, so we decided the two should be joined.

Bill had included a conservatory on the west side of the house, and he extended it to the guest house, an area to be filled with greenery with a side sitting area under a stained-glass dome. He also changed the exterior of the guest house so that it would blend with the design of the main house.

In order for the house to serve the purposes we now were seeing for it, we decided that it should be finished on all four levels.

We wanted the basement to be a recreation and service area and thought it should extend beneath the conservatory to the guest house so that people staying there could get to it without having to go through the main house. The basement would include a big sauna with dressing rooms and showers, a billiard room, a theater, an exercise room, a beauty parlor, a wine cellar, a small kitchen, a laundry, a big sitting area that could double as meeting space, a mechanical-shop room, a double garage, and other facilities.

The top level of the house would have a museum, offices, a board room, a conference room, storage areas, a small food preparation area, and access to an electronic lift that could carry several people at a time to the cupola, which could accommodate a dozen or more, both inside and on an outside widow's walk. The cupola offered a 360-degree view of the surrounding countryside more than sixty feet in the air.

As Bill was working on all of this, we decided on a contractor, selecting the area firm because it seemed more enthusiastic about getting the job. We also continued touring historic houses, because there were details about which we still had to make important decisions.

Most important among these in my mind were the columns. I knew that this would be a feature that would make the house stand out and that people would be most likely to remember. I wanted to make sure we got it right. I began a study of columns and capitals, reading everything I could find about them. But I also wanted to examine columns firsthand.

Shutters were another subject of our concern. Bill hadn't included them on his original design. Most of the historic houses we had visited had shutters, and we wanted them. But what kind?

In March, the Petersons joined us for another trip to Charleston on a historical society tour of plantation houses. We revisited Boone Hall, Middleton Place and a few others. The tour ended ninety miles from Charleston at Milford Plantation in Pineville, south of Sumter on the Santee River near the headwaters of Lake Marion.

Milford's owner, North Carolina native Richard Hampton Jenrette, a highly successful businessman, restorer, and collector of historic homes (including the Roper House in Charleston), thinks that Milford is America's finest example of Greek Revival architecture. It was built from 1839 to 1841 by a pair of twenty-two-year-olds: John Laurence Manning, son of Governor Richard Manning (John later would become governor, too, as would his son, Richard II) and his wife, the former Susan Frances Hampton, daughter of one of the South's richest planters, Wade Hampton. Its construction was financed by a large inheritance Susan had received after her father's death. The Manning family held onto the house until 1902, although it had fallen into disrepair. It was sold to the widow of a wealthy New York banker, and later was completely restored to include the original furnishings by the nephews to whom she willed it. Jenrette bought it in 1992.

Milford is without doubt one of the most beautiful historic houses we have visited. Its Corinthian columns with their ornate capitals are among the most impressive I've seen. The details of the interior design were exquisite. I took photos and made notes. The dome in the rotunda at Milford especially caught our attention, and the one in our house would end up very much like it.

I didn't realize it at the time, but I was about to become a column hunter. In coming months I would spend many Sunday afternoons driving in search of columns. I went to a lot of courthouses and other public buildings photo-graphing and measuring columns. Some of the best examples I found were not far from home: the old Davidson County Courthouse in nearby Lexington and the old Jamestown School, now the public library, in the historic Quaker town of Jamestown, adjoining High Point.

By May 10, 2001, a year after we saw the first drawing of the house, Bill had finished the fourth incarnation, the plan with which we would proceed. It included the floor plan and basic exterior design, although details such as the type of columns, shutters, and the like still had to be decided. The foyer and double grand staircase were in a rotunda with two domes: one large and the other small. The small one was in the cupola, which had been completely redesigned and enlarged. Visitors could stand in

Jack and Virginia Jackson's rock house after we restored it.

the cupola and look down through an opening in the larger dome to the exact center of the house in the entrance hall forty-five feet below. Design details for the interior still were to be done. The house ended up about the same size as the huge one we had rejected in the beginning.

In June, we hired an engineering firm in Charleston to create drawings for the foundation and steel framework. Our goal was to start site preparation by October 1, with construction to begin in November.

But as we moved into summer, the house took a backseat in our lives. Our primary attentions turned to my dad.

Fourteen

Although I was closer to my mother throughout childhood, I loved my dad deeply, had complete respect for him, honored the advice he gave me, and cherished the time I spent with him. Later in life, we formed a tight father-son bond. He was a great help and comfort to me when my marriage was breaking up. We talked a lot about how faith could guide a person through any troubles.

After my dismal experience with my first venture into business—when I had to return to live with my parents, a failure with no money and no job, my family gone—he was a rock of encouragement and hope. I borrowed money from him for months so that I could meet my bills and make support payments for the children.

We did a lot of things together after I married Linda, started to work at Analog Devices, and set my life on track again. The two of us made a trip to a ham radio convention in Atlanta and went to see Stone Mountain while we were there. I had taken flying lessons while I was at Hewlett-Packard and actually had soloed. I liked flying in small planes, something my dad never had done. So I hired a pilot I knew to fly us to West Virginia. My dad loved the mountains. He always had taken us to the mountains on vacations. This experience gave him a bird's-eye view of his cherished mountains.

By the time Alzheimer's disease was claiming my mother's mind and memory, I had joined Bill Pratt and Powell Seymour in starting RF Micro Devices. We were working day and night to build the company, and I didn't have as much time for my dad as I should have had. But we found a way to make up for that.

Whenever I wasn't traveling, I would call him on my cell phone as soon as I got to my car after leaving work, often at eleven at night or later. We chatted throughout my forty-five-minute drive home. Dad was excited about the company and wanted to know every detail of what was going on.

We continued our late night talks after my mom's death. I was concerned that Dad was so deeply lonely. He was close with his sister Frances, who lived in Archdale, and they saw each other frequently and talked by phone almost every day. After a year or so, my sisters and I became aware that Dad was spending some time with an old friend.

Throughout their marriage, my mom and dad's closest friends were Charles and Virgie Coltrane. Charles had worked with my dad laying out the foundation for the only home he ever owned and had also helped him with the carpentry. Our family made trips with Charles and Virgie's family

165

when my sisters and I were young. Charles had died a couple of years before my mom, leaving Virgie alone. My sisters and I loved her and couldn't have been happier when we discovered that she and my dad were dating and talking regularly on the phone.

A few years later, I teased Dad about Virgie.

"Well, son," he said, "you know you're in a heck of a fix when your girlfriend's eighty years old."

But Virgie looked fifteen years younger, and she was a lively, caring, and wonderfully delightful person.

Dad was pleased when he learned that Linda and I were going to be able to buy the old Kindley place, from which he had lived across the road as a teenager, and that we were planning to build a new house there. He laughed when I showed him the first plans that Bill Huey had drawn.

"Why, that looks like a place where a president would live," he exclaimed.

Having everything planned and in order was important to my dad. He and my mom had made all of the arrangements for their funerals long in advance. They had picked out caskets and vaults and paid for everything. They had chosen their side-by-side spot in the cemetery at Poplar Ridge Friends Meeting. My dad had ordered the double tombstone and footstones long before my mom died. He had laid out where they would be placed so that everything would be in balance. He had measured the exact dimensions for his grave and my mom's grave and had placed markers in the ground so there could be no question about where they were to be dug.

My dad was proud of his service in World War II. One of his requests was for a military funeral. We were talking one day after I had shown him the plans for the house and somehow the topic of the military funeral came up.

"Here's an idea," I told him. "We'll have this big house, and when you die, we can bring you over here and put you in the rotunda. We'll get a big bank of flags and an honor guard. You can lie in state just like some big general in the Capitol. What do you think about that?"

He laughed and laughed.

"Does that mean you don't want to do it?" I asked.

"No, no," he said, still laughing. "I'd love to do it. What's so funny is that you actually think I'll live long enough to see that house. That's what's funny. I don't have any chance of being alive when that house is done."

I didn't think anything about it at the time, but he would turn out to be right.

Late in the winter of 2001, my dad started having serious coughing fits.

He had coughed his entire life, no doubt due to the fine wood dust that he had breathed into his lungs during all those years of working in furniture manufacturing. His cough was so distinctive that when I heard it in church, it was the same as hearing his voice. I knew exactly where he was sitting.

But this cough was different. We thought it was just a cold at first. He took cough syrup and other over-the-counter medications. But it continued, and we took him to a clinic in Archdale. Maybe it was the flu, we all thought. A chest x-ray indicated nothing serious. He didn't have much fever. The doctor gave him some prescriptions, and the medicines seemed to work for a while.

But then the cough grew worse again. More weeks passed, and he kept thinking he would get over it, but he didn't. Some days my cousin Peggy Tilley, Aunt Frances' daughter, would sit with him. She became concerned because he would cough so hard and so long that he hardly could breathe. Those spells were difficult to witness.

Finally, he called one day in July and said, "I think I need to go to the hospital."

My sisters and I took him. I rolled him into the emergency room in a wheelchair.

A nurse who quizzed him about his medical history asked if anybody in his family had suffered breathing or lung problems. He told her about his sister Jewel dying of tuberculosis at seventeen, sixty-three years earlier. The doctors saw this information and became alarmed. They thought that dormant TB might have surfaced. They admitted him to the hospital and put him in an isolation ward. Anybody who wanted to see him had to don disposal surgical masks and gowns, every visitor increasing the hospital bills. It aggravated my dad.

We thought that TB was highly unlikely after all this time. The doctors began a battery of tests and told us it would be several days before they had results. Linda and I had previously scheduled a tour of homes in Charlotte and decided to go ahead with it.

We were on the tour when my cell phone rang. It was my sister Diane. I could tell from her voice that this was not a call I wanted to receive.

"Jerry, the news isn't good," she said. "The doctor says his lungs are full of cancer. It's inoperable." She didn't have to say more.

We drove straight back to the hospital. The doctors hadn't given my dad the news, and it was hard going in to see him, knowing what he didn't know. As always, he was happy to see me. He told me about all of the tests that he had endured. The doctors were supposed to give him the results the following day. He was fed up with coughing and suffering.

"I'm hopeful that I'm going to get good news," he said.

"I hope so, too," I told him, although they were difficult words to speak.

We were there for the scheduled session with the doctor the following day. He was forthright and held nothing back. My dad showed no emotion. He asked how long he might have. The doctor said he couldn't say.

"I understand," my dad said.

My dad loved life, but he had lived it as if every breath might be his last. If the Lord saw fit to take him, he was ready. He firmly believed that death was as natural a part of life as birth. It was not to be feared but welcomed as a transition. He had no doubt that soon he again would be with his beloved Bertie and they would be waiting for us when our times came to join them.

My dad was worried more about us than he was about his own situation. He knew that we were hurting, and he wanted to reassure us that he had no fears, no regrets. When I hugged him, he smiled and said, "Son, if you live long enough, sooner or later a doctor is going to come in and say, 'I've got some bad news.' We just have to live our lives so we'll be ready when that time comes."

We thought that Dad wouldn't get out of the hospital. He was weak, and the cancer was viciously aggressive. But I wanted him to be able to live whatever time he might have left in the little house he loved, where he had spent nearly fifty years of his life.

During the years that he was tending to my mom, the house had fallen into a state of slight disrepair. I called some of his friends who had retired from Alma Desk and now were painting as a part-time business. They agreed to drop everything else and repaint the house inside and out. They worked fast. While, they were painting, I had all the old carpet taken out and new carpet installed. I had my mom and dad's bed removed and a hospital bed put into their bedroom. Betty, Diane, and Linda cleaned the house until it was bright and spotless.

Dad was on oxygen all the time, and we brought in an oxygen generator. My daughter Annette, who has a master's degree in nursing science, set up a small pharmacy in my old bedroom where I had kept my ham gear and much of my wire. My dad was all smiles when the ambulance brought him back home. We had hired round-the-clock nurses to stay with him. But others usually were there: Virgie, Frances, my sisters, Linda and me, grand-children, friends from the church, my dad's old buddies from Alma Desk. He had no shortage of company.

Dad was suffering a lot. He was on heavy medication. His mind would come and go. He would fade in and out of sleep. I would be talking to him, and he would just drift away. A few minutes later, he'd come back and speak coherently.

He was always eager to know what was going on with the house we were planning to build. I had kept him up-to-date all through his sickness. When Bill Huey finished the final design, I brought it to my dad so he could see it. He was really impressed.

Early in August, I asked if he'd like to get out of the house and go for a ride. We could take a look at the house site, I told him. Shortly after I had bought the land, less than two years earlier, I had taken him for a tour of the property on my four-wheel-drive John Deere Gator. We'd had a lot of fun that day.

Now I began planning for another expedition. My sister Betty had a handicapped van that she needed for her husband Reese. She brought it. I got Dad into a wheelchair. We loaded up oxygen bottles and set out. We drove past Poplar Ridge Friends Meeting and the cemetery where his parents and my mom lay, and where he soon would lie beside her. That was heavy on our minds, but nobody said anything about it.

Just beyond the cemetery, we turned onto Snyder Country Road and drove the mile and a half to the spot where my dad had lived in Jeff Rush's old house when he met my mom. That property now was mine, the house long gone. Mark Peterson had owned the property but thought that I should have it and sold it to me. By this time, we had cut a rough driveway through the woods almost to the site where we planned to build the house. The entrance was only about one hundred feet from the spot where once had lain the rock on which my mom and dad had met. The rock now was a flagstone at the pump house for the well I had drilled where my dad had lived at that time.

The ride was a little bumpy, but we made it okay. Only tractor trails led up the knoll to the site where construction was expected to begin in only a couple of months. I rolled the wheelchair out of the van so that dad could have a good look around. He didn't say anything about his prediction that he wouldn't live to see this house built, but it surely was on my mind.

I could see that he was tiring quickly, and I got him back into the van so we could ride around a little more and let him see a few other nostalgic spots in this countryside that he loved so deeply.

"Any other place you want to see?" I asked.

"I think I'd better get back home," he said.

From that point, Dad grew progressively worse. He was in great pain, despite the drugs. He strained for breath even with the oxygen on high. I couldn't stand to see him suffering. He had told me many times that while he had no fear of death, no reluctance to leave life when his time came, he did fear lengthy suffering.

His condition grew so bad that we soon had to call an ambulance and take him back to the hospital. We knew that his time was close but that he might linger for weeks. We wanted him to have the maximum amount of pain medication that he could abide and ended up in disputes with doctors about it.

Virgie and family members took shifts sitting with him around the clock so somebody who loved him always would be there. Members of our congregation came regularly, as did old friends from his work days. Henry Asbury was one of them. He prayed the most beautiful prayers, absolutely poetic. I know that if my dad heard them, he loved them. He would open his eyes at times, and it was clear that he recognized us and knew that we were there, but he was getting beyond speech.

Linda and I were there with our daughter Margaret and Virgie on Sunday morning, August 12. His breathing was growing increasingly faint. My sisters had gone home to rest, and I went outside to call them on the cell phone and tell them they'd better come back. When I returned to the room, Linda met me at the door. She was crying.

She didn't need to say anything.

Virgie was still at his bedside, tears in her eyes. She and Linda had been holding his hands when he took his last breath. She had told him that she loved him and would miss him terribly.

I told them that I wanted to spend a little time with him, and they left me alone. I walked to his bedside and put a finger to his neck. He still was warm, but there was no pulse. I took his limp hand. I kissed his forehead. As I had watched him struggle for breath, I had wanted so desperately for him to die so that he could escape his suffering. But now that he was gone, a great wave of grief swept over me, like nothing I'd felt before. I thought that I might lose control, break down, but I knew he wouldn't want that. He always was a rock that everybody else could turn to for peace, assurance, and stability. And now I had to be, too.

I kept my composure as others came, some of them weeping, all of us hugging one another. People from the funeral home arrived. My grief would not relent, and I knew that I had to escape that hospital.

"I've got to go," I told Linda. "I just need to be alone. Don't worry. I'll be all right. But I've got to go."

I got in my car and drove straight to Randolph County. On the way, I remembered something my dad had told me. He had prepared a manila envelope of instructions for his funeral and told me where it would be. He wanted me to fetch it after his death.

I went first to my dad's house to get it. It was the loneliest place I'd ever set foot in. I walked past the empty hospital bed and the silent oxygen generator. On the walls were family photos of happy times long past. All the love and laughter that had filled that house were now only faint echoes in memory.

I found the envelope and sat down to read what my dad had written. He had planned everything down to the last detail, including the verses for the ministers to read and the hymns for the congregation to sing. He listed the pallbearers he wanted and had scribbled "no grandchildren" in the margin in case those he named couldn't serve. He didn't want his grandsons to suffer the grief of carrying him to his grave.

I needed to escape that house as much as I had needed to get away from the hospital. I drove to Jack and Virginia Jackson's rock house. Its restoration was complete now. I knew that nobody would be there. Nobody was apt to look for me there. I could confront my grief in private where nobody could see or hear it.

There I cried. And I didn't just cry. As wave after wave of grief swept over me, I practically convulsed. I screamed out my sorrow. I'm sure it would have frightened anybody who witnessed it. It startled me. I had no idea of the depth of my grief, but I had to face it, get it out so that I could be of comfort to others. I couldn't accept that my dad no longer would be there for me in times of distress; I couldn't face that I never again would hear his voice, his laugh.

Suddenly, I remembered something. I *could* hear his voice. Many years earlier, I had dropped by the house to see him and Mom.

"I want you to promise me something," my dad had said.

"Okay, what?"

He handed me a cassette recording.

"I made this for you. I want you to promise me that you won't listen to it until after I'm dead."

"I don't know if I can do that," I said with a grin. "You're putting me in the path of temptation. What's on here that you don't want me to know now?"

He laughed.

"Just promise," he said.

I did.

I had stashed the tape away, and I remembered that I had come across it a couple of times over the years. But where was it now?

I drove to the house. Linda hadn't got home yet. I went inside. The phone was ringing, but I ignored it. I started pulling out drawers, searching every corner. I hunted and hunted, and finally I found it.

By that time, people were arriving. The phone had to be answered. Calls had to be made. Matters had to be attended. Not until late that night did I find time for the tape. My Dodge pickup had a cassette player. I climbed into the cab, closed the door, put in the tape, and pushed the "play" button. As I sat there in the darkness, my dad's warm voice came from the speaker.

"Hello, Jerry. I've been meaning to do this for a long time, have a little chat with you on this tape. And you being over forty and me being over sixty-five, it doesn't take a genius to figure out that if I'm ever going to do it, I'd better be doing it... All of this pausing and grunting and going on will be much more apparent perhaps on this tape than it would be if you and I were talking—but nevertheless this is just your daddy and this is the way he sounded."

I later would calculate that he had made this tape in the last half of 1984, not long before my mother showed the first signs of Alzheimer's.

This was my dad's own little memoir. Not much was known about my father's family. He knew that his paternal grandfather was named Eric, and he recently had discovered that his great-grandfather, Thomas, had been lost in the Civil War, his burial spot unknown. He last had been seen near Natural Bridge, Virginia, wounded and sick.

Dad went on to recall my birth and his departure for the army three weeks later. I was fascinated when he began talking about his arrival in the Philippines, because I thought he might speak about his experiences in combat. He'd never disclosed any details. But he said only that he had been in combat three or four months.

"One day would have been a great plenty," he added.

His first time into combat had been in the mountains east of Manila. It had lasted twenty-nine days, and he'd worn the same clothes out that he wore in. He made no mention of the fighting.

If I ever flew into Manila, he said, I should look for those distinctive twin peaks that were used as navigational markers. "A lot of those mountains you'll be looking at down there, I've got holes dug in the side of 'em," he said.

He recalled a time that I didn't remember after he got back home and had bought the old '36 Chevrolet, which would hardly run. He and my mom had put quilts in the back and taken Betty and me on a camping trip to the mountains. They had left Asheville at night with a full tank of gas and less than a dollar in my dad's pocket, hoping to get back home.

"We limped on into the house," he said. He didn't know what they would have done if the car had broken down.

"Being young and being nuts is about the only combination that would cause a person to take that type of a chance. But that was our situation. I guess that's a great combination, being young and being willing to take a chance to have some fun."

He went on to recall many incidences from my childhood. My asthma. Our late-night trips to the train tracks in High Point to deal with it. My broken nose on the icy creek. All my messin' with wires. The champion steer I'd raised, and the hurt from seeing it led away to slaughter.

"If there could've been anything I could've done to relieve you in that situation, naturally, I would have. Already in life you were getting in a place where your daddy couldn't take care of one of your problems. At one time your daddy couldn't take care of a lot of 'em. Getting into a place where your daddy could just pray and hurt along with you."

He and my mom both were extremely proud of me, he said.

"I have looked at you, and actually I believe that I never saw a child do as well at taking the best of both parents that you have."

He expressed regret about not having more time to spend with my sisters and me when we were young because of the long hours he had to work.

"I'd come in at the time you children were going to bed, or come in so tired I didn't know what in the world to do with myself, had a lot of problems at work that took up energy and took up my time and wore my patience thin."

But he really had no choice. It was the only way he had to keep food on the table and clothes on our backs.

"We all were robbed of the friendship of one another back when you children were young... Life goes by so swift...

"As you get older, you'll find out that you and Linda both need each other worse when all the children are gone, been gone ten or fifteen years or something, you need each other worse right then than you need each other today.

"I mean your mama and me we see that all the time. It's just like we're one body, and if the other is not there, it's just cut out part of you. I don't think about a world without your mother. It would be a terrible problem without her, and I'm sure it would be the same with her if I was gone. So the only thing we can do is try to get a little enjoyment out of every day. Life is wonderful as long as you can enjoy, but I have no fear of it ending...no dread whatsoever about that."

He went on reminiscing and seemed to be coming to an end.

"Jerry, certainly a lot of things I've left out, but wait just a minute! Your mom's been gone to church and I think she's knocking on the door... So let me go back there and let her in."

There was a pause, and then the tape began again with a chuckle.

"Well, Jerry, got a little surprise there, wasn't your mama but it was you knocking on the back door. How you like that?"

He went on to talk about retirement, and how time and death inevitably would overtake all of us, and how he hoped that all of his children, grandchildren, great-grandchildren, and others to come would "all put our trust in Jesus Christ and be looking to a great reunion...

"Jerry, I think probably that I have talked about as long as I need to. This tape has got a few more minutes on it. So everything is going good with me. I'm happy and hope to stay that way for a while. I know I don't want anybody to have any sadness if my state of happiness on this earth does not last. After all, I have been very fortunate. I'm very thankful for what I've already seen and experienced in this life. And whatever happens and it's the Lord's will, why it's fine with me. So for the time being I'm just

My favorite photo of my dad, made shortly after I was born.

going to sign off and the best to you and yours on and on."

All I could think as I sat there in the silence and the darkness was what a magnificent gift my dad had bequeathed me in this little tape. He still was there to comfort and guide me at a moment of great need, as he would be for the rest of time.

Poplar Ridge Friends Meeting was a growing congregation. In 1971, it had built a new, spacious brick sanctuary across the road. My dad had an active interest in the construction and took many photos of it. The old building, which I had attended throughout my youth, and which my great-grandfather Edd had helped to build, had been torn apart, and the main part of it moved to another site for private use. Dad had prayed the last prayer in the old sanctuary on September 26, and the first in the new a week later.

That sanctuary was packed for his funeral.

I had discovered that arranging a military funeral wasn't easy. Once, the military branches had provided that service for any honorably discharged veteran, but no more. A group of local veterans had formed the Randolph Honor Guard. They had their own distinctive uniforms, and they agreed to come.

Dad wanted a bugler to play taps, but the honor guard only had a cassette player for that purpose. We had a heck of a time getting a bugler, but our son James finally found one in Charlotte.

The service went exactly as requested in Dad's meticulous instructions. It was a still, hot day, and at the graveside service, the honor guard snapped to attention and seven riflemen fired off three synchronized volleys. Two other members of the guard raised the flag from the coffin, stepped aside, ritually folded it, and presented it to my sister Betty. The bugler did a beautiful job.

My dad had a little surprise for those in attendance. He loved bagpipes. He had asked that we have a piper, out of sight, who would play "Amazing Grace" at the close of the graveside service. James had found the piper, too. We had placed him behind a huge oak at the edge of the cemetery. Surely nobody present will ever forget the sounds of that beautiful hymn wafting over that still afternoon, a final gift from my dad. It haunts me still.

That was not Dad's last request, though. George Sumner, whom my dad had taught in Sunday school, was standing by to take care of that.

Randolph County soil is rocky and heavy with red clay. My dad wanted no rocks, no clods of clay, no voids where water might collect in his grave, just good dirt, closely packed. He had made the same request at my mother's service. George had a tamping machine and would see to that after all of us were gone.

When we returned later, everything was neat and tightly packed. My dad was at rest beside my mom, and all was in balance.

Mom and Dad sat for this portrait shortly before my mom became ill.

175

Fifteen

Surely the first thing that needs to be understood by anybody who sets out to build a house of whatever size, style, or cost is this: it will take longer and cost more than you expect, no matter what you're told, no matter how many bids or estimates you get, and no matter the honesty and reliability of the people you hire to build it.

The same rule applies to starting a business. My partners and I had learned this lesson well through all the years of agony and questing for new supplies of cash that were required to build RF Micro Devices into a viable company. But the excitement that comes from embarking on a new dream tends to suppress wisdom gained even through harsh experience.

Unless you have so much money that you don't even know the amount and never need to be concerned with expenditures, you probably shouldn't undertake building a house of the scope we had planned unless you intend to stay on site through every minute of construction, watching every move with a parsimonious eye.

The reason is simple. You're going to see things nobody else sees just because you're paying the bills. Having to write the checks from your own account sharpens all of the senses.

Unfortunately, such realizations usually come only as afterthought following excruciating unexpected developments.

Such developments began well before we started construction. A year after RF Micro Devices' stock had hit its peak during the dot-com boom, the technology business had dived into recession. Our stock had dropped by 90 percent to $10 (a two-for-one split had taken place in the summer of 2000 cutting the price in half). The wealth that Linda and I could claim had fallen accordingly.

This had occurred before we got the final plans from Bill Huey. It certainly gave us pause. If we had waited until this point to begin planning the house, we might not have proceeded at all. But we were committed now, had put too much of ourselves into it. We had set aside enough money to build the house, based on estimates, and we decided to continue.

Over the summer, RF Micro's sales had picked up and the stock had come back somewhat. We felt confident that we were headed out of the recession. But only a month after my dad's death in August came another unexpected development, this one horrendous and devastating. Terrorists flew huge airliners into the twin towers of the World Trade Center and the

Pentagon. Like the rest of the country, we were stunned. Any personal concerns were nothing compared to the suffering going on in New York, Washington, and their vicinities.

Linda and I had a meeting scheduled with Bill Huey in Charleston several days after 9/11 and went ahead with it. Afterward we went to a Charleston church to attend a memorial service for the victims of the terrorists.

Nobody could predict how extensively these attacks would affect an already battered economy, but the consensus was that it wouldn't be good. That was borne out when stock markets reopened on September 17. The Dow took its biggest one-day drop in history, closing down 679 points. The Nasdaq fell by 116.

By the first of October, the engineering firm had finished the drawings for the steel frame of the house and turned them over to the contracting company, which began staking out the site on schedule. As soon as the layout was finished, my friend Mark Peterson and my cousin Harold Loflin began digging the basement so footings could be poured. The site preparation took several weeks, but in November sub-contractors who would handle the concrete work began building their forms.

I never missed a day checking out the progress unless I was away on travel. Sometimes I wouldn't get there until midnight and would have to examine new developments with a spotlight. Scores of people were working at the site, and I could see significant changes daily.

Footings for the house were being poured late in the fall of 2001.

In one way we were fortunate in the timing of the construction. Building had dropped off as the recession continued. Sub-contractors needed work and weren't hard to find. The cost of building supplies had fallen. We saved substantially on the steel, buying it just a few weeks before a new tariff was imposed. We got the copper for the roof and other fixtures at a good price, too.

By January, the steel erection was underway. Bare light bulbs were strung throughout, floor by floor, as the work went along, and the hilltop was lighted every night. The steel went up much faster than I imagined, even though the weather was cold and frequently nasty.

I've always loved watching construction, seeing imagination brought to physical reality, but when the construction is creating your own vision, it holds a special fascination.

By the end of February the skeleton of the house was almost intact. A topping-out ceremony was scheduled for March 5. Tables were set up out of the wind on the concrete floor of the basement for a catered lunch for all of the workers who were on hand and some guests. I invited my partners, Bill Pratt and Powell Seymour, to attend the ceremony.

It was a cold day with a brisk wind blowing. We stood in warm coats watching as the monstrous crane that had lifted all of this steel into place began raising the final short beam, which looked tiny, almost fragile, compared to all of the rest. It would be the center front beam at the top of the cupola. A bracket had been welded to it holding a flag pole from which the Stars and Stripes hung limply until the beam began to rise and wind caught the flag and snapped it to attention.

On one of the narrow beams at the top of the cupola sixty feet above, a steelworker with the agility and skill of a tightrope walker waited. As the beam swung slowly over to him, he deftly walked the narrow framework, grasped the beam with gloved hands, fitted it into place, and unhooked it from the crane's cable. We all cheered and applauded as he began bolting it down, the flag horizontal in the wind

After lunch, the crane operator offered to take Bill, Powell, and me on a ride high above the house on a small steel platform with rails around it. I love thrill rides and wasn't about to miss this one. Bill was eager, too.

But Powell checked out the platform, examined the four cables that would be lifting it, and leaned his head back to gaze at the extension on the crane more than one hundred feet above.

"I'm not about to get on that thing," he said.

"Powell, would you really want to go on living if something happened to Bill and me?" I asked.

Powell thought about it a moment. "Well, I guess not," he said, and climbed aboard.

It was quite a ride, cold and windy though it was.

Months earlier, I had gotten the tree surgeon I'd hired to remove trees for the driveway to bring his cherry picker to the top of the hill and lift me high enough to see what the view was going to be from the cupola. That had been exciting but couldn't be compared with this.

As the crane operator lifted us, we had a panoramic view of the gray-green winter forest of the Randolph County countryside and the rolling Uwharries beyond. He kept lifting us above the house, then swung us slowly out over it until we were centered above the cupola with its new flag and could look down into the framework. That may not sound like such a beautiful sight, but when you're seeing a dream taking form in steel and concrete, believe me, it is.

Only a few weeks later, scaffolding had been erected inside the house all the way to the top of the third floor. The corrugated steel that would support the concrete floors had been bolted in place, and scores of workers were pouring and finishing the concrete on the first and second floors. On March 26, I had an experience that was almost as uplifting as the topping-out ceremony and the crane ride over the framework.

I donned a hard hat, and with binoculars in hand, I climbed the scaffolding to the third floor where a tall ladder led to the cupola. From the time I had first stood atop this hill and envisioned a classical house on this spot, I had dreamed of the moment when I'd be able to go up to the cupola, walk around, and enjoy the view. Now it had come. Spring was just

A crane lifted me above the house for a bird's eye view on the day of the topping-out ceremony.

A front view of the house after the steel was erected.

beginning to tinge the winter-bare forest with pastel, and it was a grand moment indeed.

I didn't know it then, but we were about to be presented with a new purpose for the house. It came in the form of an invitation that bore the most widely recognized family name in Randolph County.

That would be Petty. Lee Petty of Level Cross became one of the first stars of stock car racing back in the late '40s and '50s when the sport was just a rough-and-rowdy passion for country boys from a few southern states, not the intensely marketed, international, high-tech phenomenon that it is today.

Lee was the first winner of the Daytona 500, and his son, Richard, went on to become known as "The King" of stock car racing, with more wins than any other driver, a record not likely to be repeated. Richard's son, Kyle, became the third generation of the family to become a racing star.

My love of stock car racing had begun when my dad and I made a tradition of listening to the Southern 500 from Darlington every Labor Day while cleaning up the shop behind the house. I always pulled for Lee Petty, then for Richard when he started driving, and after that for Kyle. Before races became televised, I often carried a tiny radio with ear plugs with me on Sunday afternoons so that I could listen to the race wherever I was and whatever I happened to be doing.

I never knew any of the Pettys, but I had read a lot about them, talked to people who did know them, and had seen them on TV. I was well aware of their reputations as friendly, caring, down-to-earth people who never let success go to their heads, people who took time for every fan, loved Randolph County, and contributed greatly to the community.

Richard became a long-time county commissioner, and his wife, Lynda, was a member of the county school board. When Richard ran for secretary of state, Linda and I went to a political gathering at his house and exchanged greetings with him, the first Petty I'd ever met.

Kyle and Pattie Petty were almost neighbors of ours. They lived only a few miles away on a big horse farm that once had belonged to the Finch family who started Thomasville Furniture Company. Although we hadn't met them, we kept up with them in the news. They were our area celebrities.

I wasn't surprised in the least when I read that Kyle and Pattie's eldest son, Adam, was becoming the first fourth-generation participant not only in stock car racing but in any American professional sport.

Adam was recognized as an open and friendly young man with a natural ability for racing. He clearly was a rising star who would maintain the Petty legacy. He had started racing go-karts at age six. At sixteen, he made his NASCAR debut, running twenty-five races in the Weekly Racing Series. The following year he moved on to the Busch Series, one step removed from the big leagues, running forty-three races and finishing three in the top five.

He became the youngest person ever to win a race at a major speedway when he won an ARCA-sanctioned event at Lowe's Motor Speedway in Charlotte in 1998. His grandfather, with whom he was very close, was waiting to greet him in the winner's circle.

On April 2, 2000, Adam started his first Winston Cup Series race—as the major league of NASCAR then was known—at Texas Motor Speedway. A blown engine ended his hopes for a good finish. Three days after that race, his great-grandfather, Lee, died from a stomach aneurysm at age eighty-six.

Nobody could have imagined then that little more than five weeks later, Adam, too, would be dead from a crash into a wall during a practice run at New Hampshire International Speedway on May 12. That came as a shock to the racing community and was shattering news in Randolph County.

I heard about it on my car radio, and it was as if it had happened to somebody I knew. I drove to my dad's house to tell him. He, too, was a big Petty fan. He was sitting in the backyard under a pecan tree. I pulled up a chair and told him that Adam Petty had been killed in a racetrack crash.

It hit him the same way it hit me, and we talked about what a tragedy it was that someone so full of promise would be struck down so young and how understanding such events probably is beyond human ability.

Later, Linda and I discussed the same thing. Our hearts went out to the Petty family, but especially to Pattie and Kyle. Losing a child is a parent's worst fear, and it's little solace that the child dies doing something he loves.

What we didn't know at the time was that Adam and his parents shared our passion for children who suffer what film star Paul Newman calls "the brutality of luck": birth defects, incurable diseases, horrible accidents. Pattie has a master's degree in child developmental psychology. Pattie and Kyle and other members of the Petty family have long contributed to and been involved with Brenner Children's Hospitals.

Their desire to help children would bring them to know Paul Newman. Newman started a line of food products to fund charities, and he got so many appeals from parents of gravely ill children that in 1986 he came up with the idea of building a free camp where these children could share the experiences that whole and healthy kids enjoy. He opened the first Hole in the Wall Gang Camp in a rural slice of northeastern Connecticut in 1988. The camp made such an impression that others followed, one in Florida.

In 1997, Kyle Petty, rode in a charity ride sponsored by Daytona Harley-Davidson for Boggy Creek Hole in the Wall Gang Camp in Florida's lake country north of Orlando. He came home talking about what a great place it was.

In 1998, the Independence Day race at Daytona International Speedway had to be cancelled because of intense forest fires in the area. It was rescheduled for October in the same period as the charity ride for Boggy Creek in which Kyle again participated. Pattie and Adam went with him and saw the camp for the first time.

Adam had been maintaining that the Petty family needed to find a charity that could become identified as their own, a charity that fans, too, could be encouraged to support. This visit gave Pattie and Adam the idea for what that charity should be—a Hole in the Wall Gang camp in Randolph County for children in the Carolinas, Virginia, and other nearby states.

They began looking into the need for such a camp and discovered that in the Carolinas and Virginia there were some 237,000 children in twenty-six ailment groups who might be able to participate in a camp experience. But when they began checking into what would have to be done to build such a camp, they encountered discouragement.

Anybody who knows Pattie Petty can tell you that if you want the impossible done, just tell her that she can't do it.

It would take $30 million even to think about building such a camp, Pattie was told. Her response: it takes $30 million to run a racing team for a year; a lot of people do that.

The idea began to blossom for a Hole in the Wall Gang Camp built around a racing theme. It would be called Victory Junction. Pattie thought that much of the money could be raised within the racing community.

Meanwhile, two hundred acres came up for sale adjoining Pattie and Kyle's farm. That would be the perfect place for the camp, they thought. It already had a big lake. The price was $1 million. No money had been raised at that time.

Adam stepped forward and said that he would buy the land for the camp. He had sponsor contracts that would give him the income over time to pay for it. He signed the contract three days before he left for the speedway in New Hampshire.

Everything stopped for the Pettys for a few weeks as they dealt with their grief after Adam's death. The land ended up being sold to another party.

But Adam's dream became a turning point for the camp. Fans found out about it and sent donations—and not just Petty fans. Hundreds of fans of other drivers sent donations in the amounts of their favorite driver's car numbers.

Adam's younger brother, Austin, took a summer job at Boggy Creek Camp after his brother's death. At the July race at Daytona, the family drove over to visit him. It was the first time Austin's grandfather, Richard, had been to Boggy Creek.

"This is not a camp," Richard said, as Pattie later remembered, "this is a resort."

That visit caused Richard and Lynda Petty to give some of their land north of Randleman as the site for Victory Junction. A donation of $1 million from the owner of New Hampshire International Speedway provided the means to hire architects to begin drawing the plans that would be necessary to raise the millions to build the camp.

I don't remember being aware of Victory Junction until sometime in 2001. Wayne and Betty Snyder were the first to mention it to Linda and me. They operate Snyder Farms Restaurant, northwest of Randleman, where we eat occasionally. Betty's mother, Lizzie Jester, was my grandmother Myrtle's best friend. The Snyders also have a catering company. One of my dad's friends from childhood, Grady Hardin, sometimes helped with the cooking for the catering service. In March 2001, Wayne and Betty began donating the proceeds of a Saturday night's receipts every month to Victory Junction.

At the beginning of April, Linda and I got an invitation to attend an event at the site where the camp was to be built.

The event was a little unusual. The James River Equipment Company of Manassas, Virginia, a huge dealer of John Deere equipment, with branches in both Carolinas, had volunteered the use of its equipment to prepare the site for the camp. The company was sponsoring a luncheon, catered by Snyder Farm, for people interested in the camp. A lot of their equipment would be on display. Nobody could have picked a better way to entice me to attend.

• • •

If pressed, I guess I'd have to acknowledge that I probably could be defined as a John Deere addict. But as much as I loved tractors, I never had a John Deere until that little 750 that I bought while I was working at Analog Devices after my granddaddy's barn burned. The second was the restored 1940 BR that I bought on an impulse at the Old Thresher's Convention in 1997, my one indulgence after RF Micro went public.

In 1998, Linda and I made a nostalgic trip back to Amish country in Pennsylvania, with a stop at the famous Civil War battlefield at Gettysburg.

"Look at that," Linda said, as we were driving along a country road near Gettysburg.

It was a field full of rusty old tractors. We stopped to have a look. I came upon a Model H there in pretty good condition and bought it on the spot, my third John Deere. Linda and I returned home, borrowed a trailer from my cousin Harold, and drove back to Pennsylvania to get it. With three, it began to look as if I were in danger of becoming a John Deere collector.

Jon Briles, who lives near Thomasville, is a master restorer of tractors. His wife Sherry is Linda's cousin. He made that Model H look brand new. Later, I would loan it to the John Deere Company museum in Moline, Illinois, where it would remain on display for a year and a half.

John Deere, I should mention, never saw a John Deere tractor. He was a blacksmith in Grand Detour, Illinois, when in 1837 he created a new plow that changed farming in the Midwest. He set up a company to manufacture the plows and in1848 moved it to Moline to take advantage of shipping on the Mississippi. From the beginning, Deere insisted that anything bearing his name have the highest quality materials and workmanship. That became the standard for the company, and that's a primary reason why I have so much respect for John Deere equipment.

In 1869, Deere's son Charles took over the business and expanded it into a wide range of other farm implements before his father's death in 1886. Charles never saw a John Deere tractor either. He died in 1907. Not until 1918 when the company took over the Waterloo Gasoline Traction Engine Works did the first John Deere tractor appear. People have been devoted to them ever since.

In the summer of 1999, I heard about an auction of antique John Deeres that was to be held in a small town in upstate New York, and I went to it. A young man who owned an equipment company had been collecting these tractors with plans to restore them. But he had come down with a brain tumor and had only a short time to live. He was at the show in a wheelchair with an oxygen bottle.

I bought two more tractors there, a Model 80 and a Model 830. After the sale, the young man's wife came up to me and said the Model 80 was her husband's favorite. She asked me to take good care of it. I promised that

Linda and I bought my third John Deere tractor on a visit to Amish country in Pennsylvania.

I would. After I painted it and put new tires and a new steering wheel on it, I sent her a photo of it.

In 1997, the John Deere Company opened the John Deere Pavilion in Moline in an old riverfront factory with an adjoining conference center, hotel, and entertainment arena. Visitors can see antique tractors and farm equipment, learn how food is grown, and experience the technological evolution of farming from 1830 to the present. In the retail store, all manner of John Deere collectibles are available.

I had wanted to visit the John Deere Commons, as the complex is called, from the time I first heard about it. But Linda and I didn't get an opportunity until the summer of 2000.

While we were there, we learned that a new facility was being developed just down the road. It was a reproduction of a 1950-era dealership to be called the Moline Plow and Tractor Company. It was to be a center for John Deere collectors. We went hoping to get a look at it and met Jeff McManus, who was creating it and would become a good friend.

He showed us all around. Technicians actually would be restoring tractors and other equipment there, he said. The earliest John Deere tractor, a 1918 model, was to be displayed, and we got a close look at it. Parts and manuals for almost any John Deere tractor would be available. This was a place after my own heart. Jeff told us that we needed to come back in August for the grand opening and the inaugural annual sale of antique John Deeres that would take place then.

Unfortunately, pressing matters at work kept me from going. Instead,

I still enjoy competing in tractor pulls.

Linda volunteered to go and buy me a really nice tractor. Our son-in-law, Don Smith, Annette's husband, agreed to accompany her to inspect the tractors beforehand and determine which were worth bidding on. He took along his brother Edward from Charlotte. Jon and Sherry Briles also went. I felt confident that the five of them would be able to pick out a good tractor.

We knew that the top collectors of John Deere tractors would be present. They are a relatively small group, and most know each other. But hundreds of people attended this first auction.

Linda set off a real buzz among the serious collectors when she showed up in her white dress and big floppy pink hat. Who was this woman with her entourage going over these tractors as if they knew what they were doing?

Even more whispering and speculation about who this mystery woman might be broke out when the bidding started and Don and his team began giving signals to Linda about specific tractors.

Later, I heard several different reports about what happened next. From what I can gather, Linda seemed to go into some kind of a bidding trance that Don and his panicked team were unable to break.

The next thing I knew, I had five more antique John Deere tractors. Don actually had given her signals to bid on only two. On the other three, he was sweating heavily and frantically trying to get her to stop bidding.

At some point, he apparently broke through to Linda, because after buying five, she called me on my cell phone to tell me that a really rare tractor was on the block, a Model 630. Only five ever were made.

"They're selling it now," she said excitedly. "You want me to bid?"

"Well, I don't know," I said. "How's the bidding going?"

"It's getting a little high," she said.

"How high?"

"Right now it's $110,000."

"Keep your hands down!" I said. "Stay in your seat. Don't make a move. Don't even blink or nod."

The 630 went for $140,000 but thankfully not to Linda.

Linda became the belle of the sale, however, and even got her full-color picture on the front page of the *Quad City Times*.

After this auction, I found myself with nine antique John Deere tractors, a solid core for a serious collection. This did create a problem, however. I kept my first five John Deeres stored in the garage and the barn, but I had no place for the new additions.

I also needed a repair facility for the farm and wanted to add a machine shop so that I could make my own parts and hardware when it was necessary. I decided to erect a big steel building that would serve as a shop and give me room to display the tractors. It was completed early in 2001. I had reserved a big room in the front to display the tractors. I wanted to open it as a museum, and I began planning an event around it.

I had become involved in tractor pulling contests, and I organized a tractor pull, as these events are called, to raise money for Poplar Ridge Friends Meeting and the Salvation Army's Boys and Girls Club. It was held in conjunction with the opening of the Neal Vintage Tractor Museum on September 8, 2001, just four weeks after my dad's death.

The event took place in a big field on the property that once had been Stonehinge Farm. We set up bleachers and tents and attracted seventy-five competitors and an audience of more than five hundred. I bought thirty trophies to be awarded and didn't win any of them. Some of the competitors offered to vote me one if I'd be willing to buy it, but I declined.

Since the opening of the museum, my John Deere tractor collection has increased to twenty-five, two of which are being restored as this is written, one by Jeff McManus. Another is awaiting restoration. My oldest tractor is a '29 Model D, which was the longest manufactured line of tractors in history. Several of my tractors are quite rare.

As much as I love my John Deeres, however, the tractor of which I'm proudest is not a Deere. After I left home, my dad sold the little odd-looking Allis-Chalmers Model G that I loved to drive as a child. A farmer who lived a few miles away bought it. The tractor was destroyed in a barn fire several years later. For more than a quarter of a century, it sat rusting away in the ruins.

My son Jerry found out about it and decided to rescue his grandfather's tractor. He convinced the farmer to sell it to him, salvaged it from the rubble, and took it to his basement. He hoped to repair it and use it himself, but the movable parts were all locked solid by massive rust. It would require heavy tools and major work. I bought it from him and moved it to the shop. I had to use torches to disassemble it to see if it could be restored to working condition. Jon Briles and I determined that it could, and he took over.

Jon did a magnificent job. The Model G looks new and runs beautifully. Jerry and I just wish that my dad could have lived to see it.

The James River Equipment Company display at the future site of Victory Junction on April 9 was especially impressive to a John Deere lover, but the dream for the camp that we were soon to learn about was even more so.

Linda and I met Pattie and Kyle Petty for the first time and posed for photos with them and Richard. Kyle joined our table to enjoy some of Wayne Snyder's fried chicken for lunch. He told a funny story about sneaking to buy his first Harley-Davidson over Pattie's objections. Kyle loves motorcycles the way I love tractors. In 1994, he and his crew chief, Robin Pemberton, decided to ride their bikes to a race in Phoenix. They attracted other riders along the way and arrived in Phoenix with about thirty in tow.

That gave Kyle the idea to start a cross-country motorcycle ride for charity, and it began the next year, two years before he visited Boggy Creek Gang Camp in Florida. The Kyle Petty Charity Ride has since become a series of events sponsored by Chic-Fil-A that attracts hundreds of riders and raises millions of dollars for children's hospitals and Victory Junction.

An early view inside my John Deere vintage tractor museum.

After lunch, we got a close look at the camp site and discovered just what an elaborate facility this was going to be. It would be more a Disney-like resort than a typical, rustic summer camp. Campers would enter through a tunnel, as race teams do at big race tracks.

The core of the camp would be built around an oval track. The dining room would be called the fuel stop, complete with race cars, video, and sound effects. One building would be in the shape of Adam's car. There children could compete in electronic virtual racing. The big, heated swimming pool would have a monstrous motorcycle in the middle of it with the most outlandish Rube-Goldberg whirling and water-spouting gizmos ever seen in this part of the country. Children in wheelchairs would be able to roll right into it.

All the aspects of other summer camps would be there, too: an arts and crafts building, a big stable for horseback riding, a climbing wall, a lake with a boat house and a big fishing pier. There also would be a gym, a theater, and a fully staffed, state-of-the-art medical center that would be capable of quickly dealing with problems that the children with their various ailments might encounter.

At this point, with land preparation about to begin, Pattie and Kyle had raised only about $10 million of the $24 million that they thought would be needed to get the camp up and running. Although much of the NASCAR racing community was lining up to support the camp, they still had a long way to go.

After seeing the plans for the camp and the passion that the Pettys had for it, especially Pattie, Linda and I knew instinctively that we had to

Linda and I met Richard, Kyle, and Pattie Petty on our first visit to the site of Victory Junction Gang Camp.

support such an incredible project as this in our own county.

What we didn't realize was how close a relationship we would come to have with Pattie, Kyle, their children Montgomery Lee, and Austin, and without ever meeting him, Adam. Neither did we know then how much their dream of seeing catastrophically ill children laughing and having fun at Victory Junction would become our own.

A few weeks later, Pattie called to ask if Linda and I would consider joining the board of directors of Victory Junction Gang Camp. We didn't have to think about it. We accepted.

One thing had been eluding me about the house we were building, and that was about to come to the forefront. Because I serve on the board of visitors for the Babcock Graduate School of Management at Wake Forest University in Winston-Salem, Linda and I often are involved in activities at the university. Early in May, our friend Melissa Combes arranged for us to tour the garden at the President's House and have lunch with Laura Hearn, wife of university president Thomas K. Hearn (who would retire in 2004).

The President's House originally was the home of businessman Ralph P. Hanes. Hanes' father, John Wesley, started a company in 1901 that would become Hanes Hosiery Mills, which consequently would become best known for introducing pantyhose in the 1960s. When Laura moved into the President's House in 1992 after her marriage to Thomas Hearn, she took a particular interest in the garden, which had been designed in 1928 by Ellen Shipman, a landscape architect who created gardens for many of America's wealthiest and best-known families in the first half of the last century.

The garden had changed radically with time. Laura closely observed it for a year and researched it intensely. She wanted to restore it as closely as possible to its original condition. She called on noted garden designer and restorer Paul Faulkner "Chip" Callaway of Greensboro to take charge of the project. They did a beautiful job. The garden is a treasure both for the university and the city.

At lunch, we talked a lot about gardens and about Chip Callaway. Laura also quizzed us about the house we were building, and we told her about our vision for it.

"What's the name of your estate?" she asked.

"Well," I said, pausing, "we don't have a name for it yet."

It was something I had been thinking about, though, and her question emphasized the necessity of coming up with a memorable name that could become identified with the causes we wanted the house to serve.

Early in June, Linda and I went to Sea Pines Resort at Hilton Head, South Carolina, for a meeting with officials of Southern Wesleyan University. Southern Wesleyan is in Central, South Carolina. I had been commencement speaker there the previous December. We were part of a group who were going to preview and offer advice on a plan for a fund-raising campaign to expand the university.

At dinner we were sitting with Ann Platz and her husband, John, from Atlanta. Ann is quite a character, an interior decorator whose work has been featured in *Southern Living* and *Better Homes and Gardens*, a public speaker, a frequent guest on radio and TV, and the author of thirteen books, including one on manners and social graces. She also is a wonderfully entertaining storyteller, and she was in fine form this night. We were having a great time.

Ann grew up on a plantation near Orangeburg, South Carolina, which has been in her family for six generations. Her father, Marshall Williams, was a state senator for fifty years before his death in 1996. Her mother, Margaret, still lives on the plantation. Ann started telling a story about her parents meeting a young couple in a restaurant on their wedding day and inviting them to spend the first night of their honeymoon at their plantation, Willbrook.

That was as far as I got. I heard "Willbrook" and something clicked in my mind. Since our conversation with Laura Hearn, I had been racking my brain to come up with a name for the house. I wanted it to honor Linda. I'd tried all kinds of combinations with her name, and nothing seemed to work. I'd even asked friends for suggestions, but none had come up with anything that seemed appropriate either.

Then I heard that word. *Willbrook*. The first few letters of the Williams name simply had been joined with brook. A beautiful brook runs right in front of the house we were building and halfway around it.

"Linbrook" flashed in my brain.

That was it!

I wanted to jump up and shout it. I didn't, but I was really happy.

Linda was quite taken with Ann, and after dinner, she approached her to tell her how much she enjoyed her stories.

"I just want to thank you," I told Ann. "You solved a big problem for me tonight."

"How's that?" she asked.

I told her about the house we were building and how long I had been searching for a name for it, how I wanted it to honor Linda, and how her story had made the right connection in my brain and "Linbrook" had leaped out.

"Oh, that's beautiful," she said.

This was the first that Linda had heard of this, and she jumped right in. "Wait a minute," she said. "I don't want it named just after me. That's not right."

"Linbrook is absolutely perfect," Ann said, "but it needs more. Linbrook something. Linbrook Manor? Linbrook Hall?"

"It has big halls," I said.

"That's it. Linbrook Hall. It flows perfectly. And it'll look so good on paper, too. You can have a beautiful logo."

"Linbrook Hall," I said, testing the sound of it.

"I disagree," Linda said. "If it's going to be named for somebody, it should be named for both of us."

Ann is no shrinking violet. She's blonde and flamboyant, even though she now is a great-grandmother. She reached out two hands flashing big diamonds, took Linda by the shoulders, and stared straight into her eyes.

"Linda," she said, "I have something important to tell you. When your husband wants to honor you, there's only one response. And you know what that is."

Linda didn't protest anymore.

Ann was curious about the house and asked lots of questions. She immediately understood our vision for it and said something that made a big impression on me.

"Your lives are going to move from success to significance," she told us, "and this house is going to be the vessel for it."

We didn't get back home until late Sunday night, and I had to be up at four for a flight to California on business. When I got back on Tuesday, I went to the on-site manager and told him that from now on this house was to be referred to as Linbrook Hall. I called Bill Huey and told him the story of how the name finally had come to me. Up to this point, Bill had been referring to the house as "the Neal residence." Henceforth, he said, all the drawings and written references would call it Linbrook Hall.

I also set a graphic artist to work creating a logo that could be designed into the weathervane on the cupola and the ironwork on the grand staircase.

One thing I hadn't counted on was how construction of the house would affect me on a day-to-day, and sometimes hour-to-hour, basis. It began to hit me hard after the roof was covered and the exterior walls started going up. Decisions had to be made every day, sometimes scores of them. All the doors and windows had to be custom made and had to arrive at certain times, and that alone required dozens of decisions. I had to make decisions about things I'd never even considered and knew little about.

I talked to Bill Huey, the architect, several times a week, often several times a day. I conferred daily with the project manager and on-site superintendent, asking and answering questions that the decisions demanded.

One major decision finally had been made. After more than a year of stalking columns all over the country, Linda and I had decided on the kind we wanted. We had been considering having the columns manufactured by a company in California that made all of the columns for Caesar's Palace in Las Vegas. The previous fall, the project manager had accompanied us to Las Vegas so that we could closely examine the workmanship on the columns at Caesar's, which offers a virtual showplace of classical columns.

That trip had helped us decide that we wanted fluted Scamozzi columns. Vincenzo Scamozzi, a brilliant architect who died in Venice in 1616, had been an apprentice to sixteenth century architect Andrea Palladio, who is credited with reviving classical Roman architecture. Linbrook Hall's fourteen columns would each be thirty-two feet tall, four feet in diameter with an eight-inch taper, on bases a little more than five feet square.

Much of the time that I had been chasing after columns, I also had been searching out gates. Wherever I went, I asked about private homes or public institutions that had big gates, and I went to examine and photograph them.

Paul O'Connor, the landscape architect, had designed a stone wall two hundred feet long and six feet high to serve as the main entrance to the house. Linda's uncle, Lloyd Bingham, had done a beautiful job constructing it. Now it needed an impressive gate. Mark Peterson's cousin, Newbern Douglas, a talented Randolph County blacksmith who has a shop near Sophia, had agreed to build it. Newbern makes ironwork bearing the imprint of Davidson County artist and designer Bob Timberlake that is sold at Timberlake's famous gallery near Lexington. Newbern and I came up with a design based on a gate I photographed at a mansion in Cleveland, Ohio. The gate would be twelve feet high, and each side would weigh nine hundred pounds. Newbern would build two other gates, almost as big, for other entrances.

But these decisions, major though they were for the impression the house would present, were nothing compared to the decisions and problems that ensnared me as construction moved into summer.

Two primary factors played into this situation. The first was time. The contractor had estimated that construction of the house would take two years. I wanted to do it in eighteen months. It would be possible by bringing in more workers, I thought, and might save money. The second factor was that Bill Huey was designing the interior of the house as construction progressed. A clash was inevitable.

By June, a slowdown occurred. Too many workers were attempting too many things at the same time, and they often were conflicting and running out of plans. The sub-contractors came up with lists of questions that had to be answered. They passed these to the project manager, who compiled them and faxed them to Bill.

Often Bill would get lists of fifty questions or more. Some needed only simple answers, while others required elaborate drawings. But the answers had to be forthcoming immediately to keep people working and meet the schedule. Many of these questions demanded more decisions on my part.

On projects of this scope, the architect often acts as a sort of on-site supervisor, but that wasn't possible with Bill living nearly three hundred miles away in Charleston. He simply was overwhelmed. He was constantly distracted from design work because of the need for additional details, and those distractions only led to many more questions down the road. The sub-contractors blamed the contractor for delays, and the contractor blamed all of the problems on Bill.

But some of the blame should have fallen on me. I had made two false assumptions. The first was that Bill and his colleague Ann Indelicato, whose specialty is interiors, only had a relatively small amount of design work left to do. The second was that construction could be speeded up without repercussions. Nobody told me that it couldn't be done when I suggested it. Neither did anybody predict that it would end up pitting key people against one another.

Later, Bill would confide that at several points he was almost at his limits. He didn't mention that at the time. He did tell me that he would do his best to protect my interests, but if it proved to be too much, he would offer to resign rather than make things worse. That was no solution so far as Linda and I were concerned. We liked Bill and his work a great deal, and we wanted him to continue. In a way, this house was as much his as ours.

At the end of June, I called a meeting of everybody involved. We walked through the house, discussing all of the problems and attempting to iron them out. I made it clear that I didn't intend to don a black and white striped shirt and serve as referee between the parties.

For a while, a ceasefire reigned and things seemed to be getting done, but that soon dissolved under new onslaughts of slowdowns, questions, and blame placing. I continued to be called upon to settle disputes and resolve issues.

Late in the summer, these problems were complicated by a new one. Costs were spiraling ever upward. No matter how much I inquired, I couldn't get any clear answers about why this was happening, although the many changes that were being made in the plans clearly were part of it. But my big concern was how high these rapidly rising costs eventually might go.

The amount Linda and I originally had budgeted to spend on the house had risen by 50 percent by the time we saw the first design. By the time construction began, the original amount had doubled. Now I couldn't determine where it might be headed.

In the meantime, the value of RF Micro Devices stock had fallen by a third in June. Although the company remained healthy and was growing, investors hadn't regained confidence in technology stocks after the dot-com bust and any setback could send prices tumbling. We were in a period of heavy research and development for new products, and those expenses cut into profits. By August, our stock price had dropped by nearly half again.

The wealth Linda and I once could claim had fallen by nearly 95 percent.

Clearly, I had to take control of these costs. I asked my friend Suzanne Rudy, the treasurer of our company, if she knew a good auditor who could look into the situation and find out what was going on. She recommended Marsha Tice, a CPA. Marsha had worked as an auditor. I met with her on September 16, and she agreed to take on this monumental task, although it would be near the end of the month before she could start.

I told her that I wanted her to do a complete audit of every cent paid to the contractor to this point. I wanted full audits of the sub-contractors as well. I told her to drill deep and keep on drilling until nothing was left to be questioned. I wanted every expense justified and documented before I paid it.

Up to this point, the contractor and I had been operating on a cost-plus agreement. My hope was that the contractor and sub-contractors would realize that I was serious about controlling costs, and that I would be able to negotiate a firm contract to limit further increases.

In the midst of these troubles, Linda and I went ahead on faith and made a substantial financial commitment to Victory Junction Gang Camp to reinforce the personal commitment we already had made.

I was really looking forward to the groundbreaking scheduled for Tuesday morning, October 9, 2002. Nearly a thousand people had been invited. Lots of the top NASCAR stars would be there, including Dale Jarrett, Bobby Labonte, Ken Schrader, Michael Waltrip, and Tony Stewart. Paul Newman, himself, would make an appearance as well, along with movie star Andie MacDowell. MacDowell, a South Carolina native, now lives in Asheville, where she started her own camp for sick children. Pattie and Kyle had helped her with fund-raising.

Excavation of the camp site had taken nearly six months and had proven difficult. The hilly land was heavily underlain by rock, and a fortune in dynamite had to be used to clear it. Huge boulders remained as evidence. Groundbreaking day turned out to be chilly with rain predicted, but hundreds of people turned out to walk around the red dirt track and see the displays showing what eventually would be built in each spot.

A big tent had been set up for the ceremonies. Pattie spoke movingly about Adam, his dream, and the family's dream for the camp, and how God was making it possible. Kyle expressed gratitude.

"For us and our families, this means everything," he said. "I can't put into words what it means for the NASCAR community as well as our local community to embrace and support us."

Paul Newman led the crowd in three cheers of "Hip, hip, hooray" for all who were making this camp possible and for the children who would attend it. Afterward, the founders and the stars all pressed their hands into wet clay to create mementoes of the day.

I was looking forward to what was to come next. Some guests were invited to lunch after the ceremonies, and Linda and I were among them. Lunch was to be served at Caraway Speedway, a track almost a half-mile in length near Sophia, where the Pettys would have a couple of their race cars.

This event, I suspect, was primarily for the benefit of Paul Newman, a veteran racer, who at age seventy-seven still was driving race cars. He wanted to take one of the Petty cars for a few turns around the track.

Kyle had promised me that after Paul got his fill, I could take the wheel for a few turns myself. To actually drive a race car was dream enough, but to be relief driver for Paul Newman was far beyond the imagination of a boy who had spent every Labor Day afternoon in the backyard workshop with his dad listening to the Southern 500.

Newman climbed into the passenger side of the famous blue and red number forty-three car so that Austin Petty could take him for an orientation turn around the track. By this time, a light drizzle had begun to fall. Austin brought the car back into the pits and crawled out of the window.

"Hurry up, guys," Newman called as he rushed to take the wheel, "we're losing to the rain."

He gunned the car onto the track and made two turns building speed. By this time, the rain was picking up. He pushed the car harder as he began his third lap.

I was suited up, helmet in hand, waiting for my chance, when I saw the famous Petty car start spinning. Every head turned in that direction. We all were cringing, and I have little doubt that everybody was thinking the same thing. Paul Newman was about to hit the wall.

Fortunately, the car spun out without making contact. Newman limped back to the pits and crawled out with a look of disgust on his face.

"Couldn't get going," he said.

Richard and Kyle clearly were relieved that no harm had been done. They ruled that the track was too wet for any more runs.

I should have known. It was just the way my luck was running.

Sixteen

Of all the historic houses that Linda and I have visited, perhaps the saddest and most forlorn of all is near Natchez, Mississippi. It is called Longwood, and it also is one of the most unusual houses we have seen.

Moorish in design, it is octagonal in shape, the biggest such house in the United States. It is four stories tall with a huge, sixteen-sided cupola, topped by an onion-like dome. Each floor was to have eight rooms built around a rotunda. A series of mirrors emanating from the dome would reflect sunlight throughout the rotunda to every level of the house.

Longwood was the dream of Haller Nutt, who was a physician, scientist, inventor, writer, and cotton planter with vast plantations on both sides of the Mississippi River, the source of his wealth. The house was designed by Philadelphia architect Samuel Sloan. Skilled northern craftsmen were recruited to build it.

Construction started in 1859, and by 1861, the exterior was largely finished. Work on the interior was underway. But on April 12, Confederate forces fired on the Union garrison at Fort Sumter in Charleston Harbor. Soon thereafter, President Abraham Lincoln issued a call for troops from every state to counter the insurrection. The craftsmen at Longwood laid down their tools and headed north to take up arms against their southern brethren.

Only the basement had been completed, and Dr. Nutt and his family moved into it. Materials to finish the house, along with furniture, sculptures, tapestries and other furnishings, and works of art had been ordered from Europe and were on their way by ship. They never would reach Longwood. Federal blockaders seized them.

Dr. Nutt and his wife, Julia, were Union sympathizers, and that perhaps saved Longwood, but Union forces still burned their fields, destroyed their farm buildings, and confiscated their livestock. His fortune lost, Dr. Nutt died of pneumonia in 1864, his spirit broken, his dream of Longwood never to be fulfilled.

Linda and I toured Longwood during the Spring Pilgrimage to Natchez's historic homes in 2002, taking the project manager and on-site superintendent of Linbrook Hall with us. The unfinished upper floors with their rough brick walls and exposed beams were ghostly and melancholy. Tools still lay where workmen had dropped them in 1861.

Those images haunted me. I was aware from my reading that Longwood wasn't the only grand house to go unfinished. These great houses take a long time to build, and circumstances can change dramatically due to all manner of misfortune and calamity.

From the beginning, my great fear was that something might happen that would prevent us from finishing Linbrook Hall. Now, only a year after we had begun construction, that prospect seemed possible.

The rapidly spiraling costs soon could create a situation that wouldn't allow us to continue. The house might well end up an empty shell known as Neal's Folly instead of Linbrook Hall. We had to get control of these costs and do it quickly.

Victory Junction Gang Camp was to be built by one of the Southeast's leading general contractors, Shelco, which is headquartered in Charlotte and has offices throughout the Carolinas. Shelco had built RF Micro Device's headquarters building and had done a great job. I had asked the contractor to bid on the house. I knew most of the top people at Shelco, and at the Victory Junction groundbreaking on October 9, I ran into Edwin Rose, the CEO, and Stuart Nunn from the Greensboro office (which later was relocated to Winston-Salem).

"How's the house coming?" Ed asked.

"Actually, we're having some serious problems," I said.

I told him about the situation, and asked if Shelco might be willing to take over the project if we were forced to drop the current contractor. The company normally was reluctant to do that, he said, but if worse came to worst, they would try to help.

I was well aware that the complexities of changing contractors would be immense. It just wasn't done unless a company failed or some other disaster intervened. I wanted to avoid that if possible.

From the beginning, I had set an absolute maximum cost for the house, but estimates of the ultimate cost were varying widely and were well beyond the maximum I had set. Trying to get a handle on the reasons was like trying to grasp Jello. It just kept shooting out through my fingers.

My hope was that Marsha Tice would be able to get enough answers about the excessive costs within a couple of weeks so that we could begin negotiating a firm contract with a final amount that was not to be exceeded. But the complexity of the situation made that impossible.

On Friday, October 18, Marsha and I met with Stuart Nunn of Shelco to go over some of the figures she had gathered so that we could try to determine if they met industry norms. That afternoon, I faxed a letter to the project manager requesting additional information and stating my desire to execute a firm contract with the same maximum cost and completion dates to which we had agreed when I authorized the second phase of construction in February.

I had scheduled a meeting with the president of the contracting company and the project managers to talk about all of this on the following Wednesday.

When I heard nothing back from the project manager on Monday, I sent an e-mail restating my desire for a contract and asking that all work by sub-contractors be stopped at the end of the week until this matter could be resolved.

The sub-contractors were informed at a meeting on Tuesday. Later that day, I got a call from Marsha about the meeting scheduled for Wednesday. She'd called a company official to get the latest figures, she said, and he told her that no numbers had been updated. He and the project manager hadn't even discussed it, he told her, and the project manager wouldn't be back in the office until later in the day and planned to be off for the rest of the week after Wednesday's meeting.

I'm not easy to anger, but I was furious. I thought the company wasn't taking my concerns seriously. I sent an e-mail to the project manager telling him that I wanted to make certain that there was no misunderstanding about the urgency of this situation and the importance of Wednesday's meeting, where I expected to see complete pricing.

"I need to see that action is being taken and progress is being made," I wrote.

Late that afternoon, I got an e-mail from a company vice president saying that he wasn't sure whether the project manager had seen my e-mail but that updates would be ready for the meeting at 9 a.m.

The president of the company, the vice-president who had responded to my e-mail, and the project manager appeared for the meeting with Marsha and me. For about an hour, I listened as figures were bandied about. But I still wasn't getting firm answers to my concerns. I was convinced that nobody actually had taken the time to come up with anything solid, that this was just something that had been hurriedly thrown together the night before to get through this meeting.

I surprised myself when I suddenly stood.

"I'm out of here," I said. "You guys have not taken this seriously. I'm not wasting any more time."

I started for the door.

"Jerry, you're obviously frustrated and upset," the company president said. "Can't we talk about this?"

"I've tried to tell you guys over and over. I've done everything to get your attention, but it's not working. You tell me you don't have any answers. Bill Huey says you haven't even talked to him in two weeks. Meanwhile, money's pouring out like a sieve, and I have no idea where it's going, or when it's going to stop. You're building a house I can't afford."

I left to silence and went back to work. Marsha remained.

I was so angry that I couldn't concentrate. I waited for my anger to abate so that I could think more clearly. That afternoon, I called in my assistant and dear friend, Kathy Adams, and told her that I needed to dictate a letter to the president of the contracting company.

"Based on performance during the last month and your inability to address my concerns, I have lost confidence in your ability to complete Linbrook Hall. Regretfully, I have decided to terminate. I deeply regret the necessity to make this drastic change."

I wanted her to personally deliver the letter to the company president, along with a copy to the project manager that afternoon. At this point, my anger had been replaced by a deep sadness, and Kathy, who can instantly read my every mood, was concerned about it. Was I sure I wanted to do this? I was.

The company president was no longer at the office when she arrived, and she left a copy for him. The project manager, whom I considered to be a friend, was there. Kathy gave him the letter. He opened it and read it as she waited.

"I'm not surprised," Kathy remembered him saying.

The company president called that night. It was clear what I wanted, he said, but this was going to be a lot of trouble for everybody.

"I have to ask," he said, "is there anything we can do to regain your confidence?"

"I don't think so," I told him.

He knew that I was preparing to leave on a business trip to Finland and wouldn't be back until late the following Wednesday. Would I grant him the courtesy of working with Bill Huey and Marsha Tice in the hope of pulling things together enough to meet my expectations by the time I got back next

The house was a forlorn place after we had to stop construction and change contractors.

week? I didn't think it would be possible, I told him, but I would grant him that courtesy.

The sadness I had felt while dictating the termination letter didn't go away. The sub-contractors stopped all work on Thursday. I went by the house that evening. Not a soul was there. The exterior brick work was not quite finished. The house was about a third complete, maybe a little more. Most of the equipment and tools were now gone with the workers. I had no idea when work might resume, or at the moment, even if it would.

A depressing loneliness had settled over the house. I walked into the empty shell, and my mind flashed back to Longwood and its empty floors, forever to go uncompleted.

We had started this house with so much hope. It was to be the fun project of a lifetime. In the beginning, we had no worry about having the money to complete it. Our greatest concern then was that we get it right and find the proper antiques and works of art to furnish it so that it would create the impression necessary to our vision for the house.

Now we had reached this low point. My sadness had turned to deep sorrow. But despite my grief and disappointment, I couldn't allow myself to accept the fear that this house might never be finished, genuine though it had become.

Earlier, I had talked to Stuart Nunn to again ask his help, and he agreed to bring a team from Shelco to inspect the construction. We met at the house on the Saturday prior to my departure for Finland. The Shelco guys went over the house pretty thoroughly.

"How much trouble am I really in?" I asked Stuart.

"None, so far as I can tell," he said.

The construction was sound. Everything looked good. He saw no problems with the warranty if we had to switch. We talked about how a turnover might take place. Shelco would try to retain the current sub-contractors, he said, but under the company's strong terms and tight controls. He foresaw no difficulty in getting new subs for any who chose not to continue. Times were tight. Work wasn't easy to find.

I left for Finland considerably heartened. I returned to find that the current contractor was taking this matter very seriously indeed. Officials had been working closely with Bill Huey and Marsha Tice. Things were getting organized. Questions were being answered. We would have a new project manager if we decided to let the original contractor finish the job. I was optimistic that we might be able to continue after all, but under tighter controls and a guaranteed price.

The company expected to have everything pulled together within a week, and we would get a proposal for a firm contract. A meeting was set for

Wednesday, November 6, but I wouldn't be able to attend. Linda and I had to fly to Memphis for a board meeting at St. Jude. Marsha would attend on our behalf.

I was on my way to the baggage claim area in the Memphis airport when I called Kathy to ask if she'd received the new proposal. She had just got it. It was twelve pages long. I told her to go straight to the base amount at the end. She read it to me.

My heart dropped. It was more than 20 percent above the absolute maximum cost to which we originally had agreed. And construction time was estimated at nearly twenty months from the point when we decided to proceed, if we did. I knew then that we would have to undergo the agony of a change in contractors if we wanted to finish the house within our resources.

I met with Marsha after our return from Memphis. She'd had time to go over the proposal carefully and had discovered errors that would increase the ultimate cost even more.

In my mind, the matter already was settled. On November 12, I notified the president of the contracting company that the proposal was not acceptable and the termination was permanent. The following day, we began working with Shelco to bring about the transition. The problems were enormous, and some had to be dealt with immediately.

Cornices were in transit from Florida, and the first columns were on their way from California. Limestone was being mined and milled in Alabama. All would have to be stored and protected until they could be installed. Randolph County's iron-red mud could permanently stain the columns if it got on them. We had to grade and gravel a level platform for them behind the house, where they could be covered and shielded from weather and mud. They arrived in a driving rain and had to be gingerly handled to prevent damage. Mark Peterson and my cousin Harold Loflin took care of that tricky job.

Stuart Nunn had warned us that the changeover would take time and that it was unlikely that any work could begin again on the house until sometime in January. The delay was inconvenient but necessary to save the house in my view.

So many matters had to be attended in that time. Sub-contractors had to be contacted; new contracts had to be drawn; insurance had to be dealt with; rented equipment had to be returned; drawings and other documents had to be collated and transferred to Shelco. Materials in transit had to be stored. Materials already stored had to be moved. Inspections had to be made. Bills had to be confirmed and paid. The work seemed endless and often aggravating, but it had to be done.

The former contractor was helpful throughout the process. In January, as work was beginning to resume on the house, the company president and

I had a face-to-face meeting, just the two of us, to iron out our differences and reach a final settlement, although it would take a few more months to clear up all of the details.

During the time that Linda and I were visiting historic houses seeking ideas for our own house, I was concentrating primarily on architectural details and landscaping. Linda, on the other hand, had been paying close attention to the furnishings. She loved antiques, and while I was buying books about architecture and gardens, she was collecting books about antiques.

We wanted to furnish the house in nineteenth century period pieces as much as possible, and it was only natural that Linda would undertake the Herculean task of searching out and purchasing the furnishings to fill such a large house.

She had been collecting things all along, but her first major pieces were bought when she took a nine-day trip to England near the end of May 2000 with Antiques Abroad, a Charlotte company that organizes buying trips to Europe. Those who take these jaunts are accompanied by experts and given access to top-line, dealer-only suppliers. Linda's friend Michelle Alvarino, accompanied her. They not only had a great time, but they brought back a lot of nineteenth century pieces, including a mahogany cabinet, a rosewood sofa, a gentleman's press and secretary, a sewing table, a wrought-iron bed made in 1817, a mahogany and brass telescope made in 1840, crystal, and leather-bound books.

But their prime find would come to grace Linbrook's entry hall. We call it the Shakespeare table. It is an intricate, twelve-sided, revolving table made by Edward Noble Courtney at Stratford-on-Avon, William Shakespeare's hometown. Its top features seven scenes in Stratford, including Shakespeare's birthplace, Ann Hathaway's cottage, and the Church of the Holy Trinity in marquetry using numerous types of wood. The table was first displayed in Stratford's town hall on Shakespeare's birthday in 1859.

I ended up making a contribution of sorts to Linda's antique collecting, but only by sheer coincidence. Erica Jenkins was a student at Guilford Technical Community College. She wasn't sure what career field she wanted to follow, and she talked to her aunt, Jill Howard, about it. Jill had been the first technician hired by RF Micro Devices, our sixth employee (as this is written, we have about 2,700 worldwide), although she later had left the company.

Jill suggested that Erica talk with Cheri Strong (later Lyons) in our Nokia Products Division about business paths she might pursue. Erica came to see her in November 1999, and Cheri ended up hiring her for a part-time job. Erica worked in the evening, and I saw her frequently because I usually worked late. She later asked to interview me for a school project and I got to know her better. After we moved into our new corporate headquarters in January 2000, we had a company gym, and Erica and I often ended up working out at the same time.

Linda was always fond of Jill Howard, and I wanted her to meet Jill's niece. Erica knew about the house we were planning to build, and I brought her to meet Linda and see the house site. Erica would become almost like a daughter to Linda and me

Erica had told us that her mother was an antiques dealer and her stepfather had a construction company. She wanted us to meet them, and we had dinner one night with Julie and Curtis Morgan. In August, we had a birthday party for Erica at the rock house. Jill Howard came and so did her sister, Linda Price. Their sister Julie made an impressive entrance, arriving on her Harley-Davidson.

We had Bill's first plans for the house at the party and showed them to everybody. Afterward, I took groups on tours of the site on my John Deere Gator.

Julie and Linda really hit it off at that party and went on to form a close and enduring friendship. Julie, who owned an antique store in downtown Greensboro, became Linda's confidante, advisor, and traveling companion to many antique auctions and other events. Julie took Linda to meet her own suppliers so that Linda could see antiques still in their crates when they first arrived from Europe.

In April 2001, Julie sold her downtown shop and opened the Antique Marketplace alongside Interstate 40 near the Greensboro airport, not far from RF Micro Devices. Antique Marketplace is a mall for many dealers, and anytime that anybody brought in a period piece that Julie thought would be appropriate for the house she bought it immediately and made it available to us.

She and Linda began filling a warehouse in Greensboro with antique treasures for the house. From the beginning, Linda had cataloged every piece she bought in what she would come to call her "furniture books," including description, size, and other details.

One great find that Linda made on her own came from P.K. "Pete" Burleson of Burlington, a craftsman of furniture and grandfather clocks who also dealt in antiques. This was a clock made in Froom, England, a place that no longer exists, by James Clark. Its hand-carved English oak case stands more than seven feet tall. Its working parts are clearly handcrafted and are of a type that ceased to be used late in the 1600s. The individual history of the clock is not known. Pete had bought it about a year earlier from a collector who was strapped for cash. It probably was made some-time after 1640 and before 1676. It would come to stand in the entrance hall at Linbrook, not far from the Shakespeare table.

• • •

From the time work began again on the house in January 2003, Linda and I were closely monitoring two Shelco projects—Victory Junction Gang Camp and Linbrook Hall—wondering which would be completed first. As time went on, it became apparent that Victory Junction was leaving us in the dust, and we couldn't be unhappy about that. The camp had a definite deadline that had to be met. We were more flexible.

More than twenty-five hundred people turned out for the grand opening ceremonies at Victory Junction on June 15, 2004.

The rush to finish the camp in time for the ceremonies proved to be quite frantic, a frenzy of work. Only a few days before the grand opening, bureaucratic red tape at the state level was preventing the camp from filling its lake. We got on the phone to state officials and told them we were prepared to send Richard Petty the seventy miles to Raleigh in one of his race cars to make a special plea to the governor, who might be embarrassed since he was supposed to speak at the grand opening. We figured Richard could get there in about twenty minutes, we said, and we felt certain we could get a TV news crew to ride along with him. We were just joking, of course, but the red tape quickly unraveled and permission was granted to pump water from a nearby stream to fill the lake shortly before the first visitors arrived.

Governor Mike Easley was just one of the dignitaries who spoke at the ceremonies. Another was Brian France, NASCAR's chairman and CEO. NASCAR made Victory Junction the first of its primary charities. Paul Newman returned and was thanked for his role in starting the Gang camps by Darren Singer, vice president of marketing for GlaxoSmithKline, the pharmaceutical company that donated $1 million for the camp's medical facility. Racing star Tony Stewart was recognized for his $1 million commitment to the camp as well.

As the invited guests toured the camp, Kyle Petty talked with reporter Mark Brumley, telling him about a group of patients from Brenner Children's Hospital in Winston-Salem who had toured the camp earlier.

"It's amazing when you look out across the camp itself...what so many people have done and what so many people have believed in," Kyle said. "But when you see the kids here, it's a totally different place. You don't pay any attention to the buildings. All you see is the kids."

That rang so true five days later when the first campers began to arrive. The wonder on their faces said it all.

I acknowledge that I am about as devoid of rhythm as it is possible for a human to be. If it's true that opposites attract, it certainly was the case for Linda and me when it comes to matters musically rhythmic. Linda is a fantastic dancer. In her youth, she was drawn to a particular dance that is peculiar to the Carolinas and Virginia. It is called the shag, and it is performed to what is called beach music, old-time rhythm and blues that has been a staple in our region for more than half a century.

Linda once spent a lot of happy weekend nights at beach music clubs where she saw many of the great rhythm and blues and old-time rock-and-roll performers. When the Public Broadcasting System did a series of concerts of so-called do-wop music, featuring many of these performers, Linda ordered the complete set of DVDs during a fund-raising campaign.

Early in September, as Linbrook Hall finally was nearing completion, we popped one of these DVDs into the player late one night and watched it from bed. It was a great show. One of the performers was Percy Sledge. He was one of Linda's favorites. His big hit, "When a Man Loves a Woman," came in 1966.

I never had kept up with that kind of music and knew little about it, but I recognized greatness when I saw it. Clearly, Percy Sledge was a terrific performer. I loved the way he sang. I loved his face. I loved his smile.

Linda fell asleep after the DVD ended, but I got up and went downstairs to the computer. I wanted to know more about Percy. I typed his name into Google and discovered that he had his own impressive Web site. As I read about him, I noticed a tab that said "booking info." I clicked on it. Anybody apparently could book the great Percy Sledge to perform. Even I?

For months, I had been thinking about a first big event for Linbrook Hall. And now I was sure that I had it. Mine and Linda's twenty-fifth anniversary would be in November. Here was a way that I could make up big-time for my lack of planning on our wedding day. What could be a better way to inaugurate the house than to have Percy Sledge singing "When a Man Loves a Woman" directly to Linda for our anniversary?

We could have a big dinner and dancing. We could invite guests with a request for a $250 per couple donation to Victory Junction Gang Camp. If four hundred people came, we could raise $50,000.

On Monday, September 9, I asked Kathy to check to see if Percy was available on a weekend close to November 16. She got a response the following day with a number to call. It turned out that Percy and The Aces Band had Friday, November 12, open. I called Pattie Petty to make sure this would be an acceptable event for Victory Junction, and she was excited and enthusiastic about it. She and the camp would help in every way possible, she said.

We had just one little problem to overcome. We still had to finish the house, furnish it, and decorate it.

Tuesday, September 14, 2004, marked a big day for Linbrook Hall.

Moving days were upon us. Although we had no certificate of occupancy yet, and much still had to be done on the house, Shelco had sent in a big cleaning team after many weeks of painting and interior finishing. We were told that it would be okay to go ahead and start bringing in stuff. I took a week off from work and rented a big truck just for shuttling incidentals. We hired movers for the bulk of the furnishings, and over the next two days, they employed two eighteen-wheelers making numerous runs back and forth to storage facilities in Greensboro.

All of the items had been marked beforehand to indicate the floors and rooms where they were to be placed. Fifteen-foot ceilings require a lot of big, stout, and weighty furnishings, and Linda and Julie had made certain that we had a sufficiency of those. The movers taped cushioned wooden panels over the marble and Brazilian cherry floors to protect them as they wheeled in these heavy pieces.

We had used three different interior decorators to get ideas for the house, but as movers spread furnishings throughout it, we relied on three others, all of whom should have had "Born to Decorate" tattooed across their biceps—Linda, Pattie, and Julie, three strong women in more ways than one.

One of my roles in all of this was to lift what I was told to lift and tote it wherever I was instructed to tote it. This frequently involved lifting and toting the same heavy item several times. My main job, though, was hanging pictures and mirrors. This was not as easy as it may sound because some of those antique mirrors weighed hundreds of pounds and I didn't even want to imagine what might ensue if I let one slip and crash to the floor.

I went to Lowe's and bought a laser leveler. One thing I can guarantee is that every painting, print, tapestry, mirror, or other wall hanging in that house is in plumb.

I've never been a person who liked to be idle; in fact, my dad used to say of my many activities, "Jerry, I get tired just watching all you do." After being around Linda, Pattie, and Julie in this house for several days, I knew exactly what he meant. They went at it hour after hour, long into the night, day after day. And the results were phenomenal.

The intuitive choices Linda had made for the antiques she bought, often with Julie's help, were amazing, especially since she had begun buying them long before she knew what the rooms would look like. Within a few days, the house began to seem like a completely different place. It was taking on warmth and a personality of its own, an aura that would become truly special.

The decorating went on for weeks, and during some of this time, Gary Johnson, an antique restorer, was at work in the basement making minor repairs and touching up some of the pieces. After all the antiques were distributed throughout the house, voids that needed to be filled became apparent, and the three decorating whirlwinds went on expeditions to furniture retailers to buy reproductions. The trucks just kept coming.

One of the trucks that arrived was at my own behest. It brought the Steinway 150th anniversary limited edition rosewood grand piano that Linda and our friend Lily Zhu had picked out in California. Lily is a concert pianist who has performed at Carnegie Hall and the White House. The two guys who brought it were professional piano movers. They pulled the truck right up to the front door.

This piano probably weighed more than eight hundred pounds, and I was concerned about possible damage to the limestone steps from the moving equipment. They told me not to worry. They had a rubber-wheeled, step-climbing dolly. This thing was manually operated, and it was a sight to behold.

My brother-in-law Mike, my cousin Harold, and I stood by in case our help was needed. When these guys started up the first step, they were straining every muscle, veins popping to the surface of their faces and arms. I thought the piano was about to get away from them. I could just see this thing lying in pieces all over the limestone steps. Mike and Harold moved to help.

"Get back! Get back!" one of the guys yelled, still straining. "Don't touch anything. We know what we're doing. We've done this hundreds of times. Just stay back."

We stayed back. Remarkably, they got it into the house in one piece, screwed the legs on, and set it up. These were two strong guys. And they did know what they were doing.

After I had gone back to my job, I'd come to the house as soon as I got away in the evening and find some rooms completely different than they had been the day before. More than a few rooms, especially bedrooms, went through several transformations. Several times I came in right in the middle of these situations and quickly resigned myself to more lifting and toting.

By early October, I had become especially concerned about one deficiency—the draperies. We had hired Mimi Fitz of Perfect Designs in Charlotte, who shared Linda's love of color, to work with us on the color scheme for the house and to help choose the rugs and draperies. She had directed us to a window covering master in Atlanta, Richard Ravan. We were told that he had many high-end customers and a long waiting list. He came to the house during the summer and later prepared elaborate drawings of draperies for the front rooms and the master bedroom suite. We had commissioned him to go ahead with those, but he'd had trouble getting some of the fabrics from Europe.

I was really anxious about the possibility of the windows still being bare for our big event on November 12. On October 4, I asked Kathy to call for a status report. The living room draperies were finished, we learned, and those for the dining room were nearly complete. I'd told Kathy to instruct him to bring what he had and begin installing them no later than Monday, October 11, so we'd at least have something up in time for the event. He and his crew showed up early that morning with the draperies for the two front rooms and went to work.

When they had finished several days later, we knew why Ravan was in such great demand. The draperies were, in a word, stunning. They brought a whole new level of elegance to the house.

Ravan and his crew returned on October 21 to do the library and the master bedroom suite. After seeing those, we commissioned him to do the window coverings for the rest of the house.

On November 3, just nine days before our opening event, we finally got a certificate of occupancy for the house, although work on it continued.

Afternoon showers were predicted for Friday, November 12. I figured they would be over well before our event and would pose no problem. Most of the event would be outside. The garden area behind the house had been designed with a big grass circle, only recently sodded, that would allow a huge tent to be erected for large functions. Dinner was to be served in the tent. If the showers came, we figured the ground would stay dry beneath the tent, where caterers already had stacked folding tables and chairs.

Diane Hough, who is director of the Kyle Petty Charity Rides, was serving as event coordinator. A florist friend of Pattie's, Becki Arrington, had agreed to do all of the floral arrangements without charge. A friend of Becki's, Debbie Baker, had come from Atlanta to help. The garage had been filled with flowers, and they had been working nonstop for two days creating some of the biggest and most beautiful arrangements I'd ever seen.

By afternoon, the house appeared to be a scene of utter chaos. It was filled with people. Workmen were coming and going. Pattie and Julie were all over the place rearranging things. A group of volunteers from Victory Junction had arrived to be instructed on their duties for the evening. They were put to work on unfinished details. A couple of guys were cutting and finishing marble tops for some of the antiques. In the midst of all of this, the band arrived and began setting up their music stands, instrument cases, speakers, and microphones on the back porch. My role was to float from crisis to crisis and be peppered with questions, for many of which I could offer no answers.

The rain came late in the afternoon. I wasn't concerned about it at first. It didn't seem bad, and I thought it would pass quickly. It didn't. It kept on and grew in intensity. Soon it was coming in torrents with no sign of stopping. My brother-in-law Mike came in to tell me we had a real problem. The tent was flooding. The water was already about an inch deep in places.

Mike quickly organized a crew, and they went out into the driving rain with mattocks, hoes, and shovels and began digging a trench in the expensive sod outside the tent in the hope of draining the water away. It didn't work. The ground was level. The trench had no elevation to allow it to drain. It just filled with water which washed back into the tent. The whole area beneath the tent was now flooded. This was beginning to look like disaster.

There was only one thing we could think to do. We could use an old carnival trick—put down straw and hope that it would absorb the water and allow people to walk without miring to their ankles. Brian Collier, who was then director of Victory Junction, said he could get some trucks and trailers from the camp. He and Mike set off to put this plan in motion.

"If this doesn't work, I don't know what we can do," I said.

"We do," one of the women volunteers replied. "We're going to pray."

A group set off to the basement to form a prayer circle.

Thirty minutes later, less than two hours before the first guests were to arrive, the rain stopped.

Where Mike and Brian managed to get the straw, I never knew, but they brought loads of it. Crews hurriedly spread it six inches deep throughout the tent and over the nearby sod. The caterers rushed to set up the tables, chairs, and serving lines in what now looked a lot like a barn—but a barn with linen table cloths and candelabra, although the candles couldn't be lit because of fire danger.

The rain had caused another big headache. We had planned for visitors to park in the grassy fields near the entrance and had arranged buses to shuttle them to the house. Those fields were now sodden, and we didn't know what might happen there.

"Don't worry about the parking," Austin Petty said. "I'll take care of it."

He quickly organized a crew of volunteers, worked out a plan, set up big mobile lights in the fields, and put tractors on standby in case anybody got stuck.

Forty-five minutes before guests were scheduled to arrive I was certain that they would be greeted by confusion and chaos. I had done all I could do. Linda had spent much of the day at the hospital where her brother was undergoing surgery and had arrived late. We had to go home to dress and leave the problems to others.

We returned not knowing what to expect and walked into a scene of serenity, elegance, and great beauty, as if we were stepping into a movie.

Somehow it all had worked out. Everything and everybody were ready, and it would turn into a lovely and wonderful evening. Nearly 450 people attended, and Victory Junction would receive more than $50,000.

After the reception and dinner, as show time neared, I took the microphone that Percy Sledge would be using and with Linda at my side welcomed everybody to Linbrook Hall. I brought on Kyle and Pattie, who spoke briefly about Victory Junction and introduced one of the campers, eight-year-old Haleigh Epperson of Brown Summit in Guilford County, a cancer victim who appeared in the first Victory Junction TV commercial.

I had written what I wanted to say next, but I spoke it instead from my heart. I told about my parents meeting on the rock up by the road as teenagers and how my family had lived on nearby land for generations. I talked about the values they and my Quaker faith had instilled in me. I told how Linda had come into my life at a low point and turned it around, and how and why we had built this house.

"Linda's heart is larger than this house," I said, "and that is why it's totally appropriate to dedicate and name it Linbrook Hall, in honor of Linda Neal. None of this would have been possible without her. My dream has come true, and now I am going to try to make her dream of using this house as an instrument to help others come true."

I had bought Linda an English car for our anniversary, a red and white Mini Cooper. I had talked with Percy earlier, and he agreed to drive it right up to the back porch at the end of my comments and surprise her with it. He did just that, lights and horn blaring, and stepped out of the car with a big smile, holding the keys high.

Later, when Percy took the stage and launched into "When a Man Loves a Woman," I led Linda onto the dance patio. It was a slow tune, thankfully, not much rhythm required.

Linbrook Hall is a work in progress, and with luck, it will continue to be. Our hope is to improve it as resources allow and put it to greater and greater uses for good. In the first year after a structure of this size and complexity is built, many kinks and problems show themselves and have to be worked out.

A year after completion of construction, we don't live in the house. We may with time, but I'm not sure about that. It's a huge place for just two people. And if we do, we probably will settle in a portion of it. For now, we are comfortable in our farmhouse.

Whenever I am at Linbrook Hall, which is often, I find myself working. I seem to be forever with tools in hand, or on a ladder. I spend a lot of time pushing my light bulb cart from floor to floor with my extension pole and plunger. You can't imagine how many bulbs burn out in a place of this size. In the summer of 2005, the blades on the fans on the back porch started sailing off. I discovered that they were incorrectly installed and fixed all of them myself. I won't even go into the problem of the latches on the back doors that consumed many hours of my time. Let's just say it was confounding.

In the spring of 2005, I made two fortuitous acquaintances that I'm sure will benefit Linbrook Hall far into the future. While on a speaking trip for Wake Forest University's Babcock Graduate School of Management, I met two fellow speakers, Dini Cecil Pickering and Lynne Ivey. Dini is the great-granddaughter of George W. Vanderbilt, who built Biltmore House, a national treasure. She and her brother, Bill Cecil Jr., operate Biltmore Estate as a family business. Lynne Ivey is the company's development director.

Dini and Lynne wanted to see Linbrook Hall, and we stopped by for a quick tour. Both understood our vision for the house immediately and have been helpful in attempts to bring it about. Dini put us in touch with E. Carlyle Franklin, a professor of forestry at N.C. State University, who developed Biltmore's forestry management program. Dr. Franklin has spent days walking the 320 acres that surround Linbrook Hall mapping different stands of trees. He is preparing a program for us similar to Biltmore's.

Dr. Franklin also has designed a series of nature trails that will meander for about five miles with varying degrees of difficulty for casual walkers. He has laid out the trails to take advantage of unusual landmarks he discovered on the property—a bubbling spring; large beds of ferns; old stone walls five feet high; erosion-control measures that may go back a hundred years or more; and most mystifying, a huge boulder that appears to have been sawed in half, the two smooth flat sides standing only inches apart.

Two of my neighbors have granted access that will allow us to extend the trails to a total of about nine miles. They will reach all the way to the Uwharrie River so that visitors can share some of the experiences that I enjoyed on my Sunday walks with Grandpa Edd long ago. One of those trails will lead to the tractor museum and to my grandparents' house across the road.

Part of my dream is to restore my grandparents' farm to the way it was in the '30s and '40s and make it, along with the tractor museum, part of a bigger rural life historical exhibit for Randolph County that would be open to the public, as the tractor museum is now, perhaps even with demonstrations on certain days. Maybe we could even have an occasional recreation of one of my grandmother Myrtle's famous Sunday dinners. With meringue-topped banana pudding.

Dini and Lynne also introduced us to Biltmore's vice president of agricultural sciences, Dr. Ted Katsigianis, who is assisting us in developing a farm plan. Our hope is to eventually make Linbrook Hall as self-sustaining as possible so that it can continue the purposes we want it to serve.

We have other dreams for the property. One is a garden that will be the equal of any in the state and will make our part of Randolph County even more beautiful and appealing to visitors from great distances.

When I stand in the cupola of Linbrook Hall watching a vivid sunset, or the approach of a dramatic lightning storm, I sometimes find it hard to believe that the dream of the house finally has become physical reality. I also become keenly conscious of the work and costs that lie ahead if it is to be enduring as a house for giving.

We only can trust in faith that it will meet that purpose and that it may serve in ways we can't even imagine now.

Seventeen

Few stories or lives are without loose ends, and the one involving my dad still bothered me. As balanced a life as he lived, my dad left one aspect slightly askew, and left me with important questions for which I sensed he never wanted to be pressed for answers. Yet, I felt a deep need to tie up this loose end, perhaps to bring understanding and balance to my own life.

From the time I was a kid, I remember my dad talking about Spencer Ahlmer. Spencer was his best friend in the Army. My dad arrived in the Philippines on Easter Sunday, 1945, with two friends with whom he had undergone basic training in Georgia. But as soon as they landed, his friends were sent to different combat units and he never saw or heard from them again.

Dad was pulled aside with several other men who soon learned that they had one thing in common. All had been involved in wood work in civilian life. They were sent to a national forest near Manila where the Army had set up a big sawmill turning trees into huge timbers to rebuild bombed bridges. My dad worked a twelve-hour shift, 11 p.m. to 11 a.m. He had reminisced about that in the tape he'd left for me.

Strangely, he didn't mention Spencer in that tape, maybe because he didn't talk about any combat experiences in it. So far as I know, he never talked about that to anyone, except for Spencer.

He and Spencer met when he was relieved from sawmill duty and taken to an airfield base camp to be reassigned to a combat unit. Spencer had arrived in the Philippines shortly after my dad. He had spent a week on mop-up operations in Manila before arriving at the base camp.

Spencer was from Honeyville, Utah. He was only nineteen, five years younger than my dad, but they quickly discovered that they had a lot in common. Both were quiet-spoken, contemplative, and deeply religious; my dad was Quaker, and Spencer was Mormon. They didn't drink, didn't chase women, didn't use swear words, and that set them apart from most of their fellow soldiers.

The experience they were about to endure would forge a friendship that created a lifetime of respect. My dad returned home months before Spencer after the war's end, and they lost touch with one another.

Nearly forty years passed before my dad, on a whim, decided to see if he could find Spencer. It wasn't hard. He knew that Spencer had lived somewhere around Ogden, Utah, and he called information there and quickly got a number. His old friend answered. They had a great time catching up with each other's lives, and afterward they made a habit of talking by telephone every Christmas.

Several years later, Spencer's daughter, Sheree, took a job in Raleigh, and Spencer called my dad and said he was coming to visit her and wanted to have a reunion. That was in September 1994, less than a year before my mom died. Dad was excited about seeing Spencer again. He asked if I would drive him to Raleigh. We met Spencer, his wife Mavis, and his daughter at John B. Umstead State Park for a picnic. The two old soldiers had a great time reminiscing.

That would end up being their only visit. After my dad's death, my sisters and I regrettably failed to think of notifying Spencer. He got worried when my dad didn't call at Christmas and he got no answer at my dad's house. He asked his daughter if she could find out if something was wrong. She called me. I later called Spencer to apologize and told him that I'd like to come for a visit and talk about his and my dad's experiences during the war. He said to come any time.

I finally found time in October of 2002. I flew to Salt Lake City, rented a car, and drove to Ogden. Spencer and Mavis were living at the foot of a mountain. Spencer had long been retired from his work as a carpenter and builder. He had constructed many houses and apartments in the area. After retiring, he had taken up painting landscapes. The living room walls were covered with his bright, colorful works.

We chatted for a long time before we got to the topic I really wanted to know about—the fighting he and my dad had faced. He had no reluctance talking about it.

My dad posed in his combat gear at Ft. Ord before shipping out to the South Pacific.

Early in May 1945, not long after they met, Spencer said, he and my dad were loaded into a truck that was part of a convoy headed east to the Sierra Madre Mountains. Japanese forces were dug in deep there in what was known as the Shimbu Line.

The 38th Infantry Division had landed in the Philippines on Pearl Harbor Day five months earlier and had retaken Bataan, where U.S. forces had been forced to surrender in 1942, and where twenty thousand American and Filipino prisoners of war had died on a horrific march to a Japanese prison camp. The 38th Division had quickly become known as the Avengers of Bataan. Now its mission was to force Japanese troops out of the mountains east of Manila. A major assault had been launched.

Woodpecker Ridge, Mount Pacawagan, Mount Binicayan, the Twin Peaks, Wawa Dam—these were the objectives. The fighting was fierce. Seven times the 152nd Infantry Battalion swept over Woodpecker Ridge, only to be counterattacked and pushed back every time—until the eighth assault when they claimed it for good. Some companies had been decimated in the fighting.

My dad and Spencer were going in as replacements, although they didn't know where or to which unit. It only was a half hour's drive from the base camp to the mountains, but from there the going got rough. Corps of Engineers bulldozer operators had pushed roads as far up the mountains as they could get.

Spencer remembered that the road they took was so steep that soldiers had to get out of the back of the truck and ride on the front fenders to give it more traction and keep it from flipping over backwards. They had to abandon the trucks when they got to the end of the bulldozer paths.

"It was raining and we had to walk," Spencer said. "Pretty soon we smelled something so bad, and we thought what in the heck is this? We got up on top of that hill and twelve Americans were laid out, all covered with ponchos, just their feet sticking out, flies thick all over 'em, hot. We went to take their places in the foxholes, and they had about two inches of water in them, scooped 'em out as good as we could with our steel helmets."

Spencer and my dad were assigned to third squad, third platoon, Company E, 149th Infantry Battalion, 38th Division. They were on Mount Binicayan, and battle-hardened Japanese soldiers were dug in all around them. They never forgot that first night.

"Don't know how you ever could have a scarier time than being in a foxhole," Spencer said. "We got in our foxholes at sundown. Anybody got out after that was shot. They told us no one gets out of that foxhole after dark. We were getting ready to cover our foxholes with ponchos for the night and a kid from over here in Roosevelt, Utah, shaking his poncho out, and the Japanese opened up and got him in the stomach. He laid all night in that foxhole, begging for medics and for morphine. All night. Next morning they drug him out and laid him on the ground."

The campaign took a month, and Spencer and my dad were in the thick of it. Their battalion would seize Mount Binicayan and Wawa Dam, which held back the Mariquina River in the gorge between Twin Peaks, one of Manila's water sources. Caves in the rocky cliffs above the dam were filled with Japanese troops and heavy weapons.

Supply lines were cut by Japanese soldiers infiltrating behind the lines, and at times, units ran short of food and ammunition. Spencer said their platoon once went three days without water, making do by cutting bamboo and allowing the sap to drip into their helmets in attempts to slake their thirsts. Air drops later brought rations, ammunition, and water purification tablets.

Their company advanced in daylight, dug in at night. Nights were always worse. Japanese troops sometimes were so close that they could hear them talking.

"Some could speak English," Spencer said. "They'd call out, 'Hey, so and so's been hurt. We've got him here. We're going to kill him.' Or they'd have a guy just screaming, hollering, 'Help, help, help.' You'd think, we need to go get him."

Infiltrators came into their lines every night. "What you'd do, you roll a hand grenade out of your foxhole if you heard one. Sometimes it was just a rat. Big rats. They'd go across the top of your foxhole and scare the heck out of you. There wasn't a night when you weren't scared."

One night their platoon faced a banzai charge, Spencer remembered. Flares were fired so they could see their targets, and they were able to kill every one, some of them close enough to see their faces.

Artillery shells also came in the night from far down the mountains aimed at Japanese targets, but one night they could hear the shells coming closer and closer until they began landing on their company, killing several soldiers. Body parts were spread all over the ground, Spencer remembered, and they had to be picked up and carried out on ponchos.

Once, their platoon was accidentally strafed by a U.S. plane. "Sometimes we wondered who was the worst," Spencer said. "We'd be laying on the ground and seeing the ground puff up around us where bullets hit. Scary times."

The hardest fighting was in the rocky cliffs above Wawa Dam. That was where Spencer was hit. A machine gunner opened up on their squad. "Rocks and bullets flying everywhere," Spencer said. "All we could do was just dive for a hole, go anywhere." He was nicked in the arm, whether by bullet or stone fragment he never knew. "Bled like crazy," he said. "Medic patched me up and we moved on."

They feared mortars more. "They [the Japanese] were experts with mortars," Spencer told me. "They could put one of those things right in your pocket."

After the taking of Wawa Dam, Company E was relieved for a rest break. Spencer and my dad had been in combat for a month. They wore the same uniforms out that they wore in, and the only baths they'd had were in a small stream where they had to pull leeches from their bodies.

"Out of forty-three guys when we went in, thirteen of us walked out," Spencer said. "Albert was one of them, me and him. Some went out with dysentery, some with malaria, some wounded, and some were killed."

Spencer had no doubt that he and my dad had survived through faith. They had carried their Bibles with them throughout the fighting, read from them whenever they could. They had prayed a lot. Frequently, he said, they recited the 23rd Psalm together. "We were so much alike in what we be-

Dad, left, with his buddy Spencer Ahlmer during a break
from combat in the Philippines.

lieved, we didn't care what else was going on," he said.

Later, Spencer and my dad went on mop-up operations, but they never again saw fighting as fierce as they experienced in the assault on the Sierra Madres. They even were fired on by mortars when they went for a week of R&R in northern Luzon near General Douglas MacArthur's summer residence, where they posed for a photo together on the backs of water buffaloes.

Even after the Japanese surrendered following the dropping of atomic bombs on Hiroshima and Nagasaki, many Japanese troops didn't get the word or refused to believe it when they did. Sporadic fighting continued for months.

My dad received six medals and ribbons for his combat service, including the Bronze Star.

Spencer ended up spending a year in the Philippines, but my dad got to leave earlier because he was married and had children.

"He was really happy," Spencer recalled. "He told me how sorry he was that he was going and I was staying. We couldn't hardly either one of us talk to each other. I just remember telling him good-bye."

I had a great visit with Spencer and his wife, who died two years later on November 7, leaving Spencer alone. We enjoyed a late lunch together. Before I left, Spencer had one more thing he wanted to tell me.

"If I ever had to go through what we went through again," he said, "I'd want Albert as my buddy."

I told him that I knew that my dad felt the same way about him.

Now that I knew what my dad had gone through in the war, I only could wonder if there were moments when he had thought he wouldn't be able to keep his pledge to my mom to come back to that house on Russell Street and drop his duffel bag in the very spot where he had left her.

After he went off to the war, his parents worried so much about him that his father was moved to go to a fortuneteller to ask what my dad's fate might be. She told him that my dad would die in the fighting, making matters far worse for my grandparents. After my dad returned home, my grandfather told him what the fortuneteller had said and how much it had worried them.

"That's what you get for placing your trust in a fortuneteller," my dad said. "Your trust needs to be in the Lord."

I know that my dad and my mom believed that their faith brought him back to us. I can't imagine what our lives would have been like if my dad hadn't returned from the war. For one thing, my sister Diane never would have been born. My own life might have taken a completely different path without his guidance.

If faith brought him back, then faith directed my life even before I was aware of it. And I only can trust that the faith of my parents, which became my own, will continue to guide me and, like their faith, enhance the lives of those I love.

Epilogue

In May 2001, while my dad was sick but before we knew his illness was fatal, I told him about a plan I had in mind. When the house we were preparing to build was finished, I was going to make a place in the garden for the rock on which he and my mom had met.

I intended to situate it on the north-south center line of the house, so it wouldn't be out of balance, and I wanted to put a bronze plaque on it so that it could tell its own story. I asked him if he would write what he wanted it to say.

He was quite pleased about this, and the next time I went to see him, he handed me a sheet of paper with a passage written in a shaky hand. Three months later he was dead.

Four years after his death, I sent those words to a plaque maker, and Linda and I scheduled a service at Linbrook Hall to honor my parents and dedicate the rock to their memory. We invited family, friends of my parents, former coworkers of my dad's, and members of Poplar Ridge Friends Meeting who knew them.

About 150 people turned out under an overcast sky on a Sunday afternoon at the end of September 2005. I had worked days preparing for this, and I wanted it to be just right and go off without a hitch.

I had set up a podium on one end of the veranda at the back of the house and hung a big U.S. flag behind it (my dad loved flags, especially the Stars and Stripes). In the entrance hall of the house, I put more flags. Tables in two rooms were filled with photos and memorabilia of my parents' lives, even a copy of my dad's patent for the rip saw guide he had invented. Rows of chairs lined the veranda, which was big enough to accommodate all who came.

I welcomed the guests and told them our purpose. Both of my sisters wanted to speak about our parents. I introduced Betty first. She spoke lovingly of our mother and her love for us and others. "I can honestly say I never heard her say anything bad of anyone. Mama had a gentle spirit and a sweet smile, but she was also a tough lady."

Betty was a daddy's girl, and she acknowledged it. "He was my hero," she said.

She recalled the treats he brought us as children and the extra treats and attention we got if we weren't feeling well. "Daddy made it almost a joy to be sick."

She also brought up Dad's worry about our safety and how he tried to protect us even into adulthood.

"Daddy was always concerned about the condition of my tires," she said. "There were more times than I can remember of Daddy checking my tires—that is until I married a man who ran a tire store. Daddy was always there for me."

As a child, Diane often accompanied Mom when she went to visit people who had troubles of one kind or another.

"Mother had a real love of people. She knew what to say or do. This was her calling. Mother could understand."

Diane not only brought up my dad's dedication to balance, recalling how he once refused to buy a car because it didn't have matching side mirrors, she also told of his fondness for autumn foliage and how he looked forward to winter.

"He loved to see it snow," she said. "He would come to my room and wake me up at the first sign of snow."

Throughout his life, he called her as soon as he saw a snowflake, unless she spotted one first and called him.

It was hard to witness his despair in the face of our mother's long illness, Diane said, especially after Mom had to go to the nursing home, but his devotion was complete to the end.

"Their marriage was really built on a rock," she said. "Praise God for a Christian mom and dad."

When my turn came, I told about my dad's long and trying journey to Randolph County by wagon with a balky cow after his family lost their farm in the Great Depression, and how unbeknownst to him it was leading him to a long and happy life. I told how he had met my mom on the rock and how later in life he'd lost track of it until one day something told him to stop and ask Clarence Rush if he knew what had become of the rock. By that small miracle, we all were gathered this day.

In preparation for this service, I had been reading through some spiral-bound notebooks in which my mom had written about things that had caught her attention. In one, in 1972, I found that she had written, "I cried and cried and cried because Jerry said some kind things to me today."

"Then at the bottom," I told the group, "she said, 'I love Jerry.' And then she said, 'A lot.' I didn't need to read in a diary that fact. I knew that my mother loved me. Never had any doubt about it.

"My relationship with my dad was every bit as close. When he was dying and we both knew that he was dying, I said, 'Dad, is there anything that we need to say to each other?' Dad said, 'We've said it all.' No unfinished business, nothing in the way. That's the kind of relationship we had.

"I'm proud to be here today as a child of Albert and Bertie and to see all of you here."

Our minister, Randal Quate at Poplar Ridge Friends Meeting, was the final speaker. He told about a man who had devoted great time and expense to building a fine sailboat, but it capsized on its maiden voyage, drowning him. Rescuers found that the keel, which is supposed to keep the boat in balance, was too small. The builder had paid close attention to everything that was visible but ignored the most crucial part beneath the surface.

"It's really what's below the waterline that makes each of us who we are," Randal said. "There's a lot that went on with Albert and Bertie below the waterline that made them who they were on the surface."

Our minister is no fan of the reality shows so popular on TV, but he wondered what a reality show based on my parents' lives would have been like. Such a show, he thought, would be striking in comparison to the others.

"The difference would be in depth. So much of what we see in our culture is driven by image. So much of what shaped Albert and Bertie was based on things called values and faith. The image life is only lived on the surface. The values-faith life is forged below the surface.

"So many of these reality shows are based on impulse, self-gratification, control, and manipulation. An Albert and Bertie reality show would reveal virtues that our society is desperately in need of, things like commitment, devotion, loyalty, trust, compassion."

The rock we were about to dedicate, Randal said, was now fully exposed, but when Albert Neal and Bertie Dorsett met there, much of it was beneath the surface, a symbol of the union they would create upon it.

"They left their mark on us all," he said.

I invited everybody to walk to the end of the garden, where the rock, now mounted on a stone base, stood upright, covered by a drop cloth. When all had gathered, Betty, Diane, and I pulled away the cover to expose the plaque with the words my dad had written:

Built on a Rock

In 1934, this stone lay beside a muddy road, affording a platform for two fourteen-year-olds to get out of the mud and talk. While getting to know each other, a romance developed that lasted a lifetime. Three wonderful children were born into this union, Betty, Jerry and Diane. Now there are grandchildren and great-grand-children, and still hoping for more, praying they will be God-fearing members of this great nation. All beginning on this solid rock. The fourteen-year-olds were Albert Neal and Bertie Dorsett.

Above these words were molded bronze images of my mom and dad taken from a faded photo. They were nineteen, in love, gazing into one another's eyes, and now they were together again on their rock.

Linda and I hope that readers of this book will consider making donations to the two charities about which we care so deeply, St. Jude Children's Hospital and Victory Junction Gang Camp. Donations may be sent to:

St. Jude Children's Hospital
501 St. Jude Place
Memphis, TN 38105

Victory Junction Gang Camp
4500 Adam's Way
Randleman, NC 27317

EST. 2004
LINBROOK HALL
is named in honor of
Linda Stewart Neal
by her husband, Jerry D. Neal,
and for the brook that flows
around the house.

Linbrook Hall is a home with
a larger purpose,
and was created to realize the vision
Linda and Jerry
share to further the support of research
and care of chronically ill children.

Photography by Victor Steel

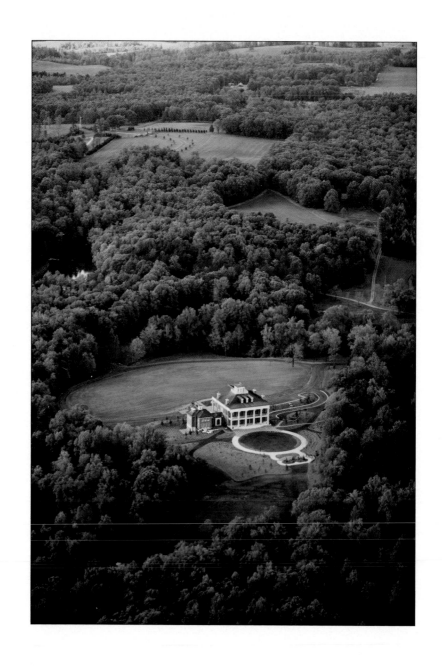